Traditional Orcharding

Traditional Orcharding
Practical Methods for Growing and Marketing Fruit

Fred C. Sears
Edited by Kary C. Davis, Ph.D.

THE LYONS PRESS
Guilford, Connecticut
An imprint of The Globe Pequot Press

The Lyons Press is an imprint of The Globe Pequot Press

10 9 8 7 6 5 4 3 2 1

Printed in the United States of America

ISBN 1-59228-002-1

Library of Congress Cataloging-in-Publication Data is available on file.

To

ROBERT W. STARR

POMOLOGIST, ADVISER AND FRIEND, THIS
BOOK IS DEDICATED BY THE AUTHOR

PREFACE

PROBABLY every teacher who studies along any one line for a series of years becomes convinced that he has learned things that would be of value to men in this line of work.

The writer offers this excuse for writing the present book, and perhaps the further justification might be added that for a number of years he has had charge of a relatively large orchard where he believes that he has sifted out his theories and discarded those that "won't work." He hopes that this belief will be shared by any who may attempt to follow his directions, and that the book may prove a real help in solving some of the problems which every orchard owner, whether experienced or inexperienced, is certain to encounter.

The writer also ventures to hope that the book may be helpful to instructors as a text for class use. He has attempted to cut out the non-essentials and to present the essentials in a reasonably brief manner and yet with sufficient detail to be followed easily when one attempts to put them into practice.

FRED C. SEARS

MASSACHUSETTS AGRICULTURAL COLLEGE,
AMHERST, January 1, 1914.

Editor's Note.

THIS book is suited to the needs of College and Short Course Classes. Its practical nature as well as its philosophical treatment makes it a book to be desired by both fruit grower and student. High schools and special agricultural schools devoting some time to the particular study of horticulture will find in this book the themes for their most profitable consideration.

The reader will be favorably impressed with the spirit of the writer throughout, particularly on questions where authorities may differ; the vigor and novelty of treatment are refreshing to those who are familiar with older works on the subject.

CONTENTS

ILLUSTRATIONS

Traditional Orcharding

CHAPTER I

THE OUTLOOK FOR ORCHARDING

IF the agricultural history of the twentieth century is ever written, the writer believes that one of the most significant features of such a history will be the account of the great interest in orcharding which developed during the latter part of the first decade of the century. That interest is still at its height. Men from all walks of life are turning toward orcharding as the one branch of farming in which they would like to engage. Wealthy men are setting out orchards (and commercial orchards) on their estates, farmers in orchard sections are enlarging their fruit plantations, while bank clerks, insurance men, and retired ministers are either investing their savings in small farms which are to be set out to fruit trees, or have bought an interest in some development scheme in the West. No wonder that there is a shaking of heads among the conservative element of our fruit growers and a wondering as to what the outcome will be. No wonder that even the most enthusiastic advocates of orcharding are speculating as to whether it may not be overdone.

A Good Occupation.—But while there has undoubtedly been a wonderful interest in the fruit business in recent years, and while many who have gone into it, without sufficient thought and preparation, undoubtedly will be disappointed, and while we may even have to admit that the price of fruit is likely to decline, yet it still seems to the writer that for the right man, in the right place and with the right methods, the growing of fruit offers a healthful and delightful occupation with at least a reasonable assurance of satisfactory financial returns. Let us examine the situation briefly and see what ground there may be for such a belief and what conditions one must fulfil if he expects to be successful.

1

The Question of Over-production.—To begin with, are we in such immediate and pressing danger from over-production? It is true that the papers are full of accounts of men who have started orchards; it is also true that any one who is supposed to know about such matters is besieged, either personally or by letter, by those who want to grow fruit, and it is probably true that where there is so much smoke there must be more or less fire. But the writer is very strongly of the opinion that the percentage of smoke is very large.

Census Figures.—There are various methods by which we may judge of the imminence of this over-production danger, none of them perhaps very accurate but all of them suggestive. The first consists of the United States figures, Uncle Sam's estimate on the subject. If we take the question of apples alone, which of course is the big end of the subject, we find first that the production has steadily declined since 1896. Here are the estimates from 1895 to 1911.

1895—60,500,000 barrels	1904—45,360,000 barrels
1896—69,000,000 barrels	1905—24,300,000 barrels
1897—41,000,000 barrels	1906—38,280,000 barrels
1898—28,500,000 barrels	1907—29,540,000 barrels
1899—58,500,000 barrels	1908—25,850,000 barrels
1900—57,000,000 barrels	1909—25,415,000 barrels
1901—26,970,000 barrels	1910—23,825,000 barrels
1902—46,025,000 barrels	1911—28,600,000 barrels
1903—42,626,000 barrels	

Are not these figures tremendously significant and do they not seem to indicate that it will be several years before we get back even to our former high-water mark? And we must not forget that at the same time that the production of apples has been declining the population has been increasing, so that it will require many more apples than 69,000,000 barrels to provide as many per capita as we had in 1896.

Another significant fact along the same line, which is brought out by the census figures, is in relation to the apple trees of the country. There were in 1910 in round numbers fifty million less bearing apple trees than in 1900 and only sixty-five million trees not yet in bearing. So that when all the trees in the country in 1910 had come into bearing, there would be only fifteen million more than in 1900, provided no trees died in the meantime. But every one knows that they are dying by the thousand every year. Even in relatively good orchard sections one may see many and many an orchard like that shown in Figure 1 which is already practically a negligible quantity so far as production is con-

Fig. 1.—One reason why orcharding will not be overdone! An orchard killed by scale and neglect. There are thousands like it.

cerned. And in the really poor sections, particularly if the San José scale is there, such orchards are the rule and not the exception.

Some Orchards Abandoned.—Passing now from Uncle Sam's estimates to the opinions of less important persons, we find it a very general opinion among people who have given the matter some thought, that a great many young orchards which were set out with high hopes a few years ago are already abandoned as hopeless. The writer himself can think of dozens. This was inevitable, considering the people who set them out, men and women who knew absolutely nothing of orcharding except what they read in the magazines or daily papers. Go into any section except our very best orchard regions and you will find plenty of examples like the orchard shown in Figure 1. One need have little fear of the competition of such an orchard as this.

Insects and Diseases.—Another thing which will help to delay this dreaded time of over-production is the constantly increasing list of orchard pests. Men have attempted to compute the loss from this source and have placed it among the millions of bushels. But whether we accept this estimate or not, no one who has seen such things at work as the bitter rot of the apple and the brown rot of the peach and plum or the codling moth of the apple and the curculio of the peach and plum can fail to realize that the loss is tremendous.

Slow Returns.—Still another factor which is always going to act as a brake on orchard setting is the length of time required to bring trees to profitable bearing. If a man starts in the dairy business he can buy a cow and sit right down and milk her (always provided of course that she is giving milk), so that his income begins at once; or if he starts in the trucking business it requires only a season to get returns. But an orchard is a long-time investment, and relatively few people are going to have the patience and the pocketbook to wait for returns (Fig. 2).

No Advertising.—If one is cataloging the hopeful factors in the orchard situation, he certainly should not omit the fact that up to date there has been almost nothing done in the way of advertising. If red apples were as persistently advertised as some patent medicines, the supply never would overtake the demand. This is one of the improvements which ought to be undertaken next, and the writer believes so emphatically in its value that he has devoted an entire chapter to the subject.

Bad Marketing.—If one wants further hope for the future of the orchard business, think of the way in which most of our fruit is marketed at the present time! If any one can think of methods better calculated to decrease consumption than those frequently in use he is a genius. Poor fruit, poorly handled and worse packed, is shipped into the market without the slightest regard for the demand at that particular time and place. What would happen to any other manufacturer if he followed the methods of many of our apple manufacturers? Bankruptcy sure and speedy! It simply shows what a good business orcharding is, that it has kept up under the methods too often in vogue.

The Right Man.—We have said that for the right people carrying on an orchard by right methods and in the right place the future is anything but dark. Let us close this brief review of the orchard situation with a word on this desirable combination. Who are the right people? Anybody with a love for the

FIG. 2.—Another reason why orcharding will not be over-done. This young orchard has been set five years and some of the trees are little if any larger than when they were set.

business and who has the knowledge, or who can hire somebody with the knowledge, to do the work. To begin with, the man brought up on the farm has an immense advantage over the man who is city born and bred. He knows already the practical details of farming. The writer is always doubtful about the success of one who knows nothing of farm life. It takes a tremendous amount of enthusiasm and hard work to overcome the handicap. Here is an example of the kind of man who ought not to go into orcharding. He wrote to our Agricultural College, saying that he expected to set a large orchard, would use fifty thousand trees, and since the nurserymen must make a lot of money out of their business did we not think it would be well for him to propagate his own trees. And in the event that we agreed with him as to the advisability of this, would it not be well for him to " start the apple seeds in the house during the winter so as to have the little trees well under way by spring." While the writer does not want to discourage unduly the city man who wants an orchard, it does seem to him that few of them can qualify as " the right man." Figure 3 represents another plan of orcharding.

Fig. 3.—Still another reason why orcharding will not be over-done. The owner of this orchard was a liveryman and wanted hay! He had the good sense not to try to raise both hay and apples on the same land.

Now while there are, of course, many exceptions, it would seem that two classes of orchard ventures are especially likely to be successful. One of these is that of the farmer in an orchard section who already has his living assured and who decides to add to his orchard plantings. And the other is that of the man who has money enough to go into orcharding on a reasonably large scale so that he can devote his time to it if he has the knowledge himself or if not can hire an expert foreman. As a rule the thing for the inexperienced man to do, if he is sure that he wants an orchard, is to work with some practical orchard man until he acquires a reasonable knowledge of the business.

Right methods are only less important than right men. The writer has tried, in the following pages, to suggest some of the things which he thinks are of importance. And even the best of men with the best of methods cannot succeed if they ignore too much the question of the right place. An uncongenial soil, a frosty location, undue exposure to fierce winds, add just so much to the unavoidable handicap of the man who grows fruit.

QUESTIONS

1. Discuss the interest in orcharding during the first decade of the twentieth century.
2. How did the production of apples vary from 1895 to 1911?
3. What are the principal factors which keep down the production of apples?
4. What type of man is most likely to be successful as an orchardist?
5. Give some examples of successful orcharding that you have seen.
6. Tell of unsuccessful orchard ventures that you have seen or read about and give the reasons for failure.

CHAPTER II

ORCHARD LANDS

WHILE there is considerable variation in the type of soil required by different classes of orchard fruits, and while in a few cases we have even worked out, with considerable accuracy, the soil preferences of individual varieties, yet it is surprising how nearly the ideal orchard conditions for most fruits agree. For example, they all agree in being subject to damage by winds, none of them thrive well on wet lands, and all of them are safer on lands which are not liable to frosts. We may therefore feel fairly safe in generalizing on orchard lands, and the following score card has been worked out for use in classes. In this is a list of the points which ought to be included in an examination of an orchard site, and an effort is made to estimate the relative importance of these different points. The score card is, of course, by no means ideal, but it does include the most important items and it ought to be suggestive to a prospective orchard planter.

Score Card for Orchard Site

		Counts.
A. Soil	30	
a. Surface soil		15
1. Fertility; chemical character; too fertile or not fertile enough.		
2. Adaptation to fruit grown.		
3. Ease of working.		
4. Sour.		
5. Humus.		
b. Subsoil		15
1. Ease of penetration by roots.		
2. Fertility; pure sand *vs.* gravelly clay.		
B. Water drainage	30	
a. Surface drainage		10
1. Good? Does water stand?		
2. Too much?		
(*a*) Washing, loss of soil and fertility.		
(*b*) Loss of water.		

Many of the points given are self-explanatory, yet a short discussion may help with most of them.

A. Soil.—*a. Surface Soil.*—1. The fertility of the soil, while not as important as the general character of the soil, is still well worth considering. If the land is " run out " it is by no means worth as much for an orchard as though it were in " good heart." Of course it can be brought up again in fertility, but this takes time and money and the writer has started enough orchards to learn that poor, run-out soil is a big handicap in developing growthy and shapely trees. To overcome it, one ought to have some barn manure available and one has to study much more carefully what kinds of commercial fertilizers to use and when to use them.

2. The adaptation of the soil to the fruit to be grown. If one is growing peaches, he prefers a light or medium loam, and if he must depart from this he would rather have a sandy soil than a

heavy clay. If he is growing pears he wants, as a class, much heavier soils than for peaches; usually a fairly heavy clay loam. This question of the adaptability of certain soils to certain classes or varieties of fruits is one which has only, within the last few years, been studied at all seriously. More and better work has been done on apple soils than any others. Near the close of this chapter the matter is discussed more in detail.

3. Ease of working the soil. One would discount a soil that was stony or rocky, or that was full of stumps or was a very heavy clay. Personally the writer thinks there is a great deal to be said in favor of rather light lands. They will not hold fertilizers as well as heavier soils, and some people think they do not hold moisture as well, though the writer doubts it. But they work so much more easily and there is so much less danger of injuring the soil or of damaging the trees if the soil isn't handled just right. With a heavy clay, one frequently has to wait days after a heavy rain before he can get on the land to work it; and there is so much more likely to be winter injury to the trees if the soil happens to have been cultivated a little too late, or if too much nitrogen has been used, or even when everything has been handled right, if the winter happens to be especially severe.

4. Is the soil sour? If it is, in most cases lime has to be applied to secure the best results. There is quite a common (and the writer believes a well-founded) prejudice in favor of soil of a limestone formation. And when one can not get this the next best plan seems to be to apply lime in some form.

5. Is there plenty of humus in the soil or has it been worked out till the physical condition has been injured? If the soil lacks humus it must be supplied. It might seem like a simple proposition to get humus back into the soil, but unless one has barn manure available he will find it an up-hill matter with either very heavy or very light soils. The catch crop intended to plow in simply will not grow. And one has a chance to exercise a lot of ingenuity and patience to get things started right. And the soil which requires all this is not as good an orchard soil, by just so much as the one which is already in shape.

b. Subsoil.—Under this head there are two main points to be considered: First, the ease of penetration by the roots of the trees, and, second, the fertility of the soil. Lands with impervious subsoils are not satisfactory for any fruits, and a good, medium, gravelly subsoil is more fertile than a pure sand. A good subsoil is a very important part of the orchard equipment. In the first place a large part of the root system is in the subsoil, and in the second place it is very difficult to improve a subsoil. Drainage is about the only thing to which one can resort.

Fig. 4.—A good orchard country. Rolling land that gives good water drainage and atmospheric drainage.

B. Water Drainage.—The score card divides this into surface and sub-drainage. In reference to the surface we have to consider whether there is enough, so that the water will not stand on the land. Even in winter standing water is objectionable (Fig. 4). Second, is there too much surface drainage so that the land is subject to washing? By washing, both soluble plant food and actual soil are lost. In times of drouth, the water from a chance shower will run off before it can soak in. A sharp slope on light lands is almost sure to suffer more from drouth than the more level lands near by, simply because the water does not have time to soak in.

Sub-drainage.—Here again it is a question of amount. Is there too little, just enough, or too much? Trees will seldom do well in a wet subsoil. The growth is poor and they are in danger of winter-killing and various other troubles. On the other hand if there is too much sub-drainage we have an exceptionally dry subsoil and consequently lack of thrift in the trees.

C. Atmospheric Drainage.—This, of course, is of importance only in sections subject to frosts, but as most of our best orchard lands are in sections where frosts may occur, it ought to be considered in choosing the orchard site. Frost is one of those intermittent troubles which one may escape for years and which then swoop down on the orchard in a night and wipe out the profits of the whole year. It is particularly comforting to know that the orchard is on lands which are not subject to this danger. And of course if one gets a crop when most of the neighbors have lost theirs, the profit is correspondingly greater. It is surprising how little elevation and how little slope are required to prevent frost. The writer has seen an elevation of not over ten feet make a difference of from 75 to 100 per cent in frost injury. The points to be considered are: (1) Is there slope enough to the field under investigation to carry off the cold air? (2) Does cold air drain down from slopes above to the orchard, *i.e.*, is the orchard at the foot of a long slope? (3) Is there any obstruction at the bottom of the orchard to hold cold air and bank it up in the orchard?

D. Aspect or Slope.—Personally the writer believes that this matter of aspect has frequently been over-worked and yet there are circumstances under which it is well worth careful consideration. If a man is an orchardist pure and simple, and wants to set out every available acre, no slope would be discarded on account of its direction. On the other hand, if one is a general farmer and wants to set one orchard on the best orchard site of the farm, then the question of slope is worthy of careful consideration. With reference to the sun, we have the ripening and coloring effects of a southern exposure which are surely worth having if they can be had without danger from frosts. But in sections and locations where frosts are a serious menace, southern and southeastern slopes ought to be avoided for all fruits like Japanese plums, which blossom very early and are frequently damaged by frosts. Lastly there is the matter of sun-scald. Where this is serious one ought certainly to avoid a southwestern slope. On the question of aspect with reference to wind it need only be said that in those sections where there are very strong winds from one or two directions, as frequently

Fig. 5.—An ideal country for orchard. Slope enough to provide good drainage, yet smooth enough to admit of cultivation.

happens, it is very desirable to avoid those slopes. Many sections, for example, are subject to very strong northwest gales and only slightly less to southwest winds. The orchardist therefore prefers to avoid these slopes, other things being equal. Frequently other things are not equal and we choose one of these slopes in spite of its direction. But such lands are not as desirable as those which do not have this handicap (Fig. 5).

E. Windbreaks.—A great deal has been said and written about windbreaks. They seem to the writer to be another factor in the orchard site question which has sometimes been over-worked and yet they are important. The one advantage of the windbreak which is likely to appeal to any man who has to get out in the orchard and do the actual work, is that it frequently enables one to work with more comfort and consequently with greater efficiency. The two operations in which this advantage will be noticed most are in pruning and spraying. Most of our pruning is done at a season of the year when the temperature is likely to be too low for real comfort. If a man is pruning some day in March in the northwest corner of an orchard on a western or northwestern slope, when there is a gale from that direction, he will very soon appreciate the value of anything that will get him out of that wind. Perhaps he resorts to the barn, but that does not get the orchard pruned. If he is lucky enough to have, as a part of his orchard, a corner which slopes to the southeast and which is, perhaps, also protected by a windbreak, he will see the practical value of shelter from winds. The case is even stronger when spraying is considered. In this operation one not only has the physical discomfort to contend with (and physical comfort or discomfort counts for a lot in getting any work done properly), but he frequently finds it a practical impossibility to get the spray where he wants it. It so happens that each of the two orchards with which the writer has most to do, has many different blocks on various slopes and with varying protections from the winds. And times without number in both orchards it has been possible to continue the work of spraying or pruning because it was possible to get away from the wind which happened to be blowing. A windbreak certainly pays in comfort and efficiency.

Kinds of Windbreak.—If one is to have a windbreak it is very desirable to choose a kind of tree for it which will harbor neither fungous diseases nor insects which might attack the trees of the orchard. For example, one would not want to have red cedar trees in a windbreak for an apple orchard, because of the cedar rust, a fungus which at one stage attacks the apple and at another the red cedar. Oaks are generally to be avoided because they harbor the tent caterpillar, and if one is unfortunate enough to live in a district infested by the brown-tail and gypsy moths both of these are also partial to oaks. On the other hand, it seems to be the common opinion that pines and spruces among evergreens, and maples among deciduous trees, are particularly suitable for this purpose.

Distance Away.—No windbreak, either natural timber or trees planted especially for the purpose, ought to be very close to the orchard. Fifty feet is near enough, and even a greater distance is better. Where the trees for the break are planted at about the same time as the orchard and come along with it there is less danger from their encroachment than where a new orchard is set out beside an old established row of trees, because in the latter case, as will be readily seen, the tree roots are already established and the fruit trees do not get a fair chance. If it is on the lower side of the orchard, the windbreak ought to be open at the bottom to allow for atmospheric drainage, otherwise there will be a frosty area next to the windbreak. Lastly, it is decidedly unwise to plant an orchard and rely for a windbreak on a block of timber owned by a neighbor. One never knows when the neighbor will decide to cut off the timber.

SPECIAL SOILS FOR DIFFERENT VARIETIES OF APPLES

Allusion has been made to the fact that the soil requirements of apple varieties have been more fully worked out than those of any other fruits. The writer wishes to close this discussion of orchard lands by quoting from a special article prepared by his friend, Mr. H. J. Wilder, of the United States Bureau of Soils, for the *Tribune Farmer.* Mr. Wilder probably knows more than any other man in the United States about apple soils, which makes his conclusions of special value.

"From agricultural experience already established, it is apparent that many of the leading special crop areas have a very definite relation to the character of the soils, and that all crops do not give equally good results on the same kind of soil. Carrying this principle further, it is purposed to point out that even the different varieties of the same crop may differ greatly in soil requirements. This is illustrated by a considerable number of varieties of apples, which have been under study for several years.

"The opinion has been frequently expressed in the past, not only in the agricultural press, but also in many horticultural books, that almost any deep, well-drained soil, on hill or slope, is adapted to apple growing. Data from a large number of orchards in many of the States east of the Mississippi show this definition of a good apple soil to be fraught with danger. Depth and good drainage of soil are, without doubt, fundamental essentials, but a very considerable percentage of soils in the Appalachian Mountain region and associated foothills is so excessively ' deep and well drained,' on account of its sandy character, that it can not compete with better soils in orchard production.

"**Unfavorable Soil Conditions.**—A still greater danger lies in the fact that so many men assume every hillside to be well drained. Shales and sandstones make up a large part of the Appalachian system. On level areas these rocks are flat, or nearly so, but on hillsides they range from gently to very steeply inclined. On such slopes erosion has prevented the accumulation of a soil covering of great depth. Much of the water from heavy rains rushes down the slopes, while that which soaks into the soil percolates down to the underlying shale, and if in excess flows along laterally and seeps out to the surface, giving rise to many spots of ill-drained soil. The same unfavorable condition is caused by a subsoil too clayey, or for some other reason too compact to allow ready downward percolation of moisture.

" Notwithstanding all that has been said, too, about selecting a deep soil, many orchards are still being planted on soils of so little depth above the underlying unbroken rock that little profit can ever come from them.

" The loss from choosing a soil for orchard planting that is not adapted to the purpose is so much more serious than a similar mistake with an annual crop that too much care can scarcely be taken in selecting the most suitable soils located on sites otherwise favorable. Because of the importance of such selection, investigations have been carried on to determine in so far as possible the types of soil most favorable to the different varieties of apples.

" It is recognized that these data are far from complete, and that the behavior of the different varieties under a range of soil conditions must be observed carefully for a long term of years before statements of adaptedness may be made positively, but enough facts have already been secured to make the indications of value to the planter; and it is hoped, in addition, so to arouse interest in the subject that growers and others will observe and collect data as occasion presents itself.

"**Baldwin Soils.**—If soils are thought of as grading from heavy to light, corresponding to the range from clay to sand, then soils grading from medium to semi-light fulfil best the requirements of the Baldwin. Following definitely the classification standards of the Bureau of Soils with reference to the proportions of clay, silt and sands, this grouping would include the medium to light loams, the heavy, sandy loams, and also the medium, sandy loams, provided they were underlain by soil material not lighter than medium loam nor heavier than a light or medium clay loam of friable structure.

" From this broad generalization it will be seen that the surface soil should contain an appreciable amount of sand. The sand, moreover, should not be all of one grade—that is, a high percentage of coarse sand would give a poor soil, whereas a moderate admixture of it with the finer grades of sand, together with sufficient clay and silt, would work no harm. In general, the sand content should be of the finer grades, but soils also occur, though comparatively rare, which would be too heavy for this variety were it not for a marked content of the coarse sands, the effect of which is to make the soil mass much more friable and open than would be expected with the presence of so much clay. Such soil dries quickly after a rain, and is not to be classed as a moist soil. It will never clod if worked under conditions at all reasonable.

" If the subsoil be so clayey or heavy that moisture does not percolate down through it readily, a Baldwin of poor color, with a skin more or less greasy, is the usual result.

" *The ideal* to be sought is a heavy, fine, sandy loam, or light, mellow loam, underlaid by plastic clay loam or heavy, silty loam. It is fully realized that the individual may not possess or easily acquire just this ideal, but the soil that most closely resembles it should be chosen. If corn be grown on such soil the lower leaves will cure down before cutting time, giving evidence of moderately early maturity. This is one of the safe criteria by which to be guided in choosing soil for this variety.

" Mention was not made in the above description of the color of the soil. The desirability of a surface soil of dark brown, the color being due to the presence of decaying organic matter, is unquestionable, and is generally recognized; and if the soil be not that color the successful orchardist will so make it by the incorporation of organic matter by means of leguminous crops or otherwise. It is often cheaper to buy soil with a good organic content, or humus supply, than it is to be compelled to put it there after purchase before good crops can be secured. Hence, this is purely an economic feature. The warning should be given, however, that soil should not be purchased or planted to apples of any variety merely because it is dark colored and rich in humus. The soil should be selected because of its textural and structural adaptation, regardless of the organic content; then if such soils happen to be well supplied with organic matter, so much the better; if not, it may be supplied.

" To modify, however, by the addition of humus, the physical condition of a sand until it resembles a sandy loam as far down as tree roots ordinarily extend is unquestionably an expensive process, and as orchards are grown for profit, the soils on which they are to be planted should be so selected for the different varieties as to furnish the most favorable condition possible before going to the additional expense of trying to change their character artificially.

" While soils so deficient in humus as to be leachy in the case of

sands, but stiff, intractable and clayey in the case of clays, clay loams and
loams, should have their humus content increased until these unfavorable
conditions for crop growth of any kind be overcome so far as possible,
it is not possible by the addition of humus so to change the physical
characteristics of a given soil that its inherent physical character be
negligiblē, so far as its adaptation to crops or to different varieties of the
same crop is concerned. The agricultural practice of the eastern part ot
the United States is replete with instances of special soil-crop-variety
adaptation.

"**Soils for the Greening.**—As the best prices for Rhode Island Greenings are usually obtained in New York City, the general aim of the
commercial grower will be to meet the preferences of that market. The
demand there for a ' green ' Greening has usually been stronger than for
one carrying a high blush, and while individual buyers may be found, it
is said, who do not discriminate against the latter, most of them do so to
the extent of 25 cents a barrel in favor of the ' green ' Greening. Of even
more importance sometimes is the fact that a ' green ' Greening will move
on a slow market when a blush Greening fails to do so. There is also, in
some markets, objection to the blush Greening, from the fact that the consumer is rarely able to distinguish it from Monmouth Pippin—a red-
cheeked green apple, which is inferior to the Rhode Island Greening and
does not serve at all well the purpose for which the latter is bought.

"To grow a ' green ' Rhode Island Greening to conform to the trade
preferring it, a surface soil of heavy, silty loam or light, silty clay loam,
underlain by silty clay loam, should be selected. Such soil will retain
sufficient moisture to be classed as a moist soil, yet it is not so heavy
as to be ill drained, if surface drainage is adequate. The soil should be
moderately rich in organic matter, markedly more so than for the Baldwin.
In contrast to the Baldwin soil in the growth of corn, it should keep the
lower leaves of the plant green until harvesting time, or at least until late
in the season. Such soil conditions maintain a long seasonal growth under
uniform conditions of moisture. It is thus seen that the soils adapted to
producing this type of Rhode Island Greening are distinct from the Baldwin standard. In fact, these two varieties, considered as standards,
differ so markedly in soil requirements that the soil adaptations of other
varieties may well be compared with them.

"If a Greening with high blush is desired, however, to meet other
market conditions, a soil somewhat warmer than that described should be
selected, a deep, light, mellow loam or productive fine sandy loam being
favorable. To secure a ' finish ' of this character soils approaching more
nearly to the Baldwin standard are best adapted.

"The Rhode Island Greening is more restricted in area than the
Baldwin, not adapting itself to climatic conditions as far south as the
Baldwin, even though suitable soils occur there. In fact, its southern

boundary may be roughly estimated as one-fourth degree north of the forty-first parallel. South of that it becomes a fall apple and keeps very poorly.

"Hubbardston Soils.—For the Hubbardston a rich, fine, sandy loam to a depth of at least a foot is preferable, and the subsoil may well be of the same texture. This variety does remarkably well on a soil of this kind in the Connecticut Valley of Massachusetts, which has been fertilized highly enough for tobacco, onions, or garden crops. The fruit is good size, well colored, and has good keeping qualities. Baldwin grown alongside is poorly colored and inferior in both flavor and keeping quality. This is undoubtedly due to the high humus content and richness of the soil, as the same soil in much poorer condition brings a better Baldwin. A subsoil containing enough clay to make the fine sandy material somewhat coherent, or sticky, is not objectionable, but there should never be enough clay present to render the subsoil heavy. If the soil is too heavy or too clayey, the fruit is liable to be deficient in both color and flavor. Compared with the Baldwin soil requirements, the heaviest soils desirable for the Hubbardston lap over a little upon the highest soils desirable for the Baldwin, while at the other extreme the Hubbardston will utilize to advantage a more sandy soil than most other varieties of the New England-New York region. This does not mean that the variety will succeed on poor, light sands, for on such soils the apple will not attain sufficient size to be of value, nor is the tree vigorous; but the soil should always be very mellow.

"Soils for Northern Spy.—The Northern Spy is one of the most exacting varieties in regard to soil requirements. To obtain good quality of fruit, i.e., fine texture, juiciness, and high flavor, the soil must be moderately heavy; and for the first two qualities alone the lighter of the 'green' Rhode Island Greening soils will be desirable. The fact that the Northern Spy is a red apple, however, makes it imperative that the color be well developed and the skin free from the greasy tendency. This necessitates a fine adjustment of soil conditions, for the heaviest of the soils adapted to the 'green' Rhode Island Greening produce Northern Spies with greasy skins and usually of inferior color. The habit of tree growth of this variety, moreover, requires careful attention. Its tendency to grow upright seems to be accentuated by too clayey soils, if well enriched, and such soils tend to promote growth faster than the tree is able to mature well. On the other hand, sandy soils, where producing good color and clear skins, fail to bring fruit satisfactory in quality with respect to texture and flavor, especially if the fruit be held for very long. The commercial keeping quality, too, is inferior to that of the Spy grown on heavier soils in the same district. Hence the soil requirements of this variety are decidedly exacting, and are best supplied apparently by a medium loam underlain by a heavy loam or light clay loam—that is, a soil as heavy as can be selected without incurring the danger of inferior drainage, for a poorly drained soil should in no case be used. It is surely best not to plant Northern Spy on a soil lighter than a very heavy, fine, sandy loam, underlain by a light clay loam, or possibly a heavy loam. Good air drainage is also very essential with this variety.

"Soils for Wagener.—The Wagener is weak in growth, and hence a soil that is deep, strong, mellow, and loamy should be selected. Stiff sub-soils are especially objectionable with this variety, and thin soils, also light sandy soils, should be avoided. The Wagener thus fits in nicely with Northern Spy in soil requirements, and its habit of early bearing makes an effective offset in this respect to the tardiness of the Northern Spy. In Massachusetts, in parts of Connecticut and New York, and in north-eastern Pennsylvania, Wagener is one of the most profitable sorts for filler purposes.

"McIntosh Soils.—The McIntosh is a variety of high quality that is now very popular in the northeastern States. Trees of sufficient age for safe comparisons are rarely available, however, over any considerable range of soil conditions, hence no positive statement is made concerning the soil preferences of this variety. The indications are, nevertheless, that the heavier of the Baldwin soils as described are desirable for the McIntosh.

"Tompkins King Soils.—The Tompkins King is fully as exacting in soil adaptation as Northern Spy. The tree with straggling tendency of growth does not develop satisfactorily on sandy soils, but succeeds best on a moist, yet well drained soil, i.e., the lightest of the 'green' Rhode Island Greening soils—a soil capable of maintaining such a supply of moisture that the tree receives no check at the approach of drouth. But the fruit grown on soils so heavy lacks clearness of skin, and the appearance is marred by the greenish look extending far up the sides from the blossom end and by the lack of well-developed color which makes this fruit, at its best, very attractive. Hence the problem is to balance these two opposite tendencies as well as possible, and soil of the following description seems best adapted to this: Light, mellow loam, the sand content thereof being medium rather than fine, thus constituting an open-textured loam rather than a fine loam. The subsoil should be of the same texture or only slightly heavier, in no case being heavier than a very light, plastic clay loam. The soil must be brought to a productive condition. Subsoils inclining toward stiffness in texture should be carefully avoided.

"Fall Pippin.—Soils adapted to the Fall Pippin are somewhat wider in range than those described for Northern Spy and Tompkins King. In fact, this variety may be very successfully grown on the soils described for the Tompkins King and Northern Spy. It is preferable, however, that the surface soil be a fine loam rather than the open-textured loam described for the Tompkins King.

"Grimes Golden Soils.—The Grimes Golden is not well adapted, it is believed, to New England and most of New York, and it is only mentioned here to show its soil relationship to other varieties. It is so similar in soil adaptation to the 'green' Rhode Island Greening that a separate description of the soils best for this variety is not given. The Grimes has been so profitable in some districts of western Maryland, Virginia, southeastern Pennsylvania, and Ohio under certain conditions of soil and climate, however, that its desirability for general planting has been widely heralded; and as a result this variety is now being planted in some sections with too little discrimination with reference to both soil and climate. The best general guide is to plant Grimes in the eastern States, where the Rhode Island Greening tends to become a fall apple. The Rhode Island Greening soil located far enough south for that variety to be undesirable for extensive planting is well adapted to, and may well be utilized for the Grimes. It should never be planted on a light or thin soil, neither on a stiff soil. The tree maintains its best growth on a well-drained, productive, moist soil, and under such conditions is a very desirable variety in its region.

"**Rome Beauty Soils.**—The Rome Beauty bears the same relation to the Grimes Golden in soil requirements as Baldwin does to the 'green' Rhode Island Greening in their respective regions. There is, however, something of an overlapping of regions. That is, the Baldwin succeeds further south than the Rhode Island Greening, and the Rome Beauty extends as far north as the Grimes; but this intraregional overlapping of the Rome Beauty and the Baldwin is largely a matter of dove-tailing, due to variations in elevation. Thus, in southern Pennsylvania, as the Baldwin in its southerly extension seeks higher elevations to offset the climatic change, so does the Rome Beauty in its northern extension seek the same soil at a lower elevation for the same reason. The Baldwin tends to become a fall variety with increasing distance south, and where this tendency is sufficiently pronounced to lessen materially its desirability it may well be replaced by the Rome Beauty, which is adapted to the same kind of soil. The Rome Beauty is grown with fairly good success in the lower Hudson Valley and at low elevations in Western New York, but there is some question whether it will become a leading commercial sort in either region.

"**Gravenstein Soils.**—The Gravenstein has given growers much trouble, but its general excellence, the high price the fruit brings, and the strong demand for it in some markets make it a tempting sort to plant. Its susceptibility to winter injury, however, is often a serious matter. There is good evidence to show that the Gravenstein should not be forced in growth, at least until it is fifteen years old or older. On rich, moist ground or with heavy fertilization with nitrogenous manures, its growth is rarely matured early enough in the season to avoid more or less winter injury. It continues to grow until freezing weather, and thus is very susceptible to injury. On a medium soil, neither too rich nor too moist, its growth may better be held in control, early annual maturity may be forced, and the color of the fruit is satisfactory. The subsoil should never be so clayey as to prevent ready downward percolation of any excess of free soil water. Annual applications of the mineral fertilizers, such as basic slag and potash, seem desirable on such soils, and a moderate amount of humus should be furnished, but nitrogenous fertilizers should be used sparingly. Fruit of good color is especially desirable with this variety, the color adding materially to the selling price. This has led to its being planted on thin or light, sandy soils in some cases, but on such land the Gravenstein is, on the whole, unsatisfactory. This is a variety for the specialist, and for such it is a very profitable sort when grown near a market—especially if within driving distance.

" **Roxbury Russet Soils.**—The Roxbury Russet is now seldom planted, but there are some commercial orchards of it in New England and New York, and many old orchards contain a few trees. The Roxbury Russet is a gross feeder, utilizing to advantage heavier applications of stable manure than almost any other variety. A deep, rich, loamy soil, with the upper subsoil of at least medium porosity, such as a fine, sandy loam or a gravelly, sandy loam, seems to be essential, though a heavier subsoil at a depth of four to six feet is not objectionable. It thrives on a much richer soil than the Baldwin, which does not color well on the best Russet soils. The 'green' Rhode Island Greening soil, on the other hand, is somewhat too clayey for the Roxbury Russet. Grown on the soil conditions described, the Roxbury tree is prolific, the fruit attains large size and good quality, its keeping characteristics are excellent and it brings a good price, especially for export trade.

" **A study of the cropping systems** practised in this country indicates that many of our important crops have reached their highest development on certain kinds of soil, and in the light of this experience it seems inevitable to conclude that soils may be selected for different crops in accordance with their relative adaptedness to the growth of such crops. In fact, there is nothing new or startling in this statement. It is simply summing up a long line of experience in the best farm practice of the country. It is only the best farm practice, the most perfect soil adaptation and the most effective soil crop management that can long survive, because no other kinds pay as well. We have been forced by competition to recognize soil adaptedness to different crops. It is a matter of economic efficiency.

" Attention has been called to the further fact that within the climatic zone favorable to certain varieties of some crops the best results have been obtained on certain definite soil conditions, and this is especially well illustrated by different varieties of apples. Little more than a beginning has been made in this line of work, and it will take time to solve the various problems relating to it, but it is already one of the promising fields for further investigation."

QUESTIONS

1. Give the main points to be considered in choosing an orchard site.
2. Give five characteristics of the surface soil.
3. What are the best subsoils for orchards?
4. Why is surface drainage needed?
5. Discuss the danger in having too much slope.
6. What are the advantages of having atmospheric drainage?
7. What are considered the best aspects or slopes?
8. What are the advantages of windbreaks for orchards?
9. What kinds of windbreaks are best for orchards?
10. Discuss the location of windbreaks.
11. What are some soil conditions that are unfavorable for apples?
12. What soils are best for Baldwin apples?
13. Discuss soils for Greenings.
14. Discuss Hubbardston soils.
15. What soils are best for Northern Spy apples?
16. What are the best soils for Tompkins King?
17. On what soils does Grimes Golden do best?
18. What are the special soil requirements of Rome Beauty?
19. On what soils does the Gravenstein succeed best?
20. Discuss soils best suited to the Roxbury Russet.

CHAPTER III
SELECTING VARIETIES AND BUYING NURSERY STOCK

HAVING selected the orchard site with due regard (so far as circumstances will allow) for the principles laid down in the preceding chapter, the next matter for consideration is what varieties shall be selected and where the stock shall be purchased. In fact, the orchardist has probably considered both of these questions, but especially the former, long before he decided on the site for his orchard, perhaps even before he bought the farm.

Let us first attack the difficult question of varieties. A common and a very convenient way of eluding this question when asked for advice is to say that " it is a personal matter." To a certain extent it is, but to a much greater extent there are certain fairly definite considerations that apply to every case. The writer favors the use of score cards, one of which has already been submitted. He has therefore attempted to reduce the principal desirable qualities of a market apple to this basis and to attach certain definite values to each quality. There are two scores, in fact; one for the general or wholesale market and the other for the special or retail market. In the latter it is supposed that the grower comes in direct or nearly direct contact with the consumer, while in the former he sells to a buyer at the orchard or to a commission man.

Score Card for a Commericial Variety of Apple

		General Market	Special Market
TREE	40		35
1. Heavy bearer		20	15
2. Early bearer		10	10
3. Health and vigor		10	10
FRUIT	60		65
4. Fair size		10	10
5. Good color		20	15
6. Good quality		12	25
7. Keeps well		10	10
8. Ships well		8	5
Totals	100	100	100	100

24

1. **Heavy Bearer.**—This might seem to need no discussion. If one does not get the fruit there is little point in having the orchard. And yet there is no question that it is a point frequently overlooked by men who plant orchards. The estimate of the variety is too often made from the fruit alone. If the fruit is handsome and of good quality (or frequently if it is merely handsome), it is assumed to be a good variety to grow. Usually this type of mistake is an individual matter but it frequently becomes almost a community matter. For example, about 1897 the Golden Russet apple had been bringing very high prices in the English markets and many orchard owners in the Annapolis Valley, Nova Scotia (where apples are grown principally for the English markets), hearing of the fine prices received per barrel by their neighbors, grafted over a large number of trees to this variety. It was only when the grafts came into bearing that they realized there was an important difference between the income per barrel and per tree. The emphasis on prolific bearing is made slightly more emphatic in the case of apples grown for the general markets than for those grown for the special markets, because the margin of profit is greater where one has a special market and his customers will pay a larger premium for good quality, so that he can afford to grow slightly less prolific varieties provided they are exceptionally good. A man might, for example, grow the Mother apple, which is rather a shy bearer, for a special market, but would never think of doing so for the general market.

2. **Early Bearer.**—This has been given equal importance in both score cards because it seemed probable that early returns would be as desirable to one type of grower as the other. And yet there may be varieties which one would be justified in waiting for in the special orchard because of their extra quality, when he would not be in the general orchard. The Spy, for example, is proverbially slow in coming into bearing, but if one has a special market that will pay him $10 a barrel for them he would be justified in setting them out, but he would not be if he had to sell them in a general market for $2 or $3 a barrel. In any case early bearing is a very desirable quality and deserves emphasis. Orcharding is a sufficiently long-time invest-

ment at best to be rather discouraging, and should not be made more so by deferred crops. It is certainly a point worth considering, whether one is to get a crop in five or six years as may happen with Oldenburg or Wagener, or must wait ten or even fifteen years, as frequently happens with the Northern Spy (Fig. 6).

3. **Health and Vigor.**—Diseases are among the most serious handicaps of the orchard. And there is frequently a very

Fig. 6.—Northern Spy apple. One of the finest varieties and, where it will grow well, profitable sort. Its principal failing is that it is exceptionally slow coming into bearing.

marked difference in the susceptibility of different varieties to different diseases. If one is in a section where apple scab is especially troublesome, then it might be better to rule out Rhode Island Greening and McIntosh altogether, because they are notoriously affected by that disease. But if fire blight is the special enemy, then McIntosh would be one of the best sorts to set, since it seems to be particularly resistant to the blight. In any case, whether one decides to set the variety under discussion or not, it is very desirable that he should know its weaknesses and give them due consideration. And a variety is certainly distinctly more valuable the more free it is from all of these troubles. One would discount for susceptibility to all diseases such as scab, blight, and canker; and for being a poor grower, the Wagener apple; or for being specially liable to overgrowing, and consequent winter-killing, as is the case with the Tompkins King and the Gravenstein apples.

4. **Fair Size of Fruit.**—It was quite a question whether this should not receive more weight in the general market than in the special, for one certainly might grow the Pomme Grise or the Lady Apple for a special market, while he would not as a rule think of growing either for the general market. But on the other hand one usually sees apples in the fruit stores (and high class stores at that) selling at prices which range directly as the size of the fruit.

If any one disagrees with the values given this point in the score card he has the writer's permission to change them, provided he can decide where the extra value taken from " size " in the special market shall be placed.

5. **Good Color** is practically synonymous with " red color." Whatever we may say about it, however strongly we may condemn people for " eating with their eyes," there is not the slightest question that they do prefer a bright red apple, and they probably always will; that is, the general public will. And since the man who grows fruit is bound sooner or later, and to a greater or less degree, to be dependent on the general public for his market, on people whose tastes have never been educated up to the high standard that they should be, it is worth while to give color due weight. Even for the special market it is easier to sell a beautiful red apple. But where one is coming into direct, personal contact with his customers, as he does in the special market, he can push an apple of fine quality, like a Palmer Greening, even though it is not red. And the more confidence his customers have in his opinion, and the finer the quality of his variety is, the more he can afford to disregard red color. But in the general market it is far different. Only the

oldest standbys, like Rhode Island Greening, have any place in that market, unless they are red. Of course there is also a difference in the attractiveness of yellow varieties, and this ought to be given due weight. One is a fine, waxy color, such as a Grimes Golden or an Ortley, while another is dull and uninteresting, as a Mann.

6. Good Quality.—This is a point which the writer likes to give special emphasis. It is astonishing what an influence quality has in the demand for apples, or any other fruit, for

that matter. Give a man a really fine apple and he wants some more at once, and incidentally he is not so particular just what he pays for it. But give him one that is indifferent or poor in quality, and he does not care just how long he has to wait for the next.

One winter the writer began on some Baldwin apples, some particularly fine Baldwin apples grown in western Massachusetts.

Fig. 7.—A Baldwin apple. Probably more people know and like the Baldwin than any other variety.

It was the custom each evening to bring up a plate of them for the family circle. It usually required two apples in his own particular case to satisfy the " demand." Later in the season, after these Baldwins were used up some rather indifferent apples of various varieties were brought forward. They were good sound apples, and well preserved, of such sorts as Rome Beauty and locally grown Stayman Winesap, but they were not of particularly high quality. It was certainly astonishing to see what a change took place in the attitude of the family toward the evening apple feast. The custom was still kept up and with fair regularity, but nobody felt very badly if it happened to be omitted, and it was nothing uncommon to have a part of an apple (and a good big part sometimes) left on a plate—something which never happened with the Baldwins (Fig. 7). Now this is exactly what will take place in practically any household under similar circumstances. Multiply this case by twenty million to learn the influence of quality on the consumption of apples in the United States. Probably not all households would be quite as particular about quality, but some would be more so. Given choice fruit, and a family will easily use ten barrels in a year. Furnish them with Ben Davis and they can get along with one barrel and not feel the loss, at least not the reduction. There are various and diverse reasons given for growing the varieties of low quality, such as the Ben Davis apple. " It is a good tree," " it bears large crops," " it has fine color and most people go by the eye anyhow," and lastly and worst of all, " it really isn't so bad in quality and a slight lowering of the quality doesn't make much difference in consumption." Now the writer wants to hasten to say that he appreciates fully the importance of good tree characteristics. But we must have quality also if we are going to increase the consumption of fruit. Nothing, in the writer's opinion, would so safeguard us against that day, so freely prophesied, when fruit is to become a drug in the market, as to grow nothing but varieties of reasonably high quality.

7. **Fruit that Keeps Well.**—This point is of far less importance since methods of storage have been so much improved. One can afford to grow the poorer keeping varieties because they can be forced to keep in the refrigerator storage. There is certainly not the importance to very late keeping that used to attach to such varieties as Roxbury Russet and Northern Spy, which would hold on till other varieties were out of the way and would then command fine prices. On the other hand, good keeping is still a very important characteristic, because it assists the storage plant in preserving the fruit in good condition. When the fruit is removed from storage the good keeper will " stand up " long after the poor keeper has gone to pieces. Moreover, one variety may hold its color and attractiveness much longer than another. The Gravenstein apple, for example, will fade

and change to a dull, unattractive red rather quickly, while the
McIntosh will hold its bright, handsome color almost indefinitely.

8. Ships Well.—This is imperative in the general market at
present, but is less important in the special market because we
wrap apples for that market and put them in smaller packages
and do various other things to make them carry better.   The
relative importance of this point is also likely to decline in both
general and special markets as we still further improve on our
methods of handling and transporting our fruit.   When ex-
pressmen are no longer allowed to handle boxes of apples as
they would pig iron it will not be so important that the fruit
should " stand up well."

So much for the qualities of varieties as shown in the score
card.

Number of Varieties.— Another question of great importance is how many varieties to set. The usual recommendation
on this point is not to set many, to keep the number down to
two or three, or four at the outside. In general, this is probably good advice. There is no question but that most men who
set out orchards of any kind find, when the trees come into
bearing, that they have some varieties that they wish they
had not planted. That is almost inevitable if one branches out
at all. Usually the more enthusiastic and inexperienced a man
is the more varieties he will set. Enthusiasm plays a very
important part in this choice of varieties. A cold and calculat-
ing attitude is probably the proper one to take. Then it is usually
possible to keep the number down where it belongs. But as soon
as most men begin to get really interested, they find one variety
after another that they think they must try, until the list soon
reaches undue proportions. One grower confessed to the writer
privately that his first order of apple trees contained ninety-
three varieties; and that he would have bought more but that
was all the nurseryman carried! A fatal mistake so far as
profit is concerned and yet one for which the writer confesses
a great deal of lenience.

The proper way to do is to separate absolutely the commercial
and the experimental ventures: Put in the former only those

varieties which have proved their right to be considered money-makers, and set in the latter a tree, or a graft even, of everything that seems interesting and promising. Even this latter would be sternly repressed by some authorities. But if one is to get the fun out of the fruit business that he ought, it is certainly allowable to have an experimental corner.

Type of Market Influences Number.—In the commercial orchard the question of number of varieties hinges very largely on the type of market to which the owner wishes to cater. If he is growing fruit, especially apples, for the general or wholesale market then he wants relatively few sorts. With apples he might even restrict his plantings to two or three varieties. Such a grower expects to sell either through a commission man or to a buyer in the orchard, and in either case he is much more likely to make a satisfactory sale if he has one hundred barrels of one variety than if he has only ten barrels each of ten sorts.

If he has a good special or retail market then it seems entirely legitimate to set as many as ten or a dozen varieties. In the case of apples, for example, he wants a succession of varieties from the very earliest to the very latest. He does not want to work up a trade on his Yellow Transparents and Williams but lose it when Gravenstein and McIntosh are in season and have to work it up again for his Baldwins. More than that, it is a good plan to have two or even three varieties available at any one time so as to give customers a choice of several sorts. One person may prefer Suttons while another one wants Kings and a third is satisfied only with Palmer Greenings. This is a doctrine which it is easy to carry too far, but, if kept within bounds, it is a rational business policy.

Self-sterile Varieties.—A point which should not be over-looked in any orchard is the fact that many varieties are more or less self-sterile, as it is called. That is, they will not bear fruit unless the blossoms are " fertilized " with pollen from some other variety. There are various reasons for this failure to produce fruit when planted alone. Sometimes it is due to defective stamens which do not produce normal pollen; in other cases the stamens do not mature their pollen when the pistils in the same blossoms are in receptive condition; while in still others, though everything appears to be normal, the pollen is impotent and will not fertilize its own pistils. A great many different factors may influence this matter of self-sterility, such as locality, weather, vigor of the tree and other influences; so no one can make hard and fast lists of self-sterile and self-fertile varieties.

Whatever the cause of self-sterility, it necessitates the mixing of varieties in the orchard. Even those varieties which are not strictly self-sterile, which may even bear good crops when planted alone, will frequently bear much better crops if there are several other sorts planted with them. This is why the family orchard usually bears abundantly while solid blocks of one sort, even a self-fertile sort, may not do so well. Even the man who is growing for the general market will do well to set at least two and preferably three varieties.

Varieties Suited to the Section.—Another point of the utmost importance is to stick to those varieties which are known to do well in the section, at least for the commercial plantings. Important as this is, it is constantly overlooked by orchardists, particularly by those who are new at the business. Just at the present time the apple business of the East gives an exceptionally good illustration of this point. There is much interest in growing apples all through the northeastern United States. Men have heard of the money that the western apple growers are making and they want to do likewise. They can not go into any city or town without seeing quantities of the fine western apples on sale. Being interested in varieties they naturally study those on sale and they say at once—'' Here, *these* are the varieties I want to grow! I do not want to plant Baldwins and Rhode Island Greenings as my neighbors do, but I want to grow Ortleys and Staymen Winesaps and King David and Delicious.'' Especially Delicious! There is something in the very name that infatuates the novice. He thinks it must be as good as it sounds and he wants to grow some at once, without reflecting that it is a new variety at best, and has never been tested in the East at all, and we can not tell for ten years to come whether or not it is a legitimate commercial variety for the section. These new sorts may have a place in the experimental end of the orchard just alluded to, but they certainly do not have a place in the commercial orchard and many of them probably never will. And the western and southern varieties ought not to be grown in the North, neither ought the northern varieties to be grown in the South.

This question of what varieties of apples are adapted to each section has been carefully studied by Dr. J. K. Shaw, of the Massachusetts Experiment Station, who has reached very interesting conclusions on the subject that are quoted here. After discussing the influence of soil, culture and climate on the apples, Dr. Shaw says:

" It is evident from the foregoing discussion that the development of the highest perfection in any given variety is closely related to most favorable mean summer temperatures. In Table I is given a list of varieties, with an estimate of the optimum temperature for each sort, and in some cases of their possible range and hardiness with respect to the cold of winter. The list of varieties includes all those that are given the double star, indicating highly successful varieties, in the list of the American Pomological Society, with a number of additions of varieties that, for various reasons, seemed worthy of consideration. Inasmuch as we consider keeping quality of considerable account with most sorts, the policy has been to prescribe about as low a temperature as will suffice to thoroughly mature a variety, leaving a margin of about 2° for seasonal fluctuations; that is, we believe that any variety may be matured when the summer mean is 2° lower than the one given. This applies more particularly to the fall and winter varieties.

" We believe, on the other hand, that any increase in the summer mean for any variety, unless it be the earliest ones, will be a disadvantage, though a very slight one, if the rise is not more than 1° or 2°. Up to a certain degree the over-maturity of the fruit in a too warm climate may be overcome if the grower will pick at the time of full maturity and put the fruit at once in cold storage. If the heat is too great, however, even with this method they will be inferior in flavor and color, and, in very extreme cases, in size. We believe that a departure of more than 2° in either direction from the temperatures given will be a noticeable disadvantage with any of the winter varieties. This remark will apply less to the fall sorts and still less to the summer varieties; or, to put it in other words, the earlier the variety the greater may be its range of temperature without marked deterioration of the fruit.

" There are doubtless errors in the case of some varieties, concerning which we have limited information. It is hoped that these may, in time, be corrected, as we are able to learn more concerning the behavior of these varieties under different conditions.

" In Table II these same varieties are grouped under their optimum temperatures for convenience in reference.

" In Table I there is also given for some varieties the range of temperature which they can stand without serious deterioration. This is, as already stated, closely connected with the season of the variety, being wide with early sorts and relatively narrow with most winter sorts. Just how much difference there is between the ranges of varieties of the same season is difficult to say. It is complicated with a variety of related questions.

" In the case of a few of the varieties given in Table I an attempt is made to give their hardiness with respect to the winter cold. Inasmuch as the ability of the tree to withstand cold depends on a variety of factors other than the temperature, it is of no use to attempt to state this in degrees. The designation Ex. H. is used for the varieties equal in hardiness to those classified as of the first degree of hardiness (by the Minnesota Horticultural Society); and the designation H., M. and T. for various degrees of hardiness below these two classes. Many of the more southern sorts are not grown far enough north on account of a lack of summer heat to test their winter hardiness in a satisfactory manner. Therefore it is impossible to make any statements regarding them, nor would there be any practical value in such statements were they possible."

TABLE I.—*Mean Summer Temperatures.*
(Dr. J. K. Shaw)

	Optimum Temperature (Degrees)	Range	Hardiness		Optimum Temperature (Degrees)	Range	Hardiness
Akin.........	52			Bismarck....	53		
Alexander...	54	.....	H.	Black Gilli-			
Arctic.......	53	.....	H.	flower.....	55		
Arkansas....	65			Blenheim....	55		
Arkansas				Blue Pear-			
Black.....	63			main......	54	.....	H.
Babbit......	57			Boiken......	57		
Bailey Sweet	58			Bonum......	65		
Baldwin.....	56	N.	M.	Borovinka...	53		
Baxter	53	.....	H.	Bough......	57		
Beach.......	65			Buckingham.	66		
Ben Davis...	64	M.	H.	Buncombe...	66		
Benoni......	59			Cabashea....	58		
Bethel	53	.....	.H.	Cannon Pear-			
Bietigheimer.	53			main......	65		

*The average of the mean monthly temperatures for March to September inclusive.

TABLE I.—*Mean Summer Temperatures—Continued.*

	Optimum Temperature (Degrees)	Range	Hardiness		Optimum Temperature (Degrees)	Range	Hardiness
Charlamoff	53	....	Ex. H.	Horse	66		
Chenango	57			Hubbardston	57		
Collins	65			Huntsman	62	N.	N.
Cooper Market	60			Hyde King	60		
Cox Orange	35			Ingraham	62		
Delicious	59			Jefferis	57		
Dominie	60			Jewett	54		
Dudley	53			Jonathan	59	N.	N.
Early Harvest	56	V. W.		July	59		
Early Joe	56			Kent Beauty	58		
Early Pennock	56			Keswick	58		
Early Strawberry	58			King David	59		
English Russet	56			Kinnaird	59		
Esopus	59	N.		Lady	58		
Ewalt	58			Lady Sweet	57		
Fallawater	60			Lankford	61		
Fall Harvey	57			Lawver	64		
Fall Orange	57			Limbertwig	66		
Fall Pippin	58			Longfield	57		
Fameuse	54	M.	H.	Lowell	58		
Fanny	63			Lowland Raspberry	58		
Flushing Spitzenburg	58			Maiden Blush	61	M.	V. H.
Foundling	54		H.	Malinda	54	N.	H.
Gano	64	M.		Mann	55	M.	
Gideon	54	....	H.	McAfee	60	....	H.
Golden Russet	56			McIntosh	56	W.	H.
Golden Sweet	58			McMahon	55		
Gravenstein	55			Melon	57		
Green Sweet	58			Milden	58	....	H.
Grimes	62			Milwaukee	54	....	H.
Haas	59			Minkler	60		
Hagloe	60			Missouri Pippin	64		
Hibernal	52			Monmouth	57		
Holland Pippin	57			Mother	58		
Holland Winter	57			Newell	55		
				Newtown Spitzenburg	60		
				Northern Spy	56	M.	H.

TABLE I.—*Mean Summer Temperatures—Continued.*

	Optimum Temperature (Degrees)	Range	Hardiness		Optimum Temperature (Degrees)	Range	Hardiness
Northwestern Greening	55	.....	V. H.	Sutton	56		
Okabena....	52	.....	Ex. H.	Swarr	58		
Oldenburg..	52	V. W.	Ex. H.	Swazie.....	55	N.	
Oliver......	64			Switzer	58		
Ontario.....	56	.....	H.	Terry	67	N.	
Ortley......	61			Tetofski.....	53	V. W.	V. H.
Paragon.....	64			Titovka....	56	.....	H.
Patten......	55	Ex. H.	Ex. H.	Tolman.....	56	M.	H.
Payne.......	62			Tompkins King......	56	M.	M.
Peck Pleasant	58			Twenty Ounce.....	58	.....	M.
Peerless.....	56	V. H.	V. H.	Twenty Ounce Pippin.......	58		
Pewaukee...	53	V. H.	V. H.	Wagener....	59		
Plumb Cider	57			Walbridge...	54	.....	H.
Pomme Grise	55	N.		Washington Royal.....	56		
Porter......	57	W.		Wealthy....	56	W.	V. H.
Primate.....	57			Westfield...	56		
Pumpkin Sweet.....	57			White Astrachan......	54		
Ralls........	62			White Pearmain......	62		
Rambo......	60			White Pippin.......	61		
Red Astrachan......	54	N	H.	Williams....	57	W.	
Red Canada.	59	M.		Willow.....	64		
Red June....	58	M.		Windsor....	55	.....	H.
Rhode Island Greening..	56	M.		Winesap....	64	M.	
Ribston.....	55	N.		Winter Banana.....	58		
Rolfe.......	56	.....	H.	Wolf River..	54	M.	V. H.
Roman Stem.	61			Yates	67		
Rome Beauty	60			Yellow Bellflower.....	61	W.	
Roxbury Russet....	57	W.	H.	Yellow Newtown......	60	V. N.	
Salome......	55	.....	H.	Yellow Transparent....	53	W.	V. H.
Scott Winter.	55	.....	V. H.	York Imperial.......	62	M.	
Shiawasse...	55	.....	H.				
Shockley....	65	N.					
Smith Cider.	61						
Smokehouse.	60						
Stark.......	62	M.	H.				
Stayman Winesap...	63						
St. Lawrence	54						

TABLE II.—*Optimum Temperatures by Groups.*

(Dr. J. K. Shaw)

Fifty-two Degrees.	*Fifty-three Degrees.*	*Fifty-four Degrees.*	*Fifty-five Degrees.*
Hibernal	Arctic	Alexander	Black Gilliflower
Okabena	Baxter	Blue Pearmain	Blenheim
Oldenburg	Bethel	Fameuse	Cox Orange
	Bietigheimer	Foundling	Gravenstein
	Bismarck	Gideon	Mann
	Borovinka	Jewett	McMahon
	Charlamoff	Malinda	Newell
	Dudley	Milwaukee	Northwestern Greening
	Pewaukee	Red Astrachan	Patten
	Teofski	St. Lawrence	Pomme Grise
	Yellow Transparent	Walbridge	Ribston
		White Astrachan	Salome
		Wolf River	Scott Winter
			Shiawasse
			Swazie
			Windsor

Fifty-six Degrees.	*Fifty-seven Degrees*	*Fifty-eight Degrees*	*Fifty-nine Degrees.*
Baldwin	Dabbit	Bailey Sweet	Benoni
Early Harvest	Boiken	Cabashea	Delicious
Early Pennock	Bough	Early Joe	Esopus
English Russet	Chenango	Early Strawberry	Haas
Golden Russet	Fall Harvey	Ewalt	Jonathan
Lowland Raspberry	Fall Orange	Fall Pippin	July
McIntosh	Holland Pippin	Flushing Spitzenburg	King David
Milden	Holland Winter	Golden Sweet	Kinnaird
Northern Spy	Hubbardston	Green Sweet	Red Canada
Ontario	Jefferis	Kent Beauty	Wagener
Peerless	Lady Sweet	Keswick	
Rhode Island Greening	Longfield	Lady	
Rolfe	Melon	Lowell	
Sutton	Monmouth	Mother	
Titovka	Plumb Cider	Peck Pleasant	
Tolman	Porter	Red June	
Tompkins King	Primate	Swarr	
Washington Royal	Roxbury Russet	Switzer	
Wealthy	Williams	Twenty Ounce	
Westfield		Twenty Ounce Pippin	
		Winter Banana	

Sixty Degrees.	*Sixty-one Degrees.*	*Sixty-two Degrees.*	*Sixty-three Degrees.*
Cooper Market	Lankford	Akin	Arkansas Black
Dominie	Maiden Blush	Grimes	Fanny
Fallawater	Ortley	Huntsman	Stayman Winesap
Hagloe	Roman Stem	Ingram	
Hyde King	Smith Cider	Payne	

TABLE II.—*Optimum Temperatures by Groups—Continued.*

Sixty Degrees.	Sixty-one Degrees.	Sixty-two Degrees.	Sixty-three Degrees.
McAffee	White Pippin	Ralls	
Minkler	Yellow Bellflower	Stark	
Newton Spitzen-		White Pearmain	
burg			
Rambo		York Imperial	
Rome Beauty			
Smokehouse			
Yellow Newtown			

Sixty-four Degrees,	Sixty-five Degrees.	Sixty-six Degrees.	Sixty-seven Degrees.
Ben Davis	Arkansas	Buckingham	Terry
Gano	Beach	Buncombe	Yates
Lawver	Bonum	Horse	
Missouri Pippin	Cannon Pearmain	Limbertwig	
Oliver	Collins	Shockley	
Paragon			
Willowtwig			
Winesap			

Choose Popular Varieties.—The grower should also choose popular varieties and in particular select sorts that are suited to the market or markets to which he expects to ship his fruit. Probably more people are partial to the Baldwin than to any other one variety. Wismer's Dessert may be a better apple, but so few people know it that the orchard man can sell a thousand barrels of Baldwins to one of Wismer's Dessert. And some markets are especially partial to certain varieties while other markets will not handle them at all. Chicago, for example, wants the Yellow Bellflower and will pay fine prices for it, while Boston and New York do not want it at all (Fig. 8). There are growers in Maine who make a specialty of growing the Bellflower for Chicago and secure high prices, but if they disregarded this point and shipped to their nearest large market, Boston, they might make little or nothing.

Buying the Stock.—Having settled on the varieties, the next thing is to buy the stock. Here are some of the points to be considered under this head: (1) Southern-grown *vs.* northern-grown stock; (2) age of trees that is best; (3) size or grade that is best; (4) price to pay.

Southern-grown vs. Northern-grown Stock.—On the first point it is a very common notion, among our northern orchard men at least, that northern-grown, and especially locally grown stock is best. This seems like a very reasonable proposition, theoretically. If a nursery tree has been grown in the same or a similar climate to that of the orchard it ought to develop into a better orchard tree than a nursery tree grown elsewhere, and particularly than a tree grown in the milder climate of a more

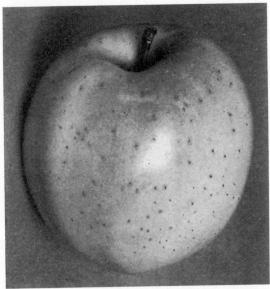

FIG. 8.—Yellow Bellflower apple. An old favorite with many people, especially popular on the Chicago market.

southern section. If that is not sound reasoning there never was any. And yet in actual practice it does not work out that way. The writer has seen nursery trees which had been grown in New York, Ontario, Nova Scotia, and Maryland set out side by side in Nova Scotia orchards and whatever difference there was in their growth was in favor of the more southern trees. He has also seen trees from New York and Maryland nurseries growing side by side in Massachusetts orchards and the southern trees giving fully as good an account of themselves as the northern trees.

There are certain advantages for really local trees, such as less freight to pay, less drying out of trees in transit, and perhaps the nurseryman feeling his responsibility more if the customer can call him up by 'phone or drop in and see him personally. But the argument of " acclimated nursery stock " has certainly been overworked. Apparently the tree has the ability during the first growing season to entirely adapt itself to the new surroundings. It has not grown long enough in the milder climate to make any permanent change in its life processes. But whatever the scientific explanation may be, the writer is thoroughly convinced of the fact that it makes little or no difference where the tree was grown so far as climatic conditions are concerned. What does make a difference is having good, thrifty stock.

Age of Trees.—On the second point, age of trees that is best, there seems to be quite a difference of opinion, the ideal of different men ranging from one to three or even more years. Very few men, however, want a tree over two years old. It is chiefly a question of one year or two year trees. Personally the writer is rather strongly in favor of the one year tree for the following reasons:

(*a*) It costs less. Out of a long list of nurserymen whose prices were compared, the difference in favor of one year trees was from nothing to $15 per hundred with an average of $6.50.

(*b*) The freight is less. This is not an important matter but is worth considering, particularly when the stock comes a long distance.

(*c*) Only thrifty trees are salable at one year; that is, a tree must be a good, growthy plant to reach a salable size in one year. This is certainly important. It is doubtful if a stunted tree ever becomes as vigorous and thrifty as one which has never had a set-back.

(*d*) The tree can be headed at any desired height while the two year tree has had its head formed by the nurseryman and it is difficult to change this height. This argument is especially important where one wants very low heads, as the writer does. If one attempts to form a very low head, say 18 inches, on a two year tree that was headed at 30 inches by the nurseryman, he does so by cutting off all the branches and leaving only 18 inches of the old trunk. He has therefore taken off all the vigorous,

FIG. 9.—Nursery tree with a poor fork. The best way to treat such a tree is to cut out all but one branch.

FIG. 10.—A nursery tree that is too heavy. Over-grown trees like this are not as good as those of medium size.

one-year-old buds and left nothing but dormant buds. The result will be that when the tree starts, instead of making a well-shaped head as a one year tree would, it throws out branches irregularly all the way up the trunk wherever there happens to be a bud that is reasonably vigorous, and one has a poor, mis-shapen tree.

(e) The younger tree will stand transplanting better than the older one. This is probably not an important point, but age seems as important with apple trees or pear trees as with cabbage plants or celery plants, where it is recognized as being of practical importance.

Older Trees.—On the other side of the question the writer has never seen but two arguments. The first and most important one is that the older trees will come into bearing more quickly. We should want considerably more evidence than is at present available before accepting this. And, second, there seems to be a feeling among the advocates of the two year tree that they are getting more for their money. When they get an orchard of two year trees set out it makes some showing, while these little, one year whips, particularly when headed at eighteen inches, certainly do not look imposing.

The Best Size or Grade of Trees.—On this point the writer is quite decidedly in favor of the medium grade or size, say a four foot, one year tree or a five to six foot two year tree. The big, overgrown tree is apt to have poorer buds on it, particularly if it is to be headed low, and it costs much more (Fig. 10). On the other hand, the trees of very small size are not thrifty and are frequently not as well shaped.

What Price Shall We Pay?—Enough to insure well-grown and well-packed stock. There is no economy in stock which is cheap in both price and quality. On the other hand, there is no use in paying the prices that are frequently asked. Of course it is assumed that any man who has ambition and sense enough to want to plant out a large orchard will have too much sense to buy his stock from a tree agent. Where one is setting only a half dozen trees he can perhaps stand the prices of these agents, but even then he can probably do better to buy direct from the firm.

The price of nursery stock, in common with the price of beefsteak, has been advancing rapidly of late years, and what constitutes a reasonable price to-day may be cheap a year from now, but at the present writing apple trees and good ones can be had at from $10 to $25 a hundred, pears $15 to $25, and peaches $8 to $15. It is very desirable, when placing an order of any considerable size, to get quotations from several different firms and to ask for sample trees. In this way one secures a definite standard of the quality or grade of stock, and from the several quotations can often save money, since one firm may be low on one part of the order while another firm is low on another part.

Order Trees Early.—Having decided on our varieties and where to buy the trees, get the order in early. This is advice often given and seldom taken, but it is good advice nevertheless. One may be sure of disappointments all along the line if he delays too long; varieties sold out, only two year trees to be had when he wants one year trees, nothing but three foot and six foot sizes left when he wants four to five foot, and so on. Get the order in by January, if it is possible to do so. Of course it is possible. It is merely a question of doing it.

QUESTIONS

1. Compare general and special markets.
2. Discuss the importance of " heavy bearing " in a variety.
3. How important is early bearing?
4. Give some idea of the importance of health and vigor.
5. How does size influence the choice of varieties for market?
6. What colors are most in demand?
7. How important do you consider " quality " in fruit?
8. Discuss the importance of good keeping quality in a variety.
9. About how many varieties should be set in a commercial apple orchard?
10. What is self-sterility? How does it influence the planting of orchards?
11. Discuss the influence of temperature on the development of the first of apple trees.
12. What is the objection to setting new varieties?
13. What are the advantages of one- and two-year-old nursery trees?
14. What is the most desirable size of nursery tree?

CHAPTER IV

ESTABLISHING THE ORCHARD

With the nursery stock ordered and the orchard site chosen, we are free to consider the question of preparing the land and setting the trees. The preparation ought to be as thorough as the circumstances will permit. In actual practice, among good growers, it will vary all the way from the man who wants to know at least a year in advance where he is going to set his trees in order that he may grow a crop on the land that will leave the soil in the best possible condition for the young orchard, to the man who plows up old pasture for his orchard, or the man who does not even insist that the land shall be fully cleared of stumps. The results will vary just as widely though not in exactly the same way. That is, the man who uses stump land may develop a fine lot of trees, provided the soil is naturally good and provided also that he takes good care of the trees. The objection to the method is the difficulty he experiences in taking good care of them, and the danger that this difficulty will discourage him. The writer very much prefers to have the land under cultivation the year before the orchard is set out, and if the crop grown on the land can be one which leaves the soil in specially good condition, such a crop as beans, or buckwheat, or even corn or potatoes, so much the better.

One Year's Preparation.—In one orchard which the writer had a hand in setting, there was a block of sixteen acres which was mostly old pasture but in one corner of which a field of about four acres had been fenced off the year previous and planted to corn. When the orchard was set this fence was removed and the whole block treated alike in preparation and set out to trees. It ought to be said also that the soil of the entire block was quite uniform, and yet when the trees began to grow those on the corn field were noticeably more thrifty than those on the old pasture and this difference was noticeable for

44

three or four years thereafter. Other similar cases might be cited, all tending to show the value of this previous treatment. Yet the writer is not prepared to say that he would defer planting for a year in order to give this preliminary treatment. In fact he knows from experience that he probably would set out the trees and attempt, by better care and more fertilizer, to bring them along satisfactorily. By using good care all along the line the trees can be made to grow very satisfactorily in most cases.

The final summing up of the case would therefore be: Get one year's previous preparation if you can, but life is too short and orchard growing too long an investment, to warrant one in delaying a whole year, except in rare cases.

Fall Plowing.—If we cannot have a year's preparatory treatment we usually can have the land plowed in the autumn, and unless the soil is in the best possible condition this is very desirable. It is particularly good on land which is a trifle heavy or in sod. But when the land has been fall plowed do not make the mistake of replowing it in the spring. It is not necessary in the first place, and if there was any trash on the land, or if it had a tough sod, there will be no end of vexatious experiences when it comes to setting the trees and cultivating the land. Let the sods and trash stay underneath where they belong and where they will decay. Of course where the field to be set has too much slope, fall plowing is out of the question on account of the washing from winter rains, but in every other case it ought to be done. And this plowing may be done at any time before the ground freezes up solid. The fact that the soil is too wet for good plowing does not matter so much in the autumn as it would in the spring, because the freezing during the winter will prevent any damage which might otherwise occur from working the soil when too wet. Heavy soil, so wet that it would be absolutely ruined for several years if plowed in that condition in the spring, may be fall plowed without injury.

Steps in Preparation.—The actual preparation of the land for setting would consist then, first, of this plowing, done either spring or fall as the circumstances will admit. This should be followed by a thorough working with the disc harrow and this probably by the spring-tooth or the smoothing harrow, whichever is available. And lastly the land should be gone over with a planker to smooth it off for laying out (Fig. 11). This can be omitted of course but it is worth the cost to secure the extra comfort in walking over the field and the greater accuracy in laying off the orchard.

There are three general methods or plans of arranging the trees in the orchard. There is first the square method in which each tree stands at the corner of a square. This is by all means

FIG. 11.—Finishing the land with a planker before beginning to lay off the orchard. This leaves the surface smooth, making it possible to stake out more easily and accurately.

the most common method and has the practical advantage that it is an easy method to lay off. Then there is the triangular or quincunx method, which is like the square with the addition that a tree is placed in the centre of each of the squares. This tree is usually a temporary one or " filler " and there are just as many of these as of the permanents. And lastly we have what is known as the hexagonal method, where each tree stands in the centre of a hexagon formed by six trees and is equally distant from each one of them. This last method has the great advantage that it best utilizes the space in the orchard. It has the practical disadvantage that it is more difficult to lay out.

Of course there are all sorts of minor variations. We may have the trees in rectangles instead of squares; and we may have the triangular method carried further by putting in fillers between the permanent trees in both directions. This last is an excellent method and the tree in the centre of the square is sometimes made a somewhat longer-lived tree than the other fillers and is then called a semi-permanent. The following diagram illustrates the method. P represents the permanents, S the semi-permanents, and F the fillers.

```
P   F   P   F   P
F   S   F   S   F
P   F   P   F   P
F   S   F   S   F
P   F   P   F   P
```

For example in using the plan we might set Baldwin for permanents, McIntosh for semi-permanents and Wealthy for fillers.

Laying off the Land.—The operation of laying off the land preparatory to setting the trees is another in which we find the greatest variation among orchard men. Some are very particular to get their rows straight and each tree in its proper place, while others are satisfied with any method that will get the trees into the ground, using a plow to lay off the rows and doing no sighting whatever. It is always surprising to see how many men are satisfied with the latter type of orchard setting. They will put more care into laying out a dog-kennel or a chicken coop that would last possibly ten years, than into laying off an orchard that will outlast their children and their children's children. The writer believes emphatically in using sufficient care to get the rows straight. It does not take a great amount of care either.

Details of a Good Method.—Various methods may be used, but the following is one which has been used with the greatest satisfaction. It is reasonably cheap, expeditious, and very accurate. The details are as follows: First, select a base line

along one side of the field to be set. This will usually be either
along the highway or a line fence (Fig. 12). Next set a stake on
this line in one corner of the field where the corner tree is to
stand. It ought to be far enough from the highway and the line
fence to allow plenty of room for turning. Twenty or twenty-
five feet is none too much. Next set a range stake at the other
side of the field and the same distance from the highway. These
two stakes establish the base line. Now begin at stake No. 1 and
set stakes along the base line and towards stake No. 2 the proper

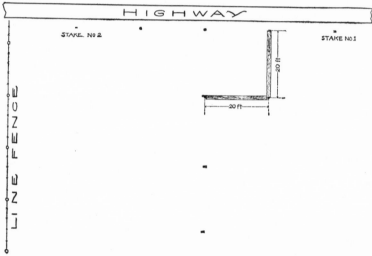

Fig. 12.—Diagram showing method of laying off a field for planting an orchard.

distance apart for the trees, say twenty feet if fillers are to be
used. Having run the line across the field, begin about the centre
of this line of stakes and lay off another line of stakes at right
angles to the first. In establishing this second line use the
carpenter's method for laying off a right angle, taking 6, 8 and
10 feet for the three sides of the right triangle. This is all the
sighting that is required by the method under discussion. The
rest of the stakes are set with two " measuring boards " which
are made as long as the desired distance between the trees. Inch
boards three inches wide will be found satisfactory for the pur-

pose. There is a notch at either end of each board. Figures 12
and 13 will serve to explain the method. The measuring boards
can be handled more easily if they are fastened together with a
small bolt.

It will surprise any one who has never seen this method used
to find how quickly and accurately the stakes can be set (Fig.
14), and it does not require high-priced labor, either. Any good
man with a little interest in his work will do it admirably. On
a farm in which the writer is interested one hundred and twenty-
five acres of orchard have been laid out by this
method and most of it was done by Polanders, many
of whom could speak no English. They were simply
" shown," and the proprietors of the orchard would be
glad to have any one who doubts the efficiency of the method
visit the place.

Planting Board.—By this method a stake is set at
every point to be occupied by a tree, and the next point
is to be sure that the tree is established in the identical
spot where the stake stood. To do this a device known as a
" planting board " is used (Fig. 15). This is simply a
board, perhaps five feet long and six inches wide, with a
notch cut in either end and one at the exact centre. This
board is placed on the ground so that the tree stake comes
in the central
notch. Then a
stake is driven
down in each of

FIG. 13.—Diagram of measuring boards. Drawn to scale.

the end notches and the board is removed and a hole dug for
the tree where the central stake stood. When it comes time to
set the tree, whether that be the same day or a week later, the
board is put back into place, the tree slipped into the central
notch, the earth shovelled in, and there the tree stands just where
it is wanted. In setting an orchard of any size it is necessary to
have several of these planting boards, and care should be taken
to see that they are all exactly alike.

Another method which the writer has used with great satisfaction and which is particularly good when the trees are a

considerable distance apart, is to begin at one corner of the field, as suggested above, and run a row of stakes along each of the four sides. This establishes the end tree in each row. Then take a gang of three men to set the rest of the stakes. One man sights in one direction, another in the other direction and the third man

Fig. 14.—Staking off the orchard by means of two measuring boards.

sets the stakes. He is " waved " into position by the two sighters as each stake is set and very soon gets it in the proper spot.

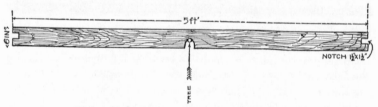

Fig. 15.—Planting board for locating tree in setting. See also Figure 19.

Heeling In.—When the trees arrive they should be heeled in at some spot convenient to the orchard site, usually on the site itself (Fig. 16). This heeling in should be done with a good deal of care, the bundles of trees being opened and the earth worked carefully in among the roots and tramped down solid.

In some cases it is worth while even to water them, especially if they are to stand here long before setting. The writer emphasizes this matter because he has so often seen trees heeled in carelessly without opening the bundles and without tramping the soil down carefully, with the result that the air passing down through the centre of the bundles would circulate freely among the roots and dry them out so as to weaken seriously, or even kill outright, a good many trees.

FIG. 16.—Heeling in nursery stock. This should be done very carefully to prevent the roots drying out.

Where trees arrive in bad condition from drying in transit, they should be taken to a brook or to a pond and soaked for a day or two, if possible having the whole tree under water. It is surprising what this will do for even the worst cases.

Another thing to guard against at the time of heeling in is damage from mice. They will frequently gain entrance to a bundle of trees, particularly if the trees are stored near the house, and girdle every tree in the bundle. Where mice are plentiful enough to be troublesome in this way, they should be guarded against by putting a pen about the spot where the trees are heeled in. A board ten or twelve inches wide will answer the purpose.

Working Out the Plan.—In actual orchard operations the entire field is usually not staked off before the digging of the

Fig. 17.—A load of nursery trees ready for the setting gang. The barrels are half full of water, which insures the trees arriving at the hole in good condition.

Fig. 18.—Gang of men setting trees. The men work in pairs and the foreman distributes the trees.

holes and setting of the trees is begun. A method which the writer has used on a fairly large orchard with entire satisfaction is the following: The setting gang consists of from six to ten men and a foreman. After the first two lines of stakes have been set (the base line and the one at right angles to it), and after some start has been made in locating the stakes with the measuring boards, which preliminary work can be done most economically by about three men, this gang goes into the field and is divided as follows: Two men continue setting stakes, the foreman and one man go after trees, and the balance of the gang begin digging holes.

The foreman and his assistant go to the spot where the trees are heeled in. They have a stone boat on which are mounted two barrels, which are half full of water, and the stone boat drawn by a single horse (Fig. 17). The trees are pulled out and the roots trimmed by taking off any broken roots and cutting back any long, straggling ones. Then the tree is put into one of the barrels. This insures the tree arriving at the hole in the best possible condition with its roots thoroughly wet. When both barrels are full, the horse is driven out to the spot where setting is to begin, and the men who are staking off and those who are digging holes, all " knock off " and go to setting (Fig. 18). The foreman distributes the trees and the men divide into pairs, one man doing the shovelling and the other setting the tree. If the subsoil is poor, it is best when the hole is dug, to put the surface soil in one pile and the subsoil in another. Then when the tree is set the surface soil may be used about the roots and thus give the tree a better soil in which to start growth. The tree should be set perhaps an inch or two deeper than it stood in the nursery, and the soil should be worked in among the roots and then very firmly tramped down (Figs. 19 and 20). This last is extremely important, as it not only keeps the soil from drying out but it brings the soil in intimate contact with the roots so that they can start growth better.

When to Plant.—The question of fall *vs.* spring planting ought to be mentioned here. There are three distinct advantages of fall planting; first, the planter is almost certain to get the varieties that he wants because he is compelled to order so early; second, the trees are ready to start growth early in the spring; and third, it gets just so much work out of the way of the " spring rush." This last is of varying importance according

Fig. 19.—Ready to set a two year apple tree. The tree is set a little deeper than it stood in the nursery.

Fig. 20.—Same tree as shown in Figure 19, set.

to the man and the farm. On many farms the autumn " rush " is fully as virulent as the spring one.

The chief objection to autumn planting is that the trees have to be dug so early, in order to insure their getting to the orchard man on time, that the nurseryman may be tempted into digging them before they are mature enough for the leaves to drop naturally. The leaves must therefore be stripped, and the stripped tree is not so good as one which loses its leaves naturally, because it is robbed of much plant food which the leaves would have supplied had they been allowed to remain on the trees. Stripping the leaves too early exposes the immature buds and uncalloused leaf scars to the weather. There is the additional objection to autumn planting that, since the roots are not well established in the soil, the tree can not withstand unfavorable winter conditions so well. Alternate freezing and thawing during variable weather is likely to make trouble, particularly if the soil is at all heavy.

The chief advantages of spring planting are that the grower gets his trees in better condition and that the danger from winter injury is avoided. The main objection to spring planting is that it is likely to be delayed until too late in the season. In the writer's experience the ideal time to set trees is just as early in the spring as the soil is in good condition to work.

Pruning after Setting.—After the tree is set it must be pruned (Fig. 21). If it is a one year whip this pruning consists merely in cutting it off or heading it at the height desired. Just what this height shall be will vary greatly with different men. The writer is very strongly in favor of a decidedly low head. The trees which he, himself, has set have been headed all the way from two feet to six inches but principally at eighteen inches. The height ought undoubtedly to vary with the variety (Fig. 22). Such very drooping varieties as the Rhode Island Greening apple, for example, ought certainly to be headed as high as two feet and might perhaps be headed higher, while with such very upright varieties as the Sutton apple and the Wickson plum there is no particular excuse for having any trunk at all.

High Heading.—As the writer has heard the matter presented, the principal arguments in favor of a high head are as follows:

1. That it makes it easier to cultivate about the trees. There is probably something in this argument but it has never seemed very strong. To begin with, the advocates of a high head exaggerate the difficulty of cultivating about a low headed tree. The branches of a high headed tree tend to come out more nearly at right angles so that they droop easily as they become heavy with the weight of a crop, while the branches of a low headed

FIG. 21.—Same tree as shown in figures 19 and 20 after pruning.

FIG. 22.—Pruning a one-year "whip." The tree is cut off at whatever height it is desired to form the head.

tree tend to take an upward slant so that they are not so much in the way as might be expected, and they do not bend so easily with their load of fruit. Then, too, the situation is very different with the modern extension implements from what it was when it was necessary for the team to get close up to the trunk of the tree. It does not make very much difference to the tree whether every weed is taken out from about the trunk or not. The feeding roots of large trees are not there to any extent, but are out some little distance from the trunk.

2. The second argument for a high head is that there is less breakage from snow. This is a sound argument and in those sections where deep snows are liable to occur and drift over the trees the heads ought to be higher.

3. The third argument for the high head is that there are less culls than with the low head, because in the latter, the lower branches are so close to the ground that they do not get enough light and air to produce fine fruit. There may be some truth in this, but it has never seemed to the writer that it was a very serious matter. The fruit on the lower branches of any tree is not so good as that from the higher branches, and there has not seemed to be a very great difference between that from low headed and that from high headed trees.

4. An argument which has been advanced in New England, and perhaps it may be used elsewhere, is that trees ought to be headed high in order to escape the deer. It

Fig. 23.—An extreme case of high heading. Most work in the orchard costs more with such trees than with low headed trees.

seems singular that such an argument should even be suggested seriously but it has been quite frequently offered where States are cursed with laws which protect the deer at the expense of the farmers. Damage from deer is a very live question with the writer, for he has seen over two thousand fruit trees, principally apple, either killed outright or so badly damaged that they had to be replaced. But deer damage is an argument for changing representatives in the Legislature and not for heading the fruit trees higher.

Low Heading.—Turning now to the arguments for the low headed tree we have the following:

1. There is less damage from winds. This would apply to mature trees where in summer the number of windfalls and in winter danger of damage from ice-storm would be reduced. It would also apply to the young trees. A tree such as is shown in Figure 23 will be much more liable to damage from winds than such a tree as is shown in Figure 24.

2. There is less danger from sun-scald. In some sections this trouble is very serious, in others it seldom occurs. In the former sections low heads ought always to be used.

3. Spraying can be done more cheaply and much more thoroughly. This latter is especially important in sections where the San José scale is abundant, but it counts with any spraying.

4. Pruning can be done more cheaply and easily.

5. It is easier and cheaper to harvest the fruit. As soon as a man has to use a ladder to do his work he adds to the expense of the operation, whatever it may be. The longer the ladder the greater the expense. With low headed peach trees all the picking can be done from the ground, and with apples, a great part of it (Fig. 24).

6. In extreme cases, like the tree shown in Figure 23, and to a less extent in less extreme cases, the fruiting of the tree is delayed when the head is raised because the oldest branches are the lowest ones and these are removed to raise the head.

Several other minor arguments are used by the enthusiastic advocates of low heads, but the foregoing are the most important and seem to justify fully the practice. The one argument of ease and cheapness of doing the work on the trees is in itself enough to settle the question.

Planting Distances.—There are several general questions which will perhaps come here as well as elsewhere. The first of these is the matter of the proper distance apart for the trees. Of course there are almost innumerable factors which influence this, the most important being the kind of trees, the individual taste of the owner, the soil and the method of pruning to be adopted.

Some varieties of apples make large trees and some never attain much size. The Spy or the Baldwin, for example, want more room than the Palmer Greening and the Wagener.

Some soils will grow large trees of a certain variety while on other soils the same variety is relatively small. The orchard shown in Figure 108, for example, is a block of Baldwins probably not far from thirty years old. They are planted at 33 feet apart and yet there is plenty of room for them. They will never make large trees.

Fig. 24.—A low headed, five-year-old, peach tree. This tree was headed at six inches.

The kind of pruning also makes a great difference. If the owner plans to give the trees free range they will need far more room than if he practises repressive pruning.

When all these points are considered the following are about the average distances recommended:

Apples .... 30 to 40 feet
Pears .... 20 to 30 feet
Peaches .... 15 to 20 feet
Plums .... 15 to 20 feet
Cherries .... 15 to 25 feet
Quinces .... 8 to 12 feet

Number per Acre.—The following table gives the number of trees per acre that can be set at the distances given. If one wishes to ascertain how many trees can be planted on an acre

Fig. 25.   Fig. 26.

Fig. 25.—An apple tree with a medium head, about thirty inches. This is a good height for many varieties, though the writer prefers a somewhat lower head.

Fig. 26.—A poor fork on a Ben Davis apple tree. Such a fork is almost certain to split down as soon as the tree begins to bear heavy crops. The two side branches should have been cut off earlier.

at other distances than those given, multiply the number of feet that the rows are apart by the distance apart of the trees in the row and then divide 43,560 by the product obtained.

8 × 8 feet—680	16 × 32 feet— 85
8 × 10 feet—544	20 × 20 feet—108
8 × 12 feet—453	20 × 30 feet— 72
10 × 10 feet—435	20 × 40 feet— 54
10 × 12 feet—363	25 × 25 feet— 69
10 × 20 feet—217	25 × 30 feet— 58
12 × 12 feet—302	25 × 40 feet— 43
12 × 20 feet—181	30 × 30 feet— 48
15 × 15 feet—193	30 × 35 feet— 41
15 × 20 feet—145	30 × 40 feet— 36
15 × 30 feet— 96	35 × 35 feet— 35
16 × 16 feet—170	35 × 40 feet— 31
16 × 20 feet—136	40 × 40 feet— 27

Orchard Fillers.—The question of the use of " fillers " in the orchard is a vexed one. A filler is a temporary tree, usually a small and early bearing one, which is planted between the permanent trees and removed (sometimes) when it begins to crowd them. Most men have very definite opinions on the filler, either condemning it altogether or favoring it with equal decision. The matter simply narrows down to this: If a man can make more money out of growing fillers in the orchard than he can out of any other crop, then they are the best crop to grow. If beans or potatoes or cabbages will bring him more money then he should grow these crops and not fillers.

The chief objection urged against the use of fillers in the orchard is that they are not cut out as soon as they should be. The owner holds onto them from year to year in order to get a revenue from them. If they have not borne much fruit he feels that he must hold onto them until they come into bearing and he " gets his money out of them." If they are bearing well then he feels that he simply cannot destroy the source of so much income. Now while the writer is strongly in favor of the filler system for his own use and believes that it ought to be possible for a man to cut the fillers out in season, yet there is no question that the method does often fail.

This filler question is in exactly the same class as the sod-mulch question. Where either one is well carried out it gives good results, but both of them tempt the owner to do what is not for the best interest of the orchard, in the one case by hauling off the hay and in the other by holding onto the fillers. As most of us yield to temptations, it is best not to put any extra ones in our own paths unless we are pretty sure that we can resist them. The man who keeps stock ought not to have a sod orchard, and the man who can not bring himself to prune a tree severely enough or to thin fruit " because it is such a waste " had better not try the filler system.

Kinds to Use as Fillers.—But for the man who can and will handle it rightly, it is a good system. If a man is going to use fillers he is most likely to be successful if he uses for the purpose

FIG. 27.—Gravenstein apple trees as permanents with cherries as "fillers." The use of fillers is advisable only when they are cut out early.

a tree which very closely resembles his permanent tree in its needs, which comes into bearing early, and which makes a small tree (Fig. 27). This means that peaches make the best fillers for peach orchards and apples for apple orchards. Many people make light of this point but others consider it a decidedly practical one. Here is an illustration of the evil effects of mixing species in setting an orchard: An apple orchard was set and peaches were used for fillers. All went well until the peaches were damaged severely one winter. Then it became desirable to help the peaches to recover and the orchard was therefore given an application of nitrate of soda, which brought them out in good condition. But the apple trees did not need this extra nitrogen. They were just coming nicely into bearing, but they at once stopped producing fruit and began to produce wood. It was years before they recovered from the extra stimulus and went to bearing again.

Now we may say that the owner was foolish; that he should have done what was best for his permanent trees and let his peach trees go. But it is human nature to try to take care of what is producing a revenue and it is certainly a weak spot in any system, whether it be orcharding or municipal politics, which requires a man to do otherwise.

Cost of the Young Orchard.—It may be well to say a word here in reference to the cost of establishing an orchard. Of course this can be only suggestive, as expenses vary greatly with different men and different sections and different years. The following figures are from the writer's actual experience in starting an orchard. They are by no means complete and leave out many factors, such as interest and taxes, which ought to be included. They may be helpful, however, and are introduced merely with that hope and with the distinct realization by the writer that they can be only suggestive.

Cost per acre of establishing and maintaining an orchard for five years.

FIRST YEAR

1. Trees—108 @ 15 cents $16.20
2. Fitting land, setting and pruning trees 6.48
3. Fertilizing 1.60
4. Cultivating 4.50
5. Cover crop—buckwheat seed and sowing 1.00
6. Clearing away trash from trees in autumn to prevent mice damage .... .50

$30.28

SECOND YEAR

1. Pruning $2.50
2. Fertilizing (same as first year except double the nitrogen) 1.75
3. Fitting the land with disc 3.60
4. Cultivation 4.50
5. Hoeing 1.00
6. Cover crop—cow horn turnips .... .75
7. Clearing away trash in autumn .... .50

$14.60

THIRD YEAR

1. Pruning $3.00
2. Fertilizing—double second year 3.50
3. Fitting the land 3.60
4. Cultivating 4.50
5. Hoeing 1.00
6. Spraying for San José scale 4.10
7. Cover crop 1.00
8. Clearing away trash .... .50

$21.20

FOURTH YEAR

Total cost only slightly more than third year.

FIFTH YEAR

1. Pruning $4.50
2. Fertilizing 5.25
3. Fitting the land 3.60
4. Cultivating 4.50
5. Hoeing 1.00
6. Spraying 5.25
7. Cover crop—crimson clover 1.20

$25.30

QUESTIONS

1. Discuss the preparation of the land for an orchard.
2. Describe three general methods of arranging the trees in an orchard.
3. Give the details of a good method of laying off an orchard.
4. What is a "planting board," and how is it helpful?
5. Describe the operation of heeling in trees.
6. Give the arguments on " fall *vs.* spring " planting.
7. Give the main arguments in favor of high heading of orchard trees.
8. What are the arguments in favor of low heading?
9. What orchards in your section would you classify as high headed? What low headed?
10. Give some idea of the best planting distances for different orchard trees.
11. Discuss the use of " fillers " in an orchard.
12. Give some idea of cost of starting a young orchard in your own section.

CHAPTER V

CROPPING THE ORCHARD

ONE of the questions which comes home very forcibly to the man who attempts to develop an orchard of any size is that of growing companion crops in the orchard while it is young. Shall this be done and if so what crops shall be used? The idea of such a crop is to help defray the cost of the orchard, and consequently it must either be a crop, such as mangels or turnips,

FIG. 28.—Late potatoes in a young peach orchard. An excellent crop when rightly managed.

which can be used profitably by the owner on the farm, or else it must be a crop such as beans or soybeans, which can be disposed of for cash. The general farmer who keeps stock has, therefore, a distinct advantage over the orchard specialist in the choice of these companion crops, because a number of the best of them are such as will work in very nicely with the plans for feeding stock or keeping dairy cows.

For several years, say four or five as a rule, it is greatly to the advantage of the young trees if the orchard is cropped, provided, of course, that the proper crops are chosen. This is especially true on general farms where there are other crops than the orchard to compete for the time of men and teams. If the potato field is in the orchard, both are cultivated together, and the trees are not only well cultivated, but receive the benefit of the fertilizer left over from the potato crop (Fig. 28). On the other hand, if the potato field is in one place and the orchard is in another, the potatoes frequently get the cultivation when labor is scarce, while the cultivation of the orchard is either deferred

FIG. 29.—Soybeans as a companion crop. This is one of the best crops for a young orchard, enriching the land and usually giving profitable returns.

to a more convenient time or omitted altogether, because the farmer knows that he will get no crop if his potatoes are not cultivated while his trees will do something even with very indifferent culture.

The ideal companion crop would have the following characteristics,. and though the ideal does not exist we can frequently come fairly close to it:

1. The crop must be profitable, either because it can be sold for cash or because it can be fed with profit to the stock on the farm (Fig. 29). This point, of course, is imperative. The list

of crops which are admissible will vary greatly with the owner's
circumstances. As already suggested the farm on which stock
is kept can profitably use a number of crops which can not be
grown on the special fruit farm. And these crops happen to be
among the most satisfactory in their relation to the orchard.
The man who is in the trucking business, or who is so situated
that he can handle truck crops, has another large selection of
crops which are almost ideal so far as the orchard is concerned,
but these crops can not usually be grown in sections far from
markets. It follows then that the orchard specialist has the
smallest number of companion crops from which to choose.

2. The crop should be one which requires cultivation. There
is absolutely no question about this unless it be in the case of
crops sown late in the season which are really cover crops rather
than companion crops. This matter of cultivation is a point
frequently overlooked by men who grow crops in their orchards,
but we are speaking of the ideal crops now. And the more
thorough this cultivation is required by the crop the better for
the orchard.

3. It ought to be a crop which does not require late stirring
of the soil, say in August or September. September work is
particularly objectionable. The philosophy of this point will be
seen on a moment's reflection, and the importance of it has been
demonstrated to the writer over and over again, though always,
he is glad to say, by other people. The young trees make their
growth early in the season and by August, and still more by
September, they are "sobering down" and thickening their
cells and beginning to get ready for winter. Now suppose one is
growing such a crop as early potatoes for example. Just at the
point where the trees want quiet the owner comes in with his
gang of men or his potato digger and gives the soil the most
thorough working it has had since the spring plowing. The result is that the trees are urged into new growth, new food is
made available for them and they go merrily forward till cold
weather comes on and checks them short. There is no time
then to prepare for the more severe weather which follows and
consequently the cambium or growing layer, between the bark

and wood, is soft and tender and no more able to resist freezing than a potato or a turnip. It is therefore killed outright or severely damaged and the next year the trees, though they may leaf out, will be found in a very bad condition. Many of them will probably die, and others might as well do so, for they will be so badly crippled as to be of little use.

4. The companion crop should be one which does not take from the soil exactly the same food elements as the trees themselves require. This is aimed especially at nursery stock, which for several reasons is a peculiarly objectionable crop, but it

Fig. 30.—Pea-beans as an orchard crop. This is another excellent crop from the standpoint of the orchard.

probably applies with more or less force to all fruit crops. Of course this is a difficulty which can be obviated to a certain extent by applying extra fertilizer, but it is far better to choose some other crop.

5. It should be an annual crop. Anyone who has ever attempted to crop an orchard with even a biennial crop like strawberries, or still worse with a perennial one like raspberries, will appreciate the importance of this point. Cross-cultivation is usually entirely prevented after the first year, the block grows more and more weedy and the trees in the block show more and more distinctly the handicap under which they are working, till

very soon one may easily pick out, at a considerable distance, the section of the orchard where the perennial crop is located by the small size of the trees and the light color of their leaves. Of course it is possible by extra effort in the way of hand labor, and by extra fertilizing with good barn manure, to overcome to a certain extent the bad effects of the crop, but these are expensive methods to use and to a very large extent they take away any profit which might accrue from the crop. Usually they are not even attempted. It is much better to use an annual crop which is cleared off the land each year and which thus allows of thorough preparation of the soil each spring.

6. Lastly, and least important, though still well worth considering, the crop should be one which makes its growth at some other time than that in which the orchard makes its most vigorous growth. This is one reason why beans, for example, are to be preferred to currants. The beans are not planted until the trees are at the height of their growth, and they do not begin to draw at all heavily on the soil moisture and plant food until the trees have come to a point where they can easily and even advantageously spare a part of both moisture and plant food. The currants, on the other hand, come along at precisely the same time as the trees and compete with them step by step for both fertility and water.

Area Reserved for Trees.—It ought to be said, before going farther, that in any scheme of cropping the orchard a certain portion of land must be reserved for the exclusive use of the trees. This will vary with different crops and with the age of the trees, but as a rule a strip six or eight feet wide along each row of trees should be reserved the first year and this should be enlarged year by year as the trees grow.

Lists of Companion Crops.—With the above requirements in mind the writer has chosen the following list of companion crops and has attempted to arrange them under three classes—good, bad and indifferent. They are also arranged in the different sections roughly in the order of their value from the standpoint of the orchard, the most objectionable ones coming last.

Good Companion Crops.—1. *Beans.*—Any variety will be satisfactory to the orchard, but especially the white pea-bean. The soybean is also admirable. There is almost no objection to these crops. They are usually profitable, are sown late, add nitrogen to the soil, and no damage arises from their use. When removed from the orchard the root systems are usually left in the soil, which adds both humus and nitrogen.

2. *Squash* is another excellent crop, coming along with a rush late in the season when the orchard ought to "sober down," never competing with the trees, and frequently giving

FIG. 31.—Squashes as an orchard crop. They are an excellent crop from the standpoint of the orchard and where the owner can handle them rightly are usually profitable.

good financial returns. It can be marketed in a wholesale way, which is not true of all crops and which is frequently a decided advantage to the orchard owner (Fig. 31).

3. *Cabbage.*—This is another decidedly satisfactory companion crop. It usually commands a fair price and can be handled in car-load lots if the orchard is of some size. It is nearly ideal so far as its effect on the trees is concerned. The only objection to it is that it requires cultivation later than the trees do, but if the strip already spoken of is reserved there is usually no trouble.

4. *Turnips and Mangels.*—These are both excellent crops from the standpoint of the orchard, but of course are not " cash " crops as a rule and must usually be restricted to the man who keeps stock. It might be possible in some cases to grow them for a neighbor who keeps stock, but generally they must be fed on the place.

5. *Late Potatoes.*—The writer would bar out early potatoes, unless a very wide strip is reserved along the tree rows, which is

Fig. 32.—Potatoes in a bearing apple orchard. They make a good orchard crop, but in this case are planted too close to the trees.

an unnecessary waste of land. But late potatoes are dug so late in the season that they do not tend to prolong the growth of the trees and they are generally a profitable and satisfactory crop. They require good cultivation and high fertilizing and it is rare that they do not show a reasonable profit (Fig. 32).

6. *Truck Crops,* such as spinach, beets, peas, and carrots, are all good crops and if handled carefully will generally give

fine results. They need good land and good cultivation, which help out the orchard trees. One difficulty with them which ought to be guarded against by the orchard owner is the fact that they usually require a good deal of barn manure and other forms of nitrogen, and it is a very easy matter to get the land too rich for the best interest of the young trees. It would probably be better not to use them year after year in the same block of orchard but to practise rotation of crops, following truck crops with squash and this with beans.

7. *Corn.*—There is some prejudice against corn, and perhaps rightly, because it is a rank feeder and is likely to get more than its share of food and moisture; also because its great height tends to shade the young trees. But if it is not grown too close to the trees and if the rows are run north and south so that the sun can get at the trees when its power is greatest, the objections will usually be overcome, and the writer knows from experience that it may work out satisfactorily. It is a crop that is usually profitable. If the farm is an orchard proposition pure and simple, the grain from corn can be fed to teams on the place and even the fodder may be used in this way in winter, if there is no winter work for the teams. Probably it would be better to restrict this crop to popcorn or to flint varieties which do not make tall stalks, and it is perhaps better not to grow corn after the third year of the orchard, though there are many exceptions to these suggestions.

8. *Buckwheat.*—This is really a combination cover crop and companion crop, but is included here because it is a reasonably satisfactory money crop to be grown in the orchard. Of course, in order to get the money out of it one has to cut the crop and remove it from the orchard, which is strictly against the rules for a cover crop. But that is something the grower has to learn to do " when necessary," if he is going to run an orchard. The difficult thing to learn is when it is necessary.

Fairly Satisfactory Crops.—9. .*Currants and Gooseberries,* if the bushes are set in rows both ways to allow for cultivation, are often quite satisfactory. The fact that they are perennial and that they make their growth each season at exactly the same time as the orchard is the chief objection to them. But they require good culture and fertilizing if they are to be profitable, which makes them acceptable to the young trees. They do not spread, which makes them at least less objectionable than some other crops.

10. *Strawberries.*—For young orchards, where there is still plenty of room, these are not bad (Fig. 33). But they tie up the land for two years at least, and with many growers much longer than that. They can not be cross-cultivated, so that the tree

Fig. 33.—Strawberries in a young peach orchard. They make a fairly good crop for very young orchards, but interfere with cross-cultivation, as they occupy the land at least two years.

rows are apt to become foul with weeds and the trees to show the lack of thorough cultivation by the second year. If the beds are held for more than one crop of berries, the damage to the trees is very markedly increased. Personally the writer would not use strawberries except during the first and second years of the orchard and even then there are many other crops to be preferred. A great point in favor of strawberries is the fact that they generally pay well. This is something that will be appreciated by the man who tries to develop a good sized orchard

11. *Asparagus* is not often used and has the serious objection that it must stand in the orchard for a number of years, yet cases are occasionally seen where it is used with very good success.

Poor Companion Crops.—12. *Raspberries and blackberries* ought practically to be debarred as orchard crops. The long period that they have to stand, the difficulty or impossibility of cross-cultivation, and the fact that they sucker so freely are the chief objections. These can be overcome by hand labor, by barn manure, and by the free use of other fertilizers. Ordinarily, however, it is the young trees that are overcome and not the difficulties.

13. *Nursery Stock.*—The growing of this crop in the orchard is seldom practised and almost always with regret so far as its effect on the orchard trees is concerned. It grows at exactly the same time as the young orchard trees, takes out the same fertilizer elements, and uses·moisture at the same time. And it usually stands two or three years. On the whole it is much better to put the nursery somewhere else.

14. *Grains* of all kinds should be strictly ruled out. They have only one redeeming feature and that is that they are annual crops. But they are not cultivated, they prevent cross-cultivation of the trees, they rob the trees of moisture, and the part of the orchard where they are grown will always show the injurious effects, at the time and frequently for several years after.

15. *Hay.*—Never use it. It is the last crop in our list and is placed there because it is regarded as "the limit." There are a few sod enthusiasts who claim to be, and probably are, successful in starting young trees in sod. But most growers, even though they resort to sod later on, start their trees under cultivation. Hay competes at every step with the young trees, robbing them of moisture and plant food when they most need them, and providing excellent conditions for injurious insects of various kinds, and when the hay is harvested the trees are liable to all sorts of accidents from the mowing machine, the rake, and the hay wagons. If you are tempted to use hay, by all means resist the temptation!

QUESTIONS

1. What are the characteristics of an ideal companion crop for the orchard?
2. How many years should such crops be used in the orchard?
3. How should the land along the tree rows be treated?

Discuss each of the following as companion crops for orchards:

4. Beans.
5. Squash.
6. Cabbage.
7. Turnips and mangels.
8. Potatoes.
9. Truck crops.
10. Corn.
11. Buckwheat.
12. Currants and gooseberries.
13. Strawberries.
14. Asparagus.
15. Raspberries and blackberries.
16. Nursery stock.
17. Grains.
18. Hay.

CHAPTER VI

ORCHARD CULTURE

Three Methods.—Having set out the orchard the next question to be decided is what type of culture it is to receive. On this point orchard men are divided into three camps: First, there are a few men like Mr. Grant Hitchings, of New York, and Mr. A. A. Marshall, of Fitchburg, Massachusetts, who practise what may be called "sod culture," that is all the grass grown in the orchard is simply cut and allowed to lie on the land as a mulch. Of course this mulch becomes thicker year by year, forming a better and better protection against the loss of moisture by evaporation and as it decays adding humus to the soil.

Second, there are the men who practise clean cultivation of the soil. By far the greatest number of really successful orchardists belong to this class. There are endless variations in the method as practised by different men, but the main features would be plowing the orchard in the spring, clean cultivation up to mid-summer, and then seeding down to a cover crop.

Lastly, there is a very large class who have their orchards in sod but who can not, by any stretch of the imagination, be said to practise sod culture. They simply have their orchards in hayfields. Perhaps it is only fair to add that there are a few men who have their orchards on relatively heavy land and who practise generous fertilizing who are quite successful in raising both hay and apples on the same land. But their conditions and their characters are so exceptional that it is dangerous to even mention them.

Methods Vary with Conditions.—There is no question whatever that the type of culture which it is best to adopt varies with conditions. Under most conditions cultivation will most emphatically give the best results (Fig. 34). And yet there are enough orchards where sod culture is practised to show that it can be made successful. And there are many cases where cultiva-

77

tion is out of the question and where sod culture must be adopted because it is the only rational method that will fit the circumstances. The great difficulty is that this method, to be most successful, requires not only peculiar soil conditions but still more a peculiar type of man, and it is rare that one finds both the man and the conditions on the same farm.

However, the question is not by any means settled, and therefore it is important to sum up the points in favor of each of these methods as advanced by their advocates.

Fig. 34.—Clean cultivation in an old renovated orchard. With most men and under most conditions cultivation will give the best results.

Sod Culture.—For sod culture the principal arguments advanced are:

1. It is not so expensive a method of caring for the soil. This is certainly correct, as the only expense is the cutting of the grass in the orchard once or twice a year (Fig. 35). But unless it can be shown that with this less expense the grower gets the same or nearly the same returns this is not a very strong argument.

2. The fruit will keep longer. This would apply to apples and pears in particular, and is probably also true. The fruit

is usually smaller than that grown under cultivation, which means a more solid flesh that naturally does not break down so soon. While keeping quality is not so important as it was when storage facilities were poorer, still it is certainly worth considering.

3. The fruit is more highly colored. Probably this will hold good as a general rule because the tree under sod culture is likely to ripen up more quickly and the fruit is therefore given

FIG. 35.—Mowing the grass in a sod orchard. The difficulty comes in resisting the temptation to rake it and put it in the barn.

the maturity which favors coloring in the autumn. Cultivated orchards sometimes are given too late cultivation or otherwise supplied with too much nitrogen, which favors late growth and consequently poor color. Also the foliage on trees that are cultivated is usually more dense, which in itself will retard coloring by keeping off the sun.

4. Trees can be headed lower when grown in sod. This may or may not be true. If the reasons for low heading already given are accepted it probably makes little difference whether

the trees are in sod or are cultivated. But with the commonly accepted notions about cultivation and height of heading, the contention is probably correct. Few people who have done the work in an orchard fail to realize the value of the low tree.

5. There is less washing on side hills. This is an argument that appeals to the writer more strongly than almost any other. There are thousands of acres all through the best apple growing sections of the United States on land which is too steep to admit of cultivation on account of the washing of the soil. If these lands are to be used for orchards, and they are frequently better adapted to orcharding than to any other purpose, they must be kept in sod.

6. The land is in better condition for the spring spraying and pruning. In sections where a spring spraying is necessary, as with San José scale, and where the weather of spring is variable, as it is in most orchard countries, this is really an important advantage and will appeal to the man who has slopped about in the mud in either spraying or pruning. It would not in itself justify one in adopting the sod method, but it certainly deserves some weight. It is sufficiently difficult to get really satisfactory work in either pruning or spraying, and anything that will assist will be welcomed by the man who has had experience along these lines.

7. The windfalls are kept in better condition. This is not of much importance with winter apples, but with early varieties and with pears it is frequently of decided importance. Men who have sod-mulch orchards claim that their windfalls are practically as valuable as the hand picked fruit and while the writer does not accept this view he does believe that a good soft mulch is a great help.

Some other claims are made, but those mentioned are really the most important ones. Those which seem to have the most weight are the prevention of washing on hillsides, the fact that the fruit is likely to have better color and to keep longer, and that the expense of caring for the orchard is less. Of course the advocates of cultivation attempt to demolish this last argument by calling the sod method a cheap affair anyway and by claiming that their method gives so much more fruit that they can afford to have the extra expense.

Cultivation.—Now let us look at the arguments which are advanced in favor of cultivation:

1. It conserves soil moisture better. It is difficult to see how any reasonable man can doubt this. The sod advocates attempt to offset it by saying that the sod will so much more effectively prevent the rains from running off that they can afford to lose some moisture, but this argument does not quite " hold water " when put to a test. As a matter of fact several of the arguments in favor of sod, such as better color and better keeping quality, are based directly on the fact that the sod orchard does not have as much moisture. When one remembers how all-important moisture is to the orchard and how frequently fruit and trees are damaged from the lack of it, he can appreciate the importance of the moisture argument as advanced by the cultivation men. It seems to be the very backbone of the cultivation side of the controversy. With light soils of poor water-holding capacity, this one argument seems about all that it is necessary to produce. The soils and locations are relatively few where lack of moisture does not, at some time during the year, interfere with the best development of a crop of fruit.

2. It renders soil fertility more available; or perhaps we should reverse that and say it renders more soil fertility available. It does this by letting in the air and moisture and generally by keeping the soil conditions favorable for chemical and bacterial action. This is a point not always conceded, but the arguments for cultivation seem very conclusive. With the high cost of fertility it is certainly a strong argument.

3. Cultivation permits the use of leguminous cover crops to furnish nitrogen for the orchard. This is also a strong argument and one not easily disproved. It is quite possible through such crops as clovers and soybeans to add all the nitrogen necessary to an orchard soil. Since nitrogen is by far the highest priced element in fertilizers, a method that " works while you sleep " is certainly welcome to the man who pays the bills. The only chance for the sod-culture orchardist in this direction is the

use of clovers in seeding down and these do not as a rule persist very long in the orchard sod.

4. There is less trouble in cultivated orchards from insects, notably borers and curculio. Take the example of a young orchard in which many trees were found to be attacked by borers. It was a cultivated orchard, but several sections of various sizes had been allowed to grow up to grass and weeds; that is, had become sod sections through poor cultivation. Without exception the trees attacked by borers were in these weedy patches. With the large number of insects which winter either in the soil or in trash upon the ground it could hardly be otherwise than that they should flourish best under a management which never disturbs the soil and which keeps a constant supply of litter to hide in. The curculio is especially happy in a sod orchard and the "red-bug" seems equally so.

Fig. 36.—A tree girdled by mice and saved by bridge grafting. This is entirely practical and any good grafter can do the work.

5. There is less danger from mice. This is another argument which it is difficult for the sod-culture advocate to disprove; in fact he usually frankly admits it and puts some sort of guard about his trees to protect them. An orchard in the Annapolis Valley, Nova Scotia, may be cited as an illustration. The owner left some grass in one corner of his orchard one winter and the next spring every tree in the acre and a quarter was completely girdled by mice. They were all bridge grafted and not a tree was lost. When visited ten years after, each tree stood on stilts, as shown in Figure 36. But one might not be so fortunate as this in every case and even with protectors

there is always danger of accidents. There are sections where mice are never troublesome, and in these localities the argument would not hold.

6. The cultivated orchard yields more fruit. This is a difficult point to prove and probably never will be proved to the satisfaction of the best sod-culture advocates. General observation and still more orchard surveys have shown that, with the rank and file, cultivation gives far better yields. After all it is the average that counts. A system may be ever so good with the exceptional man and if it falls down with the average man it is better not to attempt it, for most of us are " average."

7. Cultivated orchards yield larger and better apples. This is another point which will never be admitted by the sod culturist and doubtless is not always true. But as in No. 6 it certainly is true with the rank and file of orchard men.

Removal of Hay Crop.—There is another argument on this question of " cultivation *vs*. sod culture," which seems very important and yet which is used by both sides to support their contentions. This is the fact that *most men will not leave the hay in the orchard*. The sod men say: " We are not talking about the man who mows the grass and puts it in his barn but about the man who cuts the grass and lets it lie in the orchard." The advocates of cultivation say: " We admit that sod culture gives good results when properly carried out, but what is the use of discussing a method which only a very few men will carry out, but in which the vast majority are doomed to failure." This argument is the strongest one in the whole list and it is the one which makes many good orchardists very strong believers in cultivation. It must be admitted without argument that some of the men who use sod in their orchards are among the most successful growers. But for the rank and file of orchard men, and particularly for that great section of the fruit growing fraternity who also keep some stock, it seems much better to " remove temptation " and not to grow any hay in the orchard.

Method of Cultivation.—If, then, we are to practise cultivation in the orchard, what methods shall we use? Stated briefly the method most generally satisfactory is to plow the land, or otherwise stir it, as early in the spring as the soil is in good condition; then to cultivate it frequently up to about July 1, when the orchard is sown to some cover crop which is allowed to remain on the land until the following spring. This seems to be a simple program and if the proper implements are available to work with, and attention is given to the details, there is usually little difficulty in carrying it out. Yet there are several things that it is very desirable to look after carefully. To begin with, the land ought to be plowed, and cultivation ought to be gotten under way, just as early as possible in the spring. In fact, there are some men who advocate and practise very late fall plowing of the orchard.

Fall Plowing.—There are several good arguments in support of this practice. Here are some which have considerable weight.

1. Where land has been plowed in the autumn it can be worked earlier in the spring, not only because the operation of plowing is out of the way but because plowed land will dry out more quickly. It is always desirable to get the soil in good condition and to push the trees as early in the season as possible. Fall plowing is particularly desirable on rather heavy soils, because it is so late in the spring before they are in proper condition to be plowed.

2. It frequently, in fact usually, happens that there is less work for the teams in the autumn than in the spring. Often it is even somewhat difficult on an orchard farm to find enough team work in the autumn, and if even a part of the orchards can be plowed it keeps the teams busy and gives the comfortable assurance that at least much work will be out of the way when the spring rush comes on. To the man who has done his orchard work in an office, this may not seem to be a strong argument, but any one who really gets out and does the work, or who even " bosses the job," will find that he frequently has to modify his plans and theories to suit the case in hand. In particular he will find that the problem of keeping his teams constantly at work is by no means an easy one to solve. Too often it is solved by allowing the teams to stand in the barn, which usually means that the owner has not realized that there is any problem.

3. Fall plowing disturbs a number of insects that pass the winter in the ground. The spring canker worm, in particular, passes the winter in the soil in the pupa stage, and relatively few of them will survive if the land is fall plowed. In any case where a bad attack of canker worm is likely to occur it would seem that fall plowing might be justified for this reason alone.

4. It gets the old and diseased leaves under the ground where they will not be a source of infection for the new leaves when they come out in the spring. In apple scab, in particular, it has been shown that the disease passes the winter on the old leaves and if these can be disposed of it will aid materially in the fight for clean fruit. Where the plowing is delayed until spring most of the leaves will be blown off the land into the adjoining grass or hedge-rows where they will produce an abundance of spores. If the plowing is done in the autumn the bulk of them will be still in the orchard and will be turned under, thereby securing just so much extra humus as well as getting rid of a prolific source of infection.

The two principal arguments used against fall plowing are that the soil is more likely to wash and that there is more danger of injury to the roots of the trees by freezing. The first of these is undoubtedly correct and is a sufficient reason for not practising fall plowing in a great many cases on hillsides. Still on many farms there are one or more blocks which do not have slope enough to be damaged in this way and on most farms "every little helps," especially in the spring.

On the freezing argument there is need of more light. It would be relatively easy, with soil thermometers, to determine whether the ground will freeze more deeply in a plowed orchard than in one under sod or a cover crop. If the land were harrowed down at all there is much doubt that the plowed land would allow the frost to enter any more deeply.

Disc Harrowing.—Of course it is not always necessary that the land should be plowed. On lightish lands in particular it is often possible to fit them in the spring with some type of disc harrow. One of these disc harrows, if set so as to reach its greatest depth, will stir the soil enough. Where soils can be so handled it is usually a more expeditious method. If the disc harrow is run through the orchard in one direction and then the land is allowed to stand a few days, to be followed by a discing in the other direction, twice over the land will usually put it in good condition for the spring-tooth or some other harrow.

Early Tillage Affects Moisture.—The desirability of fitting the land as early in the spring as possible is very frequently overlooked by the orchard man, who has on the land a crop of clover or some other crop which lives through the winter. He thinks that he ought to let it grow for a time in order to get additional humus to plow under, and the temptation to get all he can in the humus line frequently gets him into serious difficulties. Of course it is expected that when the land is plowed in the spring a certain number of roots will be destroyed by the plows, but if the land is plowed each year the roots so cut will never have attained any great size and they will be replaced at once by new feeding roots which will come up into the soil which was turned over. Moreover when this is done in the early spring the tree will not feel the temporary loss of moisture, because at this time of year the loss of moisture by transpiration from the tree is relatively very small.

It ought also to be emphasized, in this connection, that the little root hairs which do most of the actual absorbing of soil moisture do not persist over winter but a new set is developed each spring. Now suppose that the orchard man, in his zeal to get extra humus, allows his cover crop to grow until June before plowing. In the first place this will seriously exhaust the soil moisture by the extra drafts made upon it to grow the cover crop; then an immense number of feeding roots and root hairs will have been developed in this surface layer of the soil which is turned over by plow. The loss of these roots, or rather of the soil moisture which they are taking in, while it would not have been felt by the tree in the least had it occurred in the early spring, is now very seriously felt, since the tree is in full leaf and giving off to the air an immense amount of moisture daily. If we add to this the further fact that this heavy layer of cover crop, both the autumn growth and the spring growth, interferes with the transference of water from the subsoil into the furrow slice which was turned over, and that therefore a considerable time must elapse before new feeding roots can be established in this surface layer, we may see at least some of the objections to deferring plowing until summer in order to grow a cover crop.

After-tillage.—Following this first "fitting" of the land there is a period of cultivating. This period varies in length with different men, all the way from not over a month to three or even four months. The principal objects of this cultivation are to keep down the weeds and to conserve the soil moisture, and individual conditions are going to very decidedly modify not only its length but its thoroughness and the implements necessary to do it. As a rule the land ought to be gone over every ten days or two weeks, but if one is so unfortunate as to have a bad case of witch grass to contend with, or if the season is especially dry, or the land, either from lack of humus or from any other cause, is not in condition to hold moisture, then it may be desirable to cultivate oftener. In particular it is well to get over all the orchard just as soon as possible after a rain, unless of course it is a rainy spell. Even then it is important to start the cultivator just as soon as the rainy spell is over. For most of this cultivation very shallow stirring of the soil is all that is necessary. It is often the practice after the land is once gotten into shape in the spring to use some harrow of the spring-tooth type for most of the work. The one shown in Figure 42 is admirably suited to this part of the work and will cover more land in a day than anything that was ever turned loose in an orchard. The acme harrow is also excellent.

The time to stop cultivation, as has been suggested, varies greatly with different men. A rather short, sharp campaign is usually best. Get the orchard under cultivation as early as possible, make the cultivation thorough, and then stop it early and sow in the cover crop. It is rare that it needs to be continued after the first of July. Several of the disadvantages of cultivation may be largely overcome by seeding down early. On land which does not hold moisture well and with a heavy crop of fruit on the trees and a dry season, late culture may be desirable

and even necessary. It must be remembered that the longer the
sowing of the cover crop is delayed the less growth there will
be of that crop, and consequently the less humus there will be to
plow under the following year, which in turn will make the land
suffer more from drouth. In other words, by prolonging cultivation we save moisture for that year at the expense of future
years.

Hand Work.—While thorough cultivation in the orchard as
a whole is desirable, it is doubtful how important it is, in older
orchards at least, that the soil close about the trees should be
stirred. And certainly it adds very greatly to the expense if one
tries to remove all the weeds and grass from close around every
tree. It means hand labor and a good deal of it, and as soon
as we resort to hand work we raise very decidedly the cost of
caring for the orchard. If, for any reason, it is thought to be
absolutely necessary to do this work, however, then as much as
possible should be done with the grape-hoe shown in Figure 43.
It is surprising how much this implement will do. The balance
may be cleared out by using a heavy hoe or a light mattock or
grub hoe.

Damage During Cultivation.—One of the annoying things
about cultivating an orchard is the amount of injury that is
pretty certain to be done to the trees by the harness and the
whiffletrees and the cultivators. Even with the best of men and
teams a certain amount of this damage is sure to occur. With
poorer men and less steady teams there is enough of it to
drive the most ardent believer in cultivation to sod culture.
Patches of bark will be scraped off the trunk by the cultivator,
the tips of branches chewed off by the horses, or the bark raked
off the branches by the hames of the harness. While one is always
more or less at the mercy of the teamster, a good many things
may be done to help him to avoid injuring the trees. The horses
may be muzzled, and harnesses with low hames ought always to
be used. We may even resort with great satisfaction to the
tugless harness shown in Figure 40. Then short whiffletrees and
doubletrees ought always to be used. It will avoid many a scar
if the outside ends of the whiffletrees are padded with burlap

Fig. 37.—A compromise method of handling the land in an orchard, sod along the tree rows and cultivation between. This method has much to commend it.

or an old sack. If extension types of implements are used, the team, at least, will be kept well away from the trees. These extension implements may be either those like the light draft harrow shown in Figure 42, which cover a wide space and consequently avoid the necessity of the team getting near the trees; or, if these are not available, the two sections of an ordinary disc or spring-tooth harrow may be separated by using a long bar or evener. In the latter case there is, of course, a strip of land in the centre each time which is not worked, but if the space between the sections is not wider than one of them the strip is cultivated on the return trip.

Sowing the Cover Crop.—When the time finally arrives for sowing the cover crop it may be sown just previous to the last cultivation which will cover the seed, except in the case of clover and turnips which are sown just after the last cultivation and either left for the next rain to cover or else lightly brushed in with a brush harrow.

It is always a satisfaction to see block after block of the orchard seeded down to the cover crop. One feels that another good job is finished and trouble (at least that particular trouble) is over for the season.

QUESTIONS

1. Outline briefly three plans of orchard management as regards culture.
2. What are the principal points in favor of sod culture?
3. Give the arguments in favor of the cultivation of orchards.
4. Outline a year's treatment of the soil in a cultivated orchard.
5. Give several reasons for and against plowing orchards in late fall.
6. Discuss the use of the disc harrow in orchards.
7. Describe the effects of early spring tillage.
8. At what time during the growing season should the cultivation cease? Why?
9. What hand work, if any, is to be recommended in the cultivation of orchards?
10. How is the cover crop started?
11. Is sod-mulch, clean culture or a modified method used in your section?

CHAPTER VII

ORCHARD IMPLEMENTS

It is a great convenience in cultivating an orchard if a man can have just the right implement for each particular part in the work and for every special combination of conditions. That is one advantage which the large orchard has over the small one. With only a few acres of orchard to care for the owner feels as though he ought to get along with the smallest equipment possible unless he has use for the implements in his other farm work. It is possible to care for an orchard with only a plow and a harrow, in fact he might even cut out the plow if his harrow were of the disc variety. But with a large orchard, the owner feels more free to add to his equipment, and if the orchard is sufficiently large he can justify quite an extensive array of implements. This is a doctrine which, like the doctrine of a fairly large list of varieties, it is easy to carry too far, and any man should keep the list down low enough so that he at least has room for every implement in the tool shed.

But since there are a great many orchard implements on the market and since slightly varying conditions may make a different one more effective than any other, it seems worth while to discuss a few of the principal types.

Plows.—As already suggested it is not always necessary to plow the orchard, but it frequently is, and when one has to plow he wants a good implement. There are about four things to be considered in selecting an orchard plow: First, the draft; second, how close it can be run to the trees; third, how much danger there is that it will damage the trees; and, fourth, its effect on the furrow slice, that is, how thoroughly it will pulverize the land as it turns it over. Any orchard plow should have a fairly abrupt mold board in order to pulverize as well as to invert the furrow slice. The type of plow which merely inverts the furrow slice without breaking it up at all will make a pretty looking field,

91

that may win in a plowing match where beauty is the main thing, but it certainly does not leave the soil in anything like as good condition as the mold board with an abrupt turn. The latter is as good as the former plus one or two harrowings.

Types of Plows.—There are four or five types of plows usually available to select from, any one of which is fairly satisfactory. First, there is the ordinary *walking plow*. This will do good work, and if the orchard is small it may be the best plow to choose. The chief disadvantages of this plow are that it is necessary to make a back-furrow and a dead furrow to each row of trees and that it is not possible to get quite as close to the trees as with some other plows, but neither one of these is a serious objection.

The former difficulty may be obviated by selecting a *hillside walking plow*. This is reversible, so that all the furrows are thrown in one direction. The plowman simply begins at one side of the orchard and goes back and forth, making neither dead nor back-furrows, until the entire orchard is plowed. The usual custom in using such a plow is to throw the land down the hill, but it is much better, unless the slope is very steep, to throw it up the hill. Hillside land which is cultivated will work down the hill fast enough without any deliberate assistance from the owner.

The principal objection to this plow is that it does not do as good work as the ordinary type of walking plow just mentioned. This is not a very serious difference, but it may be avoided by using the third type of plow, the *double-sulky plow*. This is a wheeled implement with two plows side by side, one a right-hand and the other a left-hand plow. It works exactly the same as the hillside plow but does a little better work on the soil. One can not, however, get quite so close to the trees with it. For preparing a field to set an orchard on it is the finest thing yet invented.

Orchard Gang Plow.—We have next the small orchard gang plow shown in Figure 38. This consists of three eight-inch plows and will therefore move twenty-four inches in width at one time, which means getting over the orchard in a hurry. It is built so as to get very close to the trees whether one is plowing towards them or away from them, and the draft is surprisingly small considering the surface covered. The writer has never seen an accurate draft test of this plow, but, in trying it out in orchard practice as compared with the two types of walking plows just mentioned, it did not seem that the team pulled any harder with this gang throwing twenty-four inches than with a fourteen-inch plow of the other sorts. Of course these small plows will

FIG. 38.—A gang of three eight-inch plows. One of the best implements for orchard use. The draft is light and it covers a lot of land in a day.

not throw a very deep furrow, but this is seldom wanted in an orchard. Three or four inches is usually ample. At the present writing, with only one season's experience to base the opinion on, this little plow seems to stand at the head for straight orchard work.

Orchard Disc Plow.—Lastly we have what is known as the California orchard plow, shown in Figure 39. As will be seen it consists of four large discs at one end of a long beam. The great advantage of this implement is that it does very thorough work and one can get very close to the trees with it and still have the team far enough away to avoid all danger of injury from that source. For working out the weeds and grass close about the trees it is certainly admirable.

Harrows.—Starting with the most deeply cutting types of harrows we have the *disc* and the *cutaway*. These are much alike, the only difference being that the former has a smooth edge to the discs while in the latter the edges are notched. It

Fig. 39.—A disc plow for orchard work. An excellent implement for working close to the trees without getting the team near enough to do any damage.

is claimed that these latter will cut into the soil more deeply, which is probably true. Either one is excellent for working in the orchard, and as already suggested may frequently be substituted for the plow in getting the land in shape in the spring. Even in the later cultivation it is well to have one of these harrows available for use in case the weeds get a bad start in any corner of the orchard.

. Next to the disc type of harrow comes the *spring-tooth*, and it ought to follow the disc in the season's work. It will pull the furrows to pieces and pulverize the soil well, following either the plow or the disc, and some type of spring-tooth harrow ought to be in any collection of orchard implements that is supposed to be at all complete. There is one objection to the ordinary spring-tooth harrow for young orchards and that is that it is so likely to catch on a stone or some other obstacle and jump against the trees. Careful driving will help to prevent this difficulty, and of course it does not apply in land free from stones and other obstacles. Another objection which has been made to the spring-tooth and which may be worth mentioning here, is that where an orchard has patches of witch (quack) grass in it this harrow will drag small pieces to other parts of the orchard and drop them, thus helping to spread this noxious weed. This is probably a legitimate objection but can not offset the many advantages of this type of tooth either on harrows or cultivators.

We have next the *acme harrow* shown in Figure 40. The action of this machine is to cut into the soil behind and to crush the clods in front. Where the soil conditions are right it will do as much work as anything in an orchard. But it will not work on land which is either very stony or which has much trash on it. Barring these limitations it is an excellent implement and will leave the soil in as good condition as anything on the list.

Lastly among harrows we have the *spike-tooth* or smoothing type. This is not considered a very important implement in the orchard. It is especially designed to leave the surface fine and smooth and occasionally such a tool may be needed, particularly for covering some kinds of cover crops, but this would be the first thing to strike out if one were trying to cut down the list of implements.

Cultivators.—It is difficult to draw the line between cultivators and harrows because many implements are used for both purposes. In the classification here given the cultivators are used primarily for cultivating and are more under the control of the operator than the harrows.

We have first the implement shown in Figure 41, and known technically on the market as the *orchard cultivator*. The teeth are entirely rigid and it is designed especially for use in getting the land in shape and levelling it, after it has been plowed or disced. The chief objection to it is that the frame is very rigid, so that it does not always adapt itself to irregularities

Fig. 40.—The acme harrow. An excellent orchard cultivator when soil conditions are good, but stones and trash interfere with it seriously.

Fig. 41.—An orchard cultivator with heavy, rigid teeth. An excellent implement for heavy work, either where the land is rough or the weeds are large.

in the surface, one end perhaps working too deeply and the other not deep enough. On the other hand this very rigidity makes it effective in pulling the land into shape, taking down the high

FIG. 42.—Light draft orchard cultivator. Where conditions are reasonably good (soil fairly well prepared and weeds not too large) this implement does excellent work and will easily cultivate fifteen acres a day.

places and scraping them into the low ones. And it will dig into a patch of witch grass or other troublesome weed in a way to discourage the intruder.

Next is the *light-draft orchard harrow* shown in Figure 42. It is certainly well named, as the draft is very light considering the land it covers and there are few if any implements that will get over as many acres of orchard in a day as this one. It will cheer the heart of any man with a lot of work to do. You can send a man out into a ten acre block of orchard in the morning and he is back at noon with the job done. And it does good work, too.

Fig. 43.—A grape-hoe at work in a young orchard. An excellent implement for clearing out the weeds along the tree row. It will do the work of a dozen men.

Its shortcoming is that the land has to be in pretty good condition for it to do good work. The teeth are rather light and will not work well on rough land, but once the land has been put in good condition in the spring it will certainly take care of it well and cheaply. There are two wings which enable it to work close to the trees without bringing the horses near them. A light lever attached to each of the three sections enables the operator to dump any trash that may have caught on the teeth.

A combination implement known as a *grape-hoe* is shown in Figure 43. It can be used either in the capacity of a plow or a cultivator, by changing the attachment, and is designed to save hand labor by working close to the trees. With the right man to run it, it will certainly do what it was designed to do. There is a disc for steering it, and a good husky man who has had a little practice in running it will come as near cleaning out all the weeds from about the trees as it is possible to do with anything short of a hand hoe. No orchard of any size can afford to be without one.

Then there is the common *V-shaped cultivator*. This is not strictly necessary to care for the orchard, but as soon as any of the companion crops are planted it becomes the main dependence. It is usually best to have two of them with teeth of different sizes. The large are needed for heavy work when one is unfortunate enough to get behindhand, and the small for land in better shape. In fact some orchardists have three of them in the equipment, ranging from the small, spike-toothed variety up to one with five good-sized shovels.

QUESTIONS

1. What advantages have large orchards over small ones in the matter of implements?
2. Why should the plow have an abrupt mold-board?
3. What may be said for and against the ordinary walking plow for orchard work?
4. What advantage has the hillside plow?
5. Describe a double-sulky plow and tell when you would prefer it.
6. Give the advantages of the orchard gang plow.
7. What is a "California orchard plow"? Give several points in its favor.
8. Compare the various types of harrows for use in orchards.
9. What types of cultivators are suitable for use in orchards?
10. What orchard implements are most common in your section?

CHAPTER VIII

FERTILIZERS

THE proper fertilizing of a fruit plantation is an especially difficult point to determine experimentally, because it is so difficult to determine and to control the conditions surrounding the roots of trees. When it has been determined by experiment what the best treatment for a particular orchard is, this information is of relatively little value to the owners of other orchards because the many different factors of " soil condition " are likely to vary widely. In this respect the fertilizer problem stands ahead of any other. For example, if it is a question of what to spray with, the conditions surrounding the leaves of the trees are so similar that what is best for Brown's trees will probably also be best for Smith's trees, though he may live five or ten or even one hundred miles away. But the fertilizer question is so complex, and conditions change so decidedly in going even a short distance, that what is good in the way of fertilizers for Brown's trees may not be good for Smith's though his orchard may be just across the road.

Doubtless further experiment will throw more light on the subject, and we may hope that the time will come when we shall have a generally accepted scheme of orchard fertilization. In the meantime we must use what evidence we have and do our best to gain further light for ourselves by a little personal experimenting.

The best orchardists believe in fertilizing and practise it in private orchards. But the evidence on the subject is meagre and conflicting. Three lines of reasoning should lead to the adoption of this attitude until such time as more authoritative evidence on the subject is available.

Trees Exhaust Soil.—It has been very definitely shown that apple orchards take out of the soil far more fertilizer material year by year than ordinary farm crops do. Professor I. P. Roberts has calculated that the twenty-year record of fertilizer

100

value of an acre of wheat and an acre of apples would be as follows:

Wheat, grain and straw, 20 years............. $128.23
Apples, fruit and leaves, 20 years.............. 207.45

This makes no account of the large amount of fertilizer material which is each year locked up in the roots, trunk, and branches of the tree. Now we must admit at once that the tree forages much more widely than the annual crop in search of food, but even when this is considered it seems reasonably certain that an orchard exhausts the soil faster than the wheat crop. It must be remembered further that there is no chance for rotation of crops with the orchard, but the same elements in the same ratio are taken out year after year. When we remember still further that no man who makes any pretense to being a farmer would think of trying to grow a wheat crop many years without fertilizers, it seems very reasonable that the orchard man should follow the practice of the general farmer.

Best Orchardists Fertilize.—This brings us to the second reason for thinking that orchards ought to be fertilized, and that is that the best fruit men practise fertilizing. Go into any orchard section and you will find that the most progressive and successful growers, as a rule, are the men who fertilize highly. Usually the man succeeds in proportion as he fertilizes. The man who fertilizes year after year whether he has a crop of fruit on his trees or not, is the man who usually has a crop. The man who is noted in a section as applying fertilizers in large quantity is usually also noted as a man who harvests bumper crops. This is not conclusive proof, because these men also care well for their orchards in other ways. But it is very suggestive, particularly the fact that the generous feeder usually succeeds better than the moderate feeder.

Experimental Proof.—The third point which has converted many to fertilizing their orchards is the fact that numerous experiments have shown such marked benefits from fertilizing. Of course there have been experiments that have not shown any benefit, but when, in a series of experiments, a fertilized block gives several times as much fruit as an unfertilized block, the two having been treated in exactly the same way except in the matter of fertilizers, it is difficult to avoid drawing the conclusion that the fertilizer is responsible for the difference. In the orchard fertilizer experiments at the Massachusetts Agricultural Experiment Station (with which experiments the writer has had no connection) the thing which most impresses any one who studies the results and examines the trees, is the extremely poor showing made by the trees which had no fertilizer. We may disagree decidedly as to the relative merits of muriate and sulfate of potash, or as to whether bone meal is best as a source of phosphoric acid, but none can escape the conclusion that under the conditions of this experiment *any fertilizer combination used was greatly to be preferred to no fertilizer at all.*

Influence of Nitrogen.—With so much difference in opinion as to what forms of fertilizer, if any, are required, it is hardly to be expected that there should be very general agreement as to the particular effect of the different fertilizer elements, yet all are agreed that nitrogen, in any form, is likely to produce rapid wood growth with large, dark green leaves and long terminal shoots. If the application of nitrogen is carried to excess, the wood growth is often made at the expense of fruit, though up to a certain point nitrogen is apt to increase the yield. It almost always decreases color, principally because the fruit, like the leaves, is large in size and does not reach maturity until late in the season. The heavy foliage also reduces the color by shutting off the sunlight.

Influence of Potash.—It is known that potash enters into the fruit acids and is a very large part (more than 50 per cent) of the ash of fruits. Potash has also been credited, and rightly so, with increasing the color in fruits. This effect is probably produced by the influence which potash has on the general growth of the tree. In any event fairly liberal applications of some form of potash are generally made to bearing orchards if the owner believes in fertilizing.

Influence of Phosphoric Acid.—The exact part which phosphoric acid plays in orchard development seems not to have been so well worked out, at least there is less agreement on the subject. It is certainly important in seed development and probably in the ripening of the fruit, and some men have even given it credit for improvements in the color of fruit, though this is not very generally accepted. If it occurs it is probably as a result of the control which this element exerts on the growth of the tree. Maturity and sunlight are certainly the two most important influences in producing color in fruits.

Forms to Use.—If we are to use fertilizers we have the choice of several forms of each one.

For nitrogen we have nitrate of soda, sulfate of ammonia, tankage and nitrate of potash. Nitrate of soda is probably used more than any other form and has the advantage that it is very quickly available. It is also a reasonably cheap form.

Sulfate of ammonia acts more slowly than the nitrate because it has to be changed in the soil into the nitrate form before it can be used by the plant. It also has a tendency to make the soil sour because it leaves behind the sulfuric acid. Still it is fairly popular and if lime is used to take care of the acid it is good to use in a combination where a long season of growth is wanted.

Tankage is still more slowly available and is usually reasonable in the price per unit. It is used with particular satisfaction on young trees or in any situation where a relatively long period of growth is desired. With young trees tankage in combination with nitrate of soda has given very much better results than the nitrate alone, even when two applications of the latter were given.

The nitrate of potash is hardly worth discussing because it is so seldom that one can get it. It carries about the same percentage of nitrogen as the nitrate of soda and in addition about as much potash as the muriate. It is thus a very high grade fertilizer, the highest that we have. It has the disadvantage that it requires the application of both nitrogen and potash at one time, but usually this is desirable.

We ought to add to the forms of nitrogen " cyanamid," the newly developed combination of lime with atmospheric nitrogen. It has not yet been in use long enough for its qualities to be tested, but it has this to recommend it, that it is relatively cheap.

Among *phosphoric acid fertilizers* are bone meal, rock phosphate, and basic slag. Bone meal is an old favorite among fertilizer users. Within recent years basic slag, or Thomas phosphate powder, a by-product produced in the manufacture of steel, has been used a great deal by orchard men. It has the advantage of carrying a considerable percentage of lime, but this has been reduced recently by changes in the manufacturing process. Acid phosphates or superphosphates are made from both bone and rock phosphates by treating them with sulfuric acid. This takes up a part of the lime, rendering the phosphoric acid more available. The superphosphates are specially useful with young trees where the roots are extending rapidly. They are the only form in which phosphoric acid should be applied to orchards in sod, since in such orchards one must depend on the fertilizer dissolving and being washed into the soil.

Two forms of potash are in common use, the muriate and the sulfate, the latter coming in both high and low grade. Probably the muriate is more generally used than any other form at the present time. It has the great advantage of being cheaper than sulfate, but it also has a tendency to render the soil acid by taking out the lime. This latter tendency can be overcome of course by adding lime, but that means one more thing to look after. The low grade sulfate carries about half the amount of actual potash that the high grade does, but it also has a large amount of magnesia which many consider an advantage. There is the same objection to it that there is to any low grade fertilizer, viz., that it costs more per unit of plant food to transport it and to handle it in the orchard. It is perhaps best to use the high grade sulfate altogether, until such time as it may be shown that some other form is better.

Fertilizer Formulas.—It may perhaps be helpful to include in this chapter a few fertilizer formulas which are actually in use by some of our leading orchard men.

Mr. George A. Drew, of Greenwich, Connecticut, has the following formula which is used at the rate of 400 pounds to 800 pounds per acre according to the condition of the soil. His trees are cultivated.

```
125 pounds blood  .........  16    per cent
200 pounds tankage .......  10    per cent Am. 20 per cent B. P. Lime
450 pounds bone  .........   4½  per cent Am. 50 per cent B. P. Lime
650 pounds basic slag .....  16    per cent
420 pounds sulphate potash. 48    per cent
155 pounds filler
────
2000
```

Mr. L. F. Priest, of Gleasondale, Massachusetts, grows his orchard in sod. He says: " Our best trees have a good dressing of stable manure in the fall and the following spring 600 pounds of slag and 200 pounds of sulfate of potash per acre for the largest trees, the smaller ones receiving less. All the hay we can spare is used for mulch.''

Munson and Frost, of Littleton, Massachusetts, use the following formula on their bearing apple orchard: 500 pounds basic slag, and 225 pounds high grade sulfate of potash.

Mr. A. C. Starr, of Starrs Point, Nova Scotia, writes: '' We use all the barn manure we have to spare in our orchards and we usually get over them once in about four years, giving a fair application. In addition we apply each year 400 to 500 pounds of ground bone per acre and 200 to 300 pounds of muriate of potash.''

Professor J. P. Stewart of the Pennsylvania Experiment Station, who has given a great deal of study to this question of fertilizing orchards, gives the following table of fertilizers to be used while determining by experiment what the orchard actually needs.

TABLE III.—*A General Fertilizer for Apple Orchards.*
(Amounts per Acre for Bearing Trees)

Nitrogen 30 lbs. (N)	Phosphoric Acid 50 lbs (P_2O_5)	Potash 25 to 50 lbs. (K_2O)
Carried in—	Carried in—	Carried in—
100 lbs. nitrate soda and	350 lbs. acid phosphate or in	50 to 100 lbs. muriate or in
150 lbs. dried blood or in	200 lbs. bone meal or in	
150 lbs. sulfate of ammonia	300 lbs. basic slag	100 to 200 lbs. low grade sulfate

Application.—In applying fertilizers it is much better to use a fertilizer spreader when possible. Of course where the trees are young, and the fertilizer is therefore spread over only a part of the surface, it is usually necessary to put it on by hand.

Insoluble materials, or those slowly soluble, like bone meal and basic slag, should be applied before the land is plowed or should be otherwise thoroughly incorporated with the soil. Those which dissolve readily, like muriate and sulfate of potash or nitrate of soda, may be spread upon the surface and will wash in with the first rain.

The potash and phosphoric acid salts are not readily washed out of the soil and may therefore be applied at almost any season of the year, though the orchardist should avoid a time when there are likely to be dashing rains which will carry them off in the surface water. But nitrogen is very likely to escape and should be applied after growth has started so that it may be taken up quickly.

The fertilizing of the various kinds of fruit trees will vary somewhat but there will probably not be any greater variation than might occur between two different varieties of the same kind of fruit or between two blocks of the same fruit on different soils. For example, the Wagener and Gravenstein apples will probably vary nearly as much in their fertilizer requirements as will the general classes of apples and peaches. And two blocks of Baldwin apple trees on very different soils may need quite as different fertilizers as a block of peaches and a block of apples.

QUESTIONS

1. Compare orchards with wheat in their exhaustion of soil fertility.
2. What have experiments proved in regard to orchard fertilizers?
3. What are the effects of nitrogenous fertilizers?
4. Give the effects of fertilizers rich in potash.
5. What is the influence of phosphoric acid on fruit trees?
6. Discuss the forms of fertilizer to be used in supplying nitrogen.
7. From what sources may the phosphoric acid be derived? Which are best for young trees?
8. What two forms of potash are in common use? Give an advantage of each.
9. Is orchard fertilizing practised in your section?

CHAPTER IX

COVER CROPS

WHILE most people have a fairly clear idea of what a cover crop is, it may be worth while to begin by attempting to define it so that we may have a definite idea of just what is meant by the term. In orchard parlance then, a " cover crop " is any crop grown in the orchard solely for the benefit of the trees. It is usually an annual crop and is sown in the orchard during the summer and plowed under the following spring. In actual practice we find all gradations, from the orthodox, typical cover crop, such as measures up to the definition given above, on through such plants as turnips, which are primarily cover crops but where a part of the crop may be harvested, to buckwheat, which may be grown primarily as a companion crop and sold, but which serves some of the purposes of a cover crop.

The most important purposes served by the cover crop are the following, which are arranged roughly in the order of their importance, though the order would vary under varying conditions.

Prevent Washing.—The cover crop serves to prevent washing during fall and spring rains and to make the orchard comfortable to go about in during muddy weather in the spring, that is, it serves as a cover. A crop which will really accomplish all this is difficult to find, but it ought to come as near it as possible. There is no question that the loss of soluble plant food, and of actual soil, by washing is one of the great drawbacks to cultivation on lands which are even slightly rolling, and anything which we can do to lessen this loss ought to be done. Of course the cover crop helps to prevent washing both by its roots and its tops. It is therefore important, on lands which are subject to washing, to select a plant as a cover crop that will develop a large top which will mat down on the surface of the soil and thus prevent the water from moving, and also one which has a

107

large and fibrous root system that will hold the soil particles together. Sometimes these two characteristics go together but frequently they do not and then one has to choose between them. It is difficult to say which is the more important, but a thick mat over the surface will certainly accomplish wonders.

Check Fall Growth.—The cover crop serves to check the growth of the trees in the autumn and thus force them to ripen up their wood for winter. This is often the most important function of the cover crop and is accomplished by its appropriating water and plant food that would otherwise go to the trees. When this purpose is of importance, as in sections with rather trying winter climates, one should select a crop that will develop a rank growth about the time that the trees ought to " sober down," which is at least as early as the first of September. The date of sowing the crop must of course be varied to suit its rapidity of growth and the needs of the trees. If the owner is using buckwheat, which comes on with a rush, he can afford to delay sowing much later than if he is using soybeans, which require a considerable time to develop. Another very important point in this connection is the question of whether the cover crop is hardy or is killed by frost. If it is hardy, the date of seeding may be considerably delayed, which is sometimes very desirable where the trees are carrying a large crop of fruit.

The cover crop adds humus to the soil, and where barn manure is not to be had for the orchard, which is frequently the case on special orchard farms, this purpose becomes an all-important one. With both light and heavy soils it is particularly important to keep up the supply of humus because they are both damaged much more than intermediate types when the humus content runs low. For these soils therefore one ought to select some large growing crop and be careful to secure a good growth of it. This latter is by no means as simple a matter as it might seem. Weather conditions, soil conditions, the shade of the trees, and various other factors come in to influence the result, and unless the owner looks out for all the details he is likely to find his orchard going into the winter with very little material to either prevent wash or make humus. A plan which has been tried with considerable satisfaction, on lands where it was difficult to get a good growth of cover crop, is to reserve a part or even all of the fertilizer that is intended for that block and apply it just previous to sowing the cover crop. A little nitrogen in particular applied at this time is likely to be a great help in giving the crop a start.

The cover crop takes up and holds plant food at a time when the trees are not active. The importance of this may have been over-emphasized, but it is certainly worth considering, and it is one argument in favor of those crops which are not killed by frost. With buckwheat, for example, one gets little of this effect because it is killed before the trees have stopped growing. With any plant which lives over winter we get this benefit, but the amount of it varies with the amount of root growth of the cover plant. If the soil is occupied fully by the roots there is little chance of loss.

Add Nitrogen.—A leguminous cover crop such as clover, or beans, or vetch will add nitrogen to the soil (Fig. 44). This is generally understood by all who are familiar with farm matters but is frequently overlooked in orchard practice as well as elsewhere. These plants are able, through the bacteria which live in the little nodules on their roots, to take up and " fix " the free nitrogen of the air. They thus offer to the orchard man an abundant supply of nitrogen for his orchard in return for the effort and expense of sowing the seed. In fact the writer recalls one orchard in which crimson clover was used as a cover crop for a series of years, where the soil actually became too rich in nitrogen for the best condition of the trees. They made too much growth and the fruit was under-colored. The owner suspected what the trouble was, had the soil analyzed by his experiment station, which told him that his soil was too rich in nitrogen and advised him to change cover crops. He did so, using buckwheat for a few years, and the trouble was entirely corrected. This is not a common difficulty, but is mentioned to show the possibilities of the leguminous crop. As nitrogen

Fig. 44.—Crimson clover as a cover crop. This crop makes an ideal cover where it will grow well, but it needs good soil conditions.

is by far the most expensive fertilizer to buy and as the cover crop offers a convenient method of getting it almost without cost, it is certainly a short-sighted policy of soil management which does not include leguminous plants often enough to furnish at least a large part of the nitrogen needed.

A cover crop may hold the snow and leaves in the orchard during the winter. To do this to the best advantage it must be rather a stiff, upright crop, which is not the type of crop that gives the best results on soil washing and some other things. One has to choose therefore between this character and the others. In climates where the winters are severe, and where snow is likely to blow off from the orchard, this point of holding it as a protection may be the all-important one and the orchardists may have to select an upright crop like soybeans or buckwheat or even use a mixture with corn or some other heavy plant in it, regardless of all other considerations.

Protects Fallen Fruit.—The cover crop serves to protect the fruit which drops. This is not usually considered very important and can often be disregarded altogether, but with fruit such as Yellow Transparent and Red Astrachan apples, which ripen irregularly and which have to be disposed of quickly in any case, the drops are sometimes worth about as much as the hand picked fruit.

Prevents Winter Injury of Roots.—It prevents the freezing and thawing of the soil and consequent injury to the roots during some winters. Any one who is not familiar with this effect will be surprised at the difference between a block of the orchard with a good cover crop on it such as clover or vetch, and one with no crop or with a poor one. The well covered block will stay frozen through a long rain or spell of mild weather while the bare land freezes and thaws with every change in the temperature.

In a few cases there may be other purposes served by the cover crop, but the above constitute the most important ones.

Plowing Under Cover Crops.—A point which is frequently misunderstood and which should be considered, is the importance of the crop living over winter. There is often a prejudice, for example, against crimson clover and in favor of common red clover because the former does not always live over winter, while the latter does. It is said that while there may be a fine growth of the crimson clover when winter comes on, yet by spring (in cold climates) it has been killed, and has so dried up and dwindled away that there is little left to plow under. As a matter of fact, this does not in the least affect its value as a humus producer. There will be just as much humus added to the soil in the dried remains of the crop as there would have been in succulent tissues before they were killed. The only loss has been the water which has dried out of the stalks.

A slightly different phase of the same prejudice is seen in some orchardists' opinions of crops which do live over winter. Many men will insist on delaying plowing in the spring until a new growth can be produced, no matter how rank the growth may have been in the autumn, because they say that unless they do "there is so little to plow under." It sometimes does look small in the spring, but it will make just as much humus as it would have in the autumn.

While under certain conditions there may be no objection to allowing some growth in the spring; while, in fact, it may be a distinct advantage by producing extra humus and sometimes by drying out the soil; yet there is always great danger that it will be allowed to stand too long. On heavy soils this objection is particularly strong, for a big growth of the crop will dry out the soil very rapidly and, if the weather happens to turn dry at just the right time, the soil may easily become too dry and plow up in big lumps that are very difficult to break up. On the whole a crop which makes a big growth in the autumn but does not live over winter is to be preferred because it avoids this danger.

Plants to Use.—A great many different plants are used as cover crops in the orchard, depending on the locality, the type of soil, the number of acres to be covered, the owner's pocketbook and a number of other considerations. The following table, however, includes the most common ones. It gives also the usual rate per acre, the average price (though this varies greatly in different localities and in different years) and the cost of seeding an acre.

TABLE IV.—*Amount and Cost of Cover Crop Seed.*

Crop	Rate per Acre	Price	Cost per Acre
Buckwheat...................	1 bu.	$1.50 bu.	$1.50
Cow peas.....................	1½ bu.	3.00 bu.	4.50
Cow-horn and purple top turnips......................	2 lb.	.35 lb.	.70
Dwarf Essex rape.............	2 lb.	.08 lb.	.16
Barley.......................	1½ bu.	1.25 bu.	1.88
Rye.........................	1½ bu.	1.65 bu.	2.47
Crimson clover...............	15 lbs.	.10 lb.	1.50
Mammoth red clover and common red clover.............	12 lbs.	.25 lb.	3.00
Summer vetch................	1½ bu.	3.00 bu.	4.50
Winter vetch.................	1 bu.	6.00 bu.	6.00
Soybeans—broadcast	1½ bu.	3.50 bu.	5.25
Soybeans—in drills	½ bu.	3.50 bu.	1.75
Canada field peas.............	1½ bu.	3.00 bu.	4.50

The last column is very suggestive and is well worth careful study by the orchardist. Where one has but an acre or two of orchard the cost for seed is not an important matter, but when it runs up to even ten acres the relative cost at $6.00 per acre or 16 cents per acre is certainly worth consideration.

With some crops it is possible to allow a strip along each tree row to mature seed and then, by cross-cultivation when the time arrives for sowing the cover crop, to scatter this seed over the entire surface of the orchard. There seems to be no serious objection to this practice and it will reduce materially the running expenses of the orchard.

Let us now run over the catalogue of crops given and suggest very briefly some of their good and bad characteristics, taking them in the order mentioned in the table.

Buckwheat.—This is desirable because it will grow on almost any soil, leaves the land in better physical condition than perhaps any other crop, furnishes a large amount of humus, is reasonably cheap, and starts so quickly after sowing that it will smother out many annual weeds. This last point is particularly important where one has witch grass to contend with. On the other hand buckwheat furnishes no nitrogen, makes rather a poor cover, and is killed by the first frost. All things considered the orchardist should class buckwheat as among the best three or four cover crops and one which it is difficult to do without (Fig. 45).

Cow Peas.—These are rather a southern crop and are not as good as several other crops when one gets north of Connecticut. In their own section, however, they are famous as soil improvers. They are sown in July and are killed by fall frost.

Fig. 45.—Buckwheat as a cover crop. One of the most satisfactory crops for this purpose, especially where soil conditions are not of the best.

Cow-horn and Purple-top Turnips.—The great advantage of these plants is cheapness, which certainly appeals to a man when he has fifty acres or more of orchard to cover. They also furnish an immense amount of humus, make a fairly good cover, and with the purple tops at least one may pull out and sell enough of the best turnips to far more than pay all the expense of the crop and still leave plenty on the ground for a cover. The objections to turnips are that they furnish no nitrogen, but they do have a large amount of sulfur and other ill-smelling constituents which are likely to be very offensive in the spring when the crop is rotting down and before it can be plowed under. There is a further objection that they are likely to live over winter and go to seed, making rather an unsightly appearance to people who are easily worried by such things. They have not proved a really serious weed but are merely a little too conspicuous with their gorgeous yellow flowers.

Dwarf Essex Rape.—So far as the writer's experience and observation go this is the cheapest of all covers, except weeds, and it is by no means a bad crop to use. It will grow anywhere, grows late in the autumn, and usually survives the winter, so that it catches and holds the elusive nitrates, furnishes a fine lot of humus, and makes a surprisingly good cover, as it has a very fibrous, though not a very large, root system. Where a good stand lives over winter it is sometimes rather difficult to get rid of it and it is always unsightly. These are not serious matters, however, for a cover crop is not grown for its beauty, and by using a cultivator with broad teeth it is quite possible to kill out the worst case of this. On some cultivators there is a broad, V-shaped affair in the centre called a " sweep," and two outside wings, and the combination will pretty nearly clean out anything in the weed line. Of course the rape crop gathers no nitrogen from the air.

Barley.—This is an excellent crop to use when one does not care to have a nitrogenous crop and also does not want to use buckwheat. It generally makes a good cover, particularly late in the season, is not seriously expensive, and leaves the land in very fair condition. *Oats* are sometimes used in this way but they do not leave the soil in as good condition as barley and they are therefore not included in the list.

Rye.—This is one of the greatest covers on the list when sown at the right time, but the great difficulty with it from the cover crop standpoint is that it makes very little growth during the hot weather of August and early September, so that it is of practically no value in assisting to stop the growth of the trees. It will grow almost anywhere. Sown about September first it makes a fine covering for the land over winter. When spring comes it has another shortcoming from the point of view of the orchard and that is that it stalks up very quickly and may get too tall and coarse to plow under well. It will also, on heavy land, dry out the soil very quickly and make trouble with lumps when the land is plowed. But it is fine to prevent washing of the soil, is reasonably cheap, furnishes a good supply of humus, and takes care of all soluble plant food, so that it can not be spared from the list.

Crimson Clover.—When this plant will make a good growth in the autumn it comes the nearest to the ideal of a cover crop of any plant in the list. It is reasonably cheap, and fulfils nearly all of the offices detailed at the beginning of this chapter as belonging to the ideal cover crop. It does not succeed in all climates and it very frequently makes a poor growth for the first year or two that it is tried on a particular block of land. But if the owner will persist in his efforts to grow it, it will often improve year by year until it makes a splendid growth. Another difficulty with it is that it will not grow on poor soil. The orchard must be in " good heart " before it is worth while to try any of the clovers (Fig. 44).

Mammoth Red and Common Red Clover.—Many good orchardists do not have much use for these plants as cover crops where the land is being cultivated every year, as is usually the case in orchards conducted on the cultivation plan. They seldom make any growth worth while the first autumn and therefore to get enough humus they must be allowed to grow in the spring, which, as already explained, is very objectionable. Occasionally, however, when an orchard gets to growing too much wood and the owner wants to sober it down by seeding down the land and letting it stand for two or three years, the clovers are particularly good to mix with the grass seed that is used. This is where these clovers shine, in "semi-permanent seeding."

The Vetches.—Both summer and winter vetches are splendid crops for covers and if the seed did not cost so much they would be just about perfect. But the seed does cost; and until some method is devised to bring down the cost to about one-quarter what it is at present they are going to be rather too costly for the man who has ten acres of orchard or over. It is unfortunate that this is so, as vetches are certainly about all that could be asked for the purpose in view. On small blocks of orchard, or under special conditions, they may be admissible, but as a general, commercial proposition they do not appeal to the man who pays the bills. It is to be hoped that a plan may be devised whereby the man who owns an orchard can grow his own vetch seed, but up to the present time that method has not been developed.

Soybeans.—This is a cover crop which orchardists have used with a good deal of satisfaction for a number of years, but it has to be handled quite differently from most cover crops to be entirely successful. Sown broadcast, or even in drill, at the ordinary date, it fails to make growth enough to furnish much humus or to perform any of the offices of a cover crop with conspicuous success. But if it can be drilled in about the middle of June with the rows far enough apart to admit of cultivation and then if it is cultivated two or perhaps three times before the orchard is laid by, it will do splendidly. For sowing soybeans in this way the grower may use a small five-hole drill which is used largely in the Middle West for drilling wheat in the autumn into land where corn has been grown the summer previous. Stop up all but the two outside holes and then spread the drill as wide as possible. Thus two rows at a time are drilled far enough apart to cultivate (Fig. 29). After the plants are up they are given two or three cultivations and then the land is seeded down to rape or turnips or buckwheat or rye. This makes a fine combination cover. If the beans come along nicely and ripen a good crop of seed, it may be harvested and threshed and will usually bring two and a half to three dollars per bushel wholesale. This leaves whatever else was sown on the land as a cover and the soil gets the benefit of the root-systems of the soybeans after they are mown off. On the other hand if the crop is not good enough to warrant harvesting, if the stand is poor or the frost comes before the beans are mature enough, then there is a fine crop to plow under. The common white pea-bean may be grown in much the same way, and with equal satisfaction.

Care should be taken, when this method is used on land that is subject to wash, to have the rows run crosswise of the slope. If this is overlooked they help rather than hinder washing by keeping the water in certain channels.

Canada field peas are sometimes used and will make the most humus to the square inch of anything that ever grew in an orchard. It is the only crop that really gives serious trouble in plowing it under. The vines are so rank and the stalks are so heavy that it is like trying to plow under a field of bean poles. With a good crop, the only way to get them under is to use a rolling coulter on the plow and even then they will sometimes clog up under the plow-beam. But they do furnish humus and nitrogen in abundance. When they mat down on the surface they will stop any " wash " but a cloud-burst.

Weeds.—It seems worth while to add that some orchard men make use of weeds as a cover crop. Where they can be depended upon for a good stand they are better than nothing. In fact there is probably no really legitimate objection to them, except with a very few such as witch grass. Of course they add no nitrogen.

QUESTIONS

1. What is a corn crop?
2. What are the most important uses of orchard cover crops?
3. Why should the fall growth of trees be checked? How does the cover crop assist in this?
4. What class of cover crops add nitrogen to soils?
5. Is there any advantage in having the cover live over winter?
6. Give a list of the crops most suitable for winter covers in your section.
7. Discuss the advantages of several of these.
8. What ones are legumes?
9. What ones live over winter? What ones are killed by fall frosts?
10. What is the objection to perennial crops for this purpose?

CHAPTER X

PRUNING

No other operation connected with growing an orchard can compare in interest with pruning. It requires more knowledge, more experience, and more thought than any other orchard work. Probably it is also true that we know less about it (or think we know more things that are not so) than about most other operations. Yet books have been written and might still be written about what is known of the art and science of pruning.

Fig. 46.—A young apple tree started on the wrong road by bad pruning. All the fruit spurs have been removed from the lower branches.

In the present chapter we shall attempt merely to understand a few of the most universally accepted general principles and to bring out some of the practical details of pruning our common orchard fruits.

How Trees Bear their Fruit.—One of the first things for the would-be pruner to acquire is a thorough understanding of the way in which the different orchard trees bear their fruit. Many a good apple tree has had its usefulness curtailed because the man who pruned it did not realize the vital importance of the

119

little crooked spurs along its branches, but insisted in clearing them off to make the tree look more neat. Figure 46 shows an excellent example of a young apple tree which has been thus started on the wrong road, and Figure 94 shows an old orchard which has travelled that road for years, in fact it has travelled it so long that it would be difficult to get it onto any other road.

In view of the importance of this side of the question, it may be worth while to begin by summing up briefly the method of fruit-bearing in each of the principal orchard fruits.

The apple and pear may be discussed together since their plan of bearing is practically identical. These two fruits bear almost altogether on short, crooked little branches, known techni-

Fig. 47.—An apple fruit spur. This spur is perhaps six inches long and has probably borne five apples. Yet many pruners systematically cut them off the trees.

cally as "fruit spurs." An apple spur is shown in Figure 47. This particular spur has a terminal bud on each of two very short branches. In the spring these buds expand and produce a number of leaves, perhaps a half dozen, surrounding from four to six blossoms. Under normal conditions one of these blossoms sets a fruit and the balance fall away. The growing and ripening of this apple takes about all the strength of the spur, but it usually manages to develop at one side a small leaf bud which the following year makes a very short growth in a new direction and at the end of the season produces another large, plump terminal bud. The following year this bud bears an apple, and so on. We thus have the spur bearing an apple every alternate year and continuing its slow, crooked growth for a long series of years. The spur shown in Figure 47 was about ten years old and was probably not more than six inches long. It had apparently borne at least five apples.

This is practically the only way in which apples and pears are produced, upon these little spurs, so that the man who gets enthusiastic for cleanliness and prunes off all of these little spurs from his apple and pear trees is simply spoiling his chance of getting any fruit from that particular part of the tree. Just contrast the pear branch shown in Figure 48, with its wealth of these little spurs, with the one shown in Figure 47. In the one

Fig. 48.—A pear branch well supplied with fruit spurs. Such a branch is capable of bearing a maximum crop.

case the owner stands a chance to have his tree loaded down with fruit, while in the other he can not by any possibility get fruit from that part of the tree where the fruit spurs have been cleaned away.

Two other facts in connection with these little spurs ought to be kept firmly in mind. The first is that, as already hinted, they continue to bear for a long series of years. It is nothing uncommon for one of these spurs to continue to bear for twelve or fifteen years and as it branches considerably it may produce in that time ten or a dozen apples. Think of the value of such a little spur to the man who owns the tree, and yet he is frequently the very man who cuts it off. The second point to be emphasized is that once these spurs are cut or broken away, they can never be developed again at that particular spot. The only possible way that this section of the tree can be again brought into usefulness is by developing water-sprouts on these bare

branches and then growing fruit spurs on the water-sprouts. And this is a long and difficult process.

Pruning the apple or pear tree, therefore, ought to consist in thinning out the top so as to let in enough light and air to keep it healthy, and in persistently holding on to these small spurs just as long as they remain productive.

How Peaches are Borne.— Now contrast this method of bearing and pruning with the peach. It is about as different as one can well imagine. To begin with, the peach always bears on last year's shoots instead of on these ancient little spurs (Fig. 49). Then the fruit buds, instead of being

FIG. 49.—Young peaches just set. Notice that most nodes have two peaches and a cluster of leaves.

"mixed" buds, as in the apple, which produce both leaves and blossoms, are plain blossom buds, each winter bud containing a single peach blossom. This is probably one reason why peaches are more subject to winter-killing of the fruit buds than apples. They are not nearly so well protected. And lastly the bearing section of the tree in the peach migrates along the branch, as we might say, instead of remaining practically stationary for years, as in the apple.

The whole object of the peach pruner is therefore to keep up a supply of new wood. His short, interior twigs are often useless after one year, in which case he may cut them out altogether. In any case he prunes his tree much more severely than in the apple, so as to develop new growth. Sometimes this new growth, resulting from severe pruning, is so vigorous that it does not bear much the first year but the operator knows that he can rely

Fig. 50.   Fig. 51.

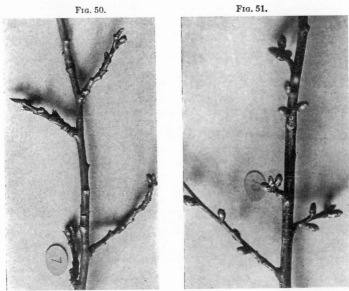

Fig. 50.—Spurs of the European plum. They differ from the apple in being straight and in not living so long.

Fig. 51.—Cherry spurs. Similar to the plum.

on its sobering down by the second year and producing a lot of good new shoots that will bear.

The " leaders " in the peach need especial attention. From the very fact that the method of bearing is progressive, there is a strong tendency for these leaders to get away and carry the tree to undue heights. This disposition is especially strong in young trees, and for several years after the tree is set the pruner has to take out practically all the leaders, even though he knows that they will be replaced by an equally strong growth.

The plums and the cherry may, perhaps, be classed together because their methods of bearing, though differing in many minor details, are essentially the same. They all agree in bearing their fruit not only on the sides of shorter or longer spurs, but also from the lateral buds of last year's growth. These spurs, which may be seen in Figures 50 and 51, differ from those of the apple in that they produce their fruit from lateral buds and also in that they do not live nearly so long as the apple spurs. These fruits also agree fairly closely in the character of the winter blossom bud, which is about half way between that of the peach and the apple. There are usually two or more blossoms in each

Fig. 52.—Blossoms of the Japanese plum. These bear on short, plump spurs which carry a large number of blossom buds and consequently set fruit very abundantly.

winter bud and one or more leaves, though the leaves are frequently rather rudimentary (Figs. 52, 53 and 54).

In pruning these trees the orchardist adopts a middle course. They are not pruned as severely as in the peach because the spurs are going to bear for three or four or even more years, but they are pruned more severely than the apple because the bearing wood has to be renewed more frequently.

The Quince.—It remains to speak briefly of the quince, which has a method of fruit bearing entirely its own. There are not any winter fruit buds whatever; but each spring, shoots arise from lateral buds on last year's wood, and after these shoots have grown from one to six inches they produce a single, terminal blossom, which of course stops any further growth in that direction. The pruning ought therefore to aim at keeping the tree growing with reasonable vigor, and at keeping up a supply of new wood.

General Principles of Pruning.—It seems worth while to notice next a very few general principles which apply with greater or less force to the pruning of any tree.

FIG. 53.   FIG. 54

FIG. 53.—Blossoms of the European plum. Notice the blossoms and small or rudimentary leaves from each winter bud.

FIG. 54.—Cherries just set. Notice that only one (or two) in each cluster is developing. The rest will be crowded out in the struggle for existence.

Heavy Pruning and Vigorous Growth.—The first, and by all means the most important of these, is that a heavy pruning of the top during the dormant season will tend to cause a very vigorous wood growth the following season. This is exactly what might be expected and is easily explained if one will think the matter over a little. When the tree goes into the winter there is normally a balance between the top and the root system. Each one has grown enough so that when spring comes 'round again and growth begins, the roots can supply the food and water that will be needed to make a natural, typical growth of the top. Now comes along the pruner and takes off twenty-five to fifty per cent of that top. The result is that there remains one hundred per cent of roots to support fifty per cent of top, and of course the top is going to be better supported. It is going to make a tremendous growth to try and take care of all the food that the root is supplying. This is an especially important principle in renovation work, which is discussed in Chapter XVI.

Rank Growth Opposed to Fruit-bearing.—A second general principle which ought to go with this first one, though it is not strictly a principle of pruning, is that rank wood growth is opposed to fruit-bearing. One will rarely find a tree which is growing very vigorously that is also bearing heavily. The two things simply do not go together. The young tree, so long as it remains vigorous and growthy, does not come into bearing. In general it is those varieties, like the Wagener and Oldenburg apples, which are not vigorous growers, that bear early in life, while the strong growing sorts like Gravenstein and Spy require more time to come into fruit. So it is with the heavily pruned old tree. It at once starts a very vigorous growth of top but does not bear fruit until it has had time for this growth to subside.

The lesson which these two principles teach is very frequently overlooked by the man who does the pruning. He gauges his success by the amount of wood he takes out of the tree, and then when the tree fails to bear the following year he blames the practice of pruning instead of the operator.

Influence of Summer Pruning.—A third principle is that when pruning is done in the winter the tendency is to promote a strong growth of wood, while pruning done in the summer tends in the opposite direction, or towards the production of fruit. There can be no question about the first part of this. It is the same fact that was given in the first principle, only stated a little differently. The strength of the tendency will correspond exactly to the severity of the pruning. Prune a tree very severely during the dormant season and you will develop a very strong tendency towards wood growth the following year; prune it very moderately and the tendency to wood will be moderate. The other side of the principle, the influence of summer pruning towards the production of fruit, is not so well established and doubtless depends considerably on the nature and extent of such pruning. If a large amount of wood is

FIG. 55.   FIG. 56.

FIG. 55.—A Sutton apple tree. A very upright growing tree and one that is difficult to prune into a satisfactory shape.

FIG. 56.—Bradshaw plum tree. Like many other varieties of European plums the Bradshaw makes strong leaders which need to be cut back each year to keep the tree down.

removed in the summer pruning, and particularly if this is done rather early in the season, it is very doubtful whether there is much, if any, tendency towards fruit. In fact such pruning will usually result in developing secondary shoots which may produce quite as much growth as the original shoot would have done. But if the pruning is delayed until rather late in the season, and if it then consists in merely taking out the growing tip of the leaders, then it ought to have a considerable influence towards fruit-bearing.

This seems to be a reasonable explanation. We have said that rank growth does not favor fruit, while moderate growth does. This is because it is necessary to have plenty of elaborated plant food, such as starch and sugar in the cells to produce the fruit bud. It is the lack of this elaborated plant food which forces the little apple spur to produce merely a leaf bud the year that it bears an apple. Now if the summer pruning is delayed until rather late in the season so that plenty of leaf surface has been developed to manufacture starch and sugar, and if we then merely take out the growing tip we develop exactly the conditions that will tend towards fruit. We have taken away that part of the plant which was forming new leaves and new wood and which was therefore using a large amount of plant food (far more than it was itself producing), and we have left the manufacturing end of the tree practically the same as it was before. There is nothing left for the tree to do but to develop fruit buds.

Different Pruning for Old and Young Trees.—It is perhaps worth while to give one more general principle and that is that the habit of growth is quite different in a young tree from that in an old tree, and consequently the young tree requires a different kind of pruning. This difference is shown in various ways. In the first place the young tree grows more rankly, producing longer shoots and larger leaves.

In the second place young trees of most varieties tend to make a much more upright growth while young than when they get older. This is especially true of certain varieties of plums, apples, and pears, but it applies more or less to nearly all kinds of tree fruits except a certain few, like the Burbank and Satsuma plums, which are persistent sprawlers from the start (Fig. 57). Now if one of these close-growing young trees is thinned out during the first few years to what may seem the proper degree of density, then, when it comes into bearing, and the branches spread, as they naturally will, with the load of fruit the top is entirely too open. The pruner ought, therefore, to understand his variety and if it is an upright grower, as the Bartlett pear, it should be allowed to remain somewhat too thick while young, knowing that when it comes into bearing it will correct this difficulty of itself.

Pruning Tools.—Let us turn now to some of the practical details of pruning the orchard. The first thing to do is to provide a suitable outfit of pruning tools. This, of course, is going to vary with the type of pruning that one is doing, but for

Fig. 57.—A Burbank plum tree; one of those sprawling growing varieties which need to have the side leaders cut back every year.

general pruning, for doing all the different kinds that one is likely to be called upon to do, there should be at least several different saws, a good pair of hand shears, and a knife. Possibly we might add the pole pruner, though it is rare that it is needed and then it is unsatisfactory, as it can not be made to take off a branch properly. The one place where a pole pruner is really useful is in heading back side branches that are out of reach from the ground. The knife will be used the least of any part of the equipment, barring the pole pruner, but still the

FIG. 58.—A well-shaped Baldwin apple tree. Such a tree will carry a very heavy load of fruit and still not break down.

workman does occasionally find a place where nothing is quite so satisfactory as a good knife—in removing side shoots from the trunk of a young tree, for example.

Pruning Saws.—It is a singular thing, but the writer has never found a pruning saw upon the market that exactly suited him for serious orchard work. The fact that nine-tenths of the pruning saws on the market are of the two-edged type lends strength to the argument that there are at least very few good pruning saws to be had (Fig. 59). This two-edged pruning saw is a relic of barbarism which probably comes down from the days of the two-edged sword when men were not particular how much they mutilated the remains of their victims. Certainly no man who has ever done any pruning, and who has any regard for the tree he is at work upon, would ever use such a saw the second

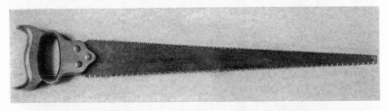

Fig. 59.—The two-edged saw. An abomination that ought to be banished from the orchard.

time if it could be avoided. After a good deal of thought and some experimenting, and after many consultations with practical orchard men, the writer has developed the series of saws shown in the accompanying pictures (Figs. 60, 61 and 62), which, if they are not entirely satisfactory, are at least a great improvement over anything that could be bought in the open market. They were all made up on special orders, by one of our large saw manufacturers.

The largest saw is designed for renovation work primarily, and any one who has " fiddled along " with one of the ordinary small pruning saws, or who has in desperation resorted to a big, clumsy carpenter's saw, will be delighted with the way this saw works. It was modelled after an old carpenter's saw that had been filed so often it had been reduced nearly to a point, and the narrowness at the point of this saw shown will be appreciated by the orchard renovator who gets into a narrow place. The specifications of the saw will be found beneath the picture. In developing this saw the large type of tooth was first tried; this is known technically as the lumberman's tooth, and is shown in the cut of the two-edged saw. This tooth was tried because it seemed reasonable that a large tooth, on a saw of this

Fig. 60.   Fig. 61.   Fig. 62.

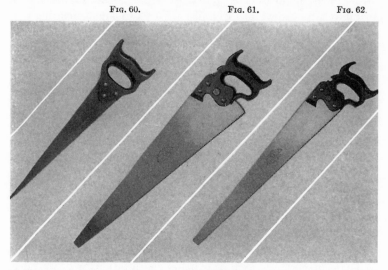

Fig. 60.—A good saw for small trees. It is 14 inches long, three inches wide at the butt, with seven teeth per inch.

Fig. 61.—An excellent saw for heavy pruning. It is 26 inches long, 6 inches wide at the butt, 1 inch wide at the tip and has five teeth per inch.

Fig. 62.—A good saw for ordinary pruning. It is 24 inches long, 4 inches wide at the butt, 1 inch wide at the tip, with five and one-half teeth per inch.

type, would cut faster than a small one, but in actual orchard work it was found that it required more effort to cut off a branch with the coarse-toothed saw than with the finer type. The saw simply did not have weight enough to carry such heavy teeth.

The second and third saws are intended for use on trees which have been well cared for and regularly pruned and which therefore do not need to have any very large branches taken out.

The writer is still experimenting on both of these sizes and may develop some slight changes, but they are very satisfactory just as they stand. The small saw, Figure 60, is intended primarily for work in young trees, but it will do excellent work on any ordinary fruit tree. It simply means a little more work to get off a large limb with this saw than with those shown in Figures 61 and 62.

Pruning Shears.—Next to a saw, a good pair of hand shears will be found most useful. In fact where the orchardist is pruning fairly young trees, say up to six or seven years, and where he has a large pair of shears, of the type shown in Figure

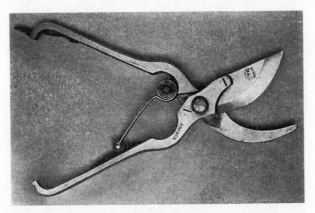

FIG. 63.—An excellent type of pruning shears. A large part of the pruning on many trees may be done with a shear of this type.

63, it is surprising how seldom it is necessary to resort to the saw. The shears shown are imported, being made in France. They are known technically as the " French wheel-spring shears." It seems unfortunate to be obliged to recommend an imported article; perhaps the writer has been unfortunate in the American shears he has used, but he has tried many makes and none of them have stood up under hard usage like this French make. In buying such shears get good-sized ones for heavy work. A ten-inch size of this pattern is none too large when one is going to do a lot of heavy pruning. For example: A foreman used one of these ten-inch shears for pruning about

three thousand peach trees four and five years old, and an equal
number of apple trees varying from one to five years; after which
the shears were still in good working order.

A good knife completes the outfit for most work. A heavy
knife, with a wide blade and a good hook on the end of the
blade, is best. The one shown in Figure 64 suits the work admirably, though a man will use a pair of shears a thousand times

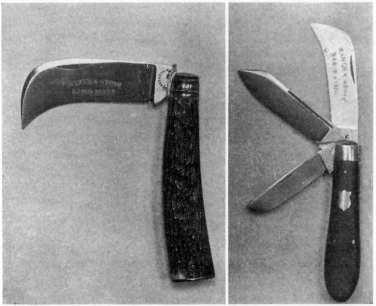

Fig. 64.—A good type of pruning knife. Long hooked blade and large enough for heavy
work.

Fig. 65.—A good combination knife; pruning, budding and ordinary blades.

for every time he uses a knife. The second knife shown in
Figure 65 is a good one, with a budding blade and an ordinary
blade, in addition to the pruner. Where a man wants to do
various things with the knife it is probably worth having.
Usually, however, the workman prefers to have his blade in
different handles, and carry only the type of knife for which he
has immediate use.

Actual Pruning.—Now let us sally forth with our newly acquired pruning tools and do some actual pruning. Every different tree will prove to be a different problem. This is one thing that makes pruning interesting. It is not the province of this chapter to suggest all the types of problems that the pruner will encounter. Two of these will have to suffice.

Young Trees.—The first is the young tree. Like training children this is the most important and the most difficult stage. At the time of setting, the tree is given a severe pruning as outlined in chapter four. The next season and for several years thereafter something like the following program is followed:

First.—The head of the tree is examined to see that the main branches are satisfactory in number and in position. There ought to be from three to five of these main scaffold branches and they should be well distributed about the tree, not coming out at the same height and not too many of them on any one side. This is a more serious problem than some might think, particularly with certain varieties such as the Wealthy apple, which do not tend to form good heads naturally. It will require ten times the effort on this one point to shape up satisfactorily a block of Wealthy trees that it will to develop a similar block of McIntosh trees. In any case, but particularly with wayward growers, it is well worth while to look after this matter of main branches during the growing season, and it ought to be settled just as early in the life of the tree as possible. Yet with all one's care it often happens that branches simply will not develop in the right place at the start, and the pruner must keep at the tree until he gets a reasonably satisfactory top. Frequently he has to forego a scaffold branch at one point and train out secondary branches from adjoining main branches to supply the deficiency.

Second.—Examine the leaders, particularly the leaders in the top of the tree, and shorten them in, if they need it, as they usually do. In most cases the side leaders may be allowed to grow as much as they will, for at this stage one wants to develop a good big tree. It is only with such sprawling growers as the Burbank plum that one needs to head back the side leaders.

Third.—Look for poor forks on all the main branches. This is not quite so important as the forks at the main trunk, but it is well worth looking out for, especially with varieties which tend to develop these poor forks frequently, and it does not require a great amount of time.

Fourth.—Take out crossing branches, particularly those which tend to grow back into the centre of the tree where they do not belong. As a rule these crossing branches may be left till the second year without any damage, unless they are very vigorous, and one will find that it requires much less time to do the necessary pruning if only two-year wood is considered. This is really a point of a good deal of practical importance where one has many trees to prune. With a half dozen trees to look after the owner can afford to look at every twig. With a half dozen hundred it is a different matter.

Fifth.—Thin out the rest of the top where this may be needed. Usually there is little left to do after the first four points have been looked after.

Sixth.—Never take out the small shoots so long as they remain healthy. This rule has few exceptions. If the top is too thick take out small branches with their attached shoots but do not take the shoots alone.

Bearing Trees.—The second illustrative pruning problem we want to discuss is the tree at bearing age. Of course this is going to vary greatly even with different varieties, and still more with different classes of fruits, and yet there are a good many things which are common to all trees. Here is the program:

First.—Preserve the fruit spurs. Never strip a branch of small shoots, whether they are spurs or not. This has already been discussed under the various fruits and also under the young tree and it need not be further elaborated here, but it is of crucial importance.

Second.—Thin the top uniformly by taking out relatively small branches. It is a very common mistake to prune out too large branches while removing the same total amount of wood from the tree. This means that in some parts of the top we have made large holes where there is no wood whatever, while in other parts the top is as thick as before. Branches the size of a man's finger are the ideal size. This kind of pruning requires more work, in some cases much more work, but it is worth the extra effort. And the tendency to overdo the pruning is less.

Third.—Cut out dead or diseased or broken branches. This needs no discussion except to say that in some diseases, like black knot and canker, it is not always possible to remove all the affected branches. Sometimes the branch is of so much importance that it must be cured if possible.

Fourth.—Shorten back the leaders where they are going too high or are spreading too far. In doing this do not leave a straight stub but take them back to a side shoot. The importance of keeping the trees down where they can be sprayed and picked and pruned easily can hardly be overestimated.

Fifth.—Take out the water-sprouts altogether where they are not needed and shorten them back severely where they are needed. In this type of tree, the well-cared-for, bearing tree, there are usually few water-sprouts and no need of preserving them. But if they are needed it is merely to reclothe a branch with bearing wood and they should therefore be cut back each year to one or two buds. This ought to gradually cause the formation of fruit spurs. If it does not they should be taken out altogether.

Sixth.—Cut out crossing branches or such as tend to grow back into the tree. There are not likely to be many of these where the pruning is attended to each year, yet there are always a few.

Seventh.—Thin the balance of the top where it is needed. As with the young tree, there is usually not much left to thin after all the other points are looked after.

Time to Prune.—It remains to discuss briefly a few general questions which are sure to come up where the subject of pruning is being discussed. The first of these is the season of the year at which pruning should be done. It does not make much difference. Summer and winter pruning have already been discussed, and barring the difference brought out in that discussion, there is little choice as to seasons so far as the effect on the tree is concerned. There is this objection to autumn pruning that the wounds made then have to stand a long time before they can begin to heal, which means, of course, that they dry out and die back further than they would if made at any other time of year. And yet other considerations may entirely offset this objection. For example, renovation pruning is frequently done in the autumn, because the owner wants to begin the fight on the San José scale,

Fig. 66.   Fig. 67.

Fig. 66.—A long stub left in pruning. Such a stub is sure to decay before it can heal over.

Fig. 67.—An old stub beginning to decay. It is impossible for such stubs to heal over and every one is a menace to the tree.

and this can not be done to the best advantage until the dead and half-dead branches have all been removed. It ought also to be said here that there is no harm to the tree from pruning when the wood is frozen. It may harm the *pruner* but not the pruned. There is also probably little harm to the tree from bleeding, though it is best to avoid it if possible. It produces more favorable conditions for disease germs and possibly weakens the tree slightly.

There are two very strong reasons why pruning is usually done during the dormant season, the first being that there is usually more time at that season of the year, and the second that a workman can judge better what branches ought to be removed, because there are no leaves to interfere. It will be seen, therefore, that the time for pruning is chosen largely from the standpoint of convenience. Do it when it will best fit in with the other farm work.

How to Prune.—The best way to make the cuts in pruning is of far more importance than the time of making them. To

FIG. 68.   FIG. 69   FIG. 70

FIG. 68.—A well-made wound. Such a wound will heal over if some dressing is used to preserve the heart wood.

FIG. 69.—A well-made wound beginning to heal. With proper care such a wound will heal over completely in a few years.

FIG. 70.—A well-made wound that has entirely healed over.

begin with, every branch that is removed, whether it be small or large, ought to be cut just as close to the limb from which it is taken as possible (Fig. 68). There is no exception to this rule. A large collection of these wounds was made in getting up an exhibition on pruning, for a "better farming" train. Without any exception the wounds where long stubs had been left were not healing well. Those that were old enough had already begun to decay (Fig. 67). Those which had been cut close were healing nicely. Some of these wounds are shown in Figures 68 and 69. Cutting back close like this is going to enlarge the wound considerably, but do not worry about that. Cut close, and the tree will do the rest.

It is also desirable to leave the wound as smooth as possible, to which end one should not use an axe but should use a sharp saw. It rarely pays, however, in commercial work to smooth a wound up with a knife. Leave that for the amateur. Occasionally, when the best healing is very important and when, in some way, a rough cut has been made, it may be worth while to take a knife and smooth up the edges along the cambium layer.

Dressings for Wounds.—All sorts of things are used for this purpose, from mixtures of clay and cow-dung to grafting wax or shellac. The ideal dressing ought to be durable, waterproof, harmless to the tree, reasonably cheap and easily applied. If it can be antiseptic so much the better. In the writer's opinion there are just two classes of dressings that are worth using. These are paints of various kinds and the tar and creosote mixtures. For nearly all wounds, paint is the best material by far and comes very near to possessing all of the desirable points just enumerated. It is best to mix your own paint rather thick, using white lead and raw linseed oil. Also add a little raw sienna, enough to make the paint about the color of the bark. This does not make it any better dressing, but the wounds you are making will worry the neighbors less. This is particularly important on renovation work where many and relatively large wounds will have to be made. Tar or creosote are preferred on large wounds simply because these substances are better preservatives than paint, and the heartwood of the large wound will have to stand many years before it is completely healed over. One reason why tar preserves better than paint is because it strikes in more deeply. It therefore damages the cambium layer more, and for this reason, on large wounds which it is very desirable to have heal well, the pruner will sometimes tar the center of the wound and use oil and lead paint around the outside over the cambium layer. This takes considerable time but is worth it in important cases. Pruners are sometimes advised to take a paint pot into the tree when pruning and paint the wounds at once. There are two objections to this: First, the pruning tools are all that he wants to be bothered with at one time; and, second, the wounds will take the paint much better if they are allowed to dry out a little. It is usually much better to delay the painting for two or three weeks.

QUESTIONS

1. Explain why the pruner should understand how trees bear their fruit
2. Describe the method of fruit-bearing of pear and apple trees.
3. What should be the object of the orchardist in pruning these trees?
4. Describe the method of fruit-bearing in the peach.
5. Give the differences in pruning between the peach and the apple.
6. Compare the plum or the cherry with the apple in method of bearing fruit.
7. How would the pruning differ?
8. How does the quince differ from the others in its fruit-bearing?
9. Explain the general relation between heavy pruning and vigorous growth.
10. Why is rank growth opposed to fruit-bearing?
11. What are the influences of summer pruning as compared with winter pruning?
12. Why should the pruning of young trees differ from that of old ones?
13. Give a list of pruning tools for orchard work.
14. What are some of the desirable points in a pruning saw?
15. Describe the best shears for orchard pruning.
16. Give specific directions for the pruning of young trees for the first few years.
17. Discuss the problems involved in pruning trees of bearing age.
18. Give cautions and directions regarding the pruning operations.
19. How should wounds be dressed? Why is this done?
20. Have you seen old orchards that were not properly pruned? What was the effect of such neglect?

CHAPTER XI

ORCHARD INSECTS

IT is not expected that this chapter will include, by any means, all of the insects with which the orchard owner is likely to have dealings. To do that would require a volume in itself. An endeavor has been made to select merely those insects which experience and observation have shown were almost certain to be commercially important to the man who grows an orchard. And they have been treated in the briefest possible way and principally from the standpoint of fighting them in the orchard, only enough of their life history being included to give a key to the most effective line of treatment.

Following the custom of almost every one who writes on this subject, the writer wishes to lay down certain general principles, a knowledge of which ought to enable the orchardist to select, with a fair degree of certainty, the remedies that should be most successful. Of course the details will vary slightly with each case, but it should be possible for anyone to select the general line of attack.

The first general rule is that if an insect actually devours the tissues of the plant, so that anyone can see very evidently where it has been at work and that some of the tissue has disappeared, then the cheapest and best remedy is some kind of poison applied to that part of the plant where the insect is feeding. In other words, it is cheaper to poison an insect by means of the food it eats than it is to kill it in any other way; but you are able to kill it in this way only when it chews off a piece of the leaf or fruit and swallows it.

Take the *tent-caterpillar* as an example of this class of insects. Almost every one is familiar with its work. The tree attacked looks more and more ragged as its leaves are eaten until finally it may be entirely stripped of foliage. It ought to be evident to anyone that these insects are devouring the plant tissues and can be killed through their food. Some sort of poison

142

is used to kill them, such as Paris green or arsenate of lead, and not such a substance as lime, or sulfur or copper sulfate.

If a man were attempting to poison a skunk or a weasel that was killing his chickens he would not expect to do it by putting out a bait covered with sulfur, but would use some form of strychnine or arsenic. Precisely the same rule holds with insects. They are merely smaller animals. They take the poison along with the plant tissue into the stomach and are killed.

Now contrast with this the *aphis,* which is a conspicuous example of an altogether different type of insects. Most orchard owners are entirely too familiar with the way this insect works. If the owner is on the watch for it he sees first a few little green or black lice on the under side of the leaf, or even on the opening bud, waiting for the leaf to appear. These increase rapidly in number and the leaf begins to curl up because the under surface, where the insects are sucking the sap of the leaf, is thereby retarded in its growth, while the upper surface, being less affected, continues to grow normally or nearly so. But the leaf, while it is distorted, does not disappear. It is all there except the juice and no amount of poison applied to it will have any effect on the aphis. It would be exactly as reasonable to expect to kill a mosquito, by putting Paris green on one's hand, as to destroy the aphis with such a poison. The beak of either insect would be pushed through the layer of poison and into the tissues on which it wished to feed and it would draw in the blood of the man or the sap of the plant without any poison whatever.

Insects of the aphis type have to be attacked in an entirely different manner. And it is a much more expensive method. They must be treated with some substance which will either stop up the pores along the sides of the abdomen through which the insect breathes or else (either by entering those pores or by working on the surface of the insect) will corrode the tissues and destroy the insect. Soapy substances work in the former manner, while the oils and similar substances actually attack the tissues.

These may seem like very simple statements and so they are. But they are fundamental and are inserted here because so often they are not understood. Indeed, at meetings of fruit growers one often hears some intelligent orchard man recommend the use of Bordeaux mixture for the tent-caterpillar, or condemn arsenate of lead because it did not kill the aphis.

APPLE INSECTS

The following list comprises those insects which the apple grower has to reckon with year in and year out. Of course they do not all come in any one season, but he has to be on the watch for them, and when they do come they make serious trouble. They are arranged roughly in the order of their importance, though seasons, localities and even varieties influence this point.

The San José scale and the codling moth are rivals for first place on the list of the apple grower's insect troubles. Either one is bad enough but the scale is considered first because of its ability in actually killing the trees. In its damage to the fruit itself the codling moth is far in the lead, for a wormy apple is seriously damaged, while the apple with scale on it is not hurt much for cooking and even for eating raw, a few scales will not particularly affect the flavor.

There are three things which make the scale an insect specially dreaded by the orchardist.

Inconspicuous.—The first of these is its inconspicuous character. Unless the owner is very familiar with it, the first notice he has of its presence on the tree may be the dying of some of the branches. An insect which is spectacular in its attack, such as the tent-caterpillar or the fall web-worm, has little chance of escaping notice. But the San José scale is so small, and looks so much like the bark of the tree, that even one who is entirely familiar with it may go by an affected tree day after day and never notice it. The writer confesses with chagrin that he has proved this point in his own garden.

Breeds Rapidly.—The second difficulty in combating the scale is the fact that it breeds continuously and rapidly throughout the season. Beginning some time in the late spring or early summer, at a date varying with the locality, the young scales are produced up to late autumn. And they are produced with surprising rapidity. Investigations have shown that so rapidly are the young produced and so quickly do they reach maturity, that starting with a single female in the spring we might reasonably expect that by the close of the breeding season there would be a family of something like a billion, if there were no accidents. Fortunately there are many accidents, but, even so, the rate of increase is tremendous. This "continuous performance" in production means that while the grower may clean up the trees in the early spring and have relatively few live scales, yet if he leaves any at all, he may expect that by autumn the trees will be in bad shape again.

Attacks Many Kinds of Plants.—The third difficulty in keeping the scale down comes from the fact that it feeds on so many different trees and shrubs. The orchardist may get it out of his apple trees, but an adjoining currant patch or some Japanese quinces or thorn trees or dog-woods on a neighbor's lawn, or even willow trees along the brook, may furnish a new source of supply. It is therefore a constant fight in a scale neighborhood.

Hard to Recognize.—The first point in this fight is to learn to recognize the pest. The easiest way to do this with apple trees is to watch the young apples as they develop. The young scales seem to be particularly partial to the fruit and are especially conspicuous on it, so that if there are any great number of scales on the trees one is sure to find them sooner or later on the apples. They usually collect at the blossom or calyx end of the fruit, and frequently, though not always, produce a bright red spot, the scales themselves varying in color from nearly white on through gray to practically black. One will therefore find a white, gray or black central speck surrounded by a bright red ring. The scale itself is easily scraped off, leaving the red ring with a light center. On the twigs and branches the appearance is frequently described as resembling ashes thrown upon the tree, and this is as good a description as can be given. The bark will be roughened, and on scraping it with the thumb nail or the back of a jack-knife a wet, yellowish streak is produced by the crushing of the insects. Also if the observer cuts into

the twig, the inner bark, which is normally green, will be found
to be stained red.

Remedies.—In fighting this insect the two standard remedies,
at the present time, are the lime-sulfur washes and the miscible,
or so-called "soluble," oils, which are fully described in
Chapter XIV. Many other things are used, and doubtless
new remedies will be constantly put upon the market, but these
two have stood the test of time and seem likely to stand it for
some time to come. It is usually not possible to keep the scale
entirely under control without giving two sprayings per year.
Not being able to decide which of the above remedies is the
better, the writer has developed the plan of using oil in the
autumn, as soon as the leaves are off the trees, and lime-sulfur
in the spring just before the buds break. The bulk of the
insects are thus killed by the autumn treatment while many
of them are young and less resistant, and one gets the advantage
of the " creeping " of the oil. Also the operation is less disagreeable, which is worth considering. And lastly, the tree
does not have to exhaust itself by supporting all these insects
over winter. Then by using the lime-sulfur in the spring, the
orchardist not only kills what scales were left but also gets the
advantage of the fungicidal effect of the wash.

Thorough Spraying.—The one fundamental thing in the application of insecticides for scale is thoroughness. Keep everlast-
ingly after the men who are doing the work and insist on their
reaching every part of the trees. This is more important with
scale than with any other insect, though it is always of importance. Take the codling moth for example. Suppose the
orchardist sprays only half of the apples—he has protected those,
at least in a section like New England where there is but one
brood. But if he is going to hit only half of the apples in fighting
scale, he might better save his time and money, and go to a ball
game, for both will be absolutely thrown away on this spraying.
The scales will continue to breed on the unsprayed areas and
will soon reinfest the whole tree.

Perhaps a little experience may be worth relating here, as it
serves to show just where a grower is likely to get into trouble.

It was in spraying for scale on some old apple trees at the Massachusetts Agricultural College. These trees had been used for a number of years for testing new, and for the most part worthless, sprays for scale. Many of the trees had become completely covered with scale and were dying rapidly, and though they were not very valuable in themselves, they were a constant menace to other trees that were valuable. It did not look well for the college to have such a disreputable orchard around, even for experimental purposes. So it was decided to clean it up. It was sprayed as here outlined, oil in the autumn and lime-sulfur in the spring, and the work was done with a reasonable degree of thoroughness. The next season the trees were examined from time to time through the summer, and at first everything looked well, and we said, "What a fine thing it was to get those old trees cleaned up." But gradually we began to see a few scales, and then more and more, till finally we were back about where we started. Too many of the tips of the branches had been missed in spraying. The next year the same program was followed, only these tips were looked after, and out of thirty trees that were literally alive with scale only two or three were found that had any scale at all, and these had very few indeed.

Some Varieties Injured more than Others.—A point which is worth mentioning in this connection is the varying degree to which different varieties are injured by the scale. Any neglected orchard that is suffering from scale will show this. Rhode Island Greening trees will be found half-dead, while Kings and Baldwins, under the same conditions, are in fairly good condition.

Codling Moth.—This is the insect that is responsible for the wormy apple, and no one can visit our markets without having it borne in upon him what a fearful responsibility it is. Simple as the treatment for this insect is, and long as the life history has been well understood, the pest is still allowed to do a tremendous amount of damage.

The moth itself is small and inconspicuous and is seldom seen by the orchard man. It deposits its eggs sometimes on the fruit but more often on adjoining leaves or even on the bark of twigs and branches, where they hatch in a short time and the little " worms," or larvæ, soon attack the young apples, in most cases entering at the blossom end. Once inside the apple, they feed for about a month, principally on the inside (but occasionally working on the surface). When it has reached full size the larva emerges and forms its cocoon usually in some crevice in the bark. From this point the life history varies with different parts of the country. In most of New England there is only a partial second brood, that is most of them pass the winter in the cocoon stage. A few pass through this stage and emerge as moths which deposit their eggs, producing the second brood of " worms." The future history is practically the same as before, except that the later broods of the season do more feeding on the surface of the apples, especially where two apples hang together or where a leaf rests upon an apple.

In States farther south there are two or more complete broods in a season.

The all-important remedy in fighting the codling moth is spraying with poison, and usually it is the only remedy attempted. In sections where the codling moth is very troublesome the following additional methods are practised:

First, the rough bark is scraped from the trees so as to reduce the number of hiding places for the larvæ when they emerge.

Second, bands of burlap are put about the trees as traps under which the larvæ will spin their cocoons. These bands are removed from time to time and the insects which are found under them are killed.

Third, the windows of storage houses are kept screened so as to prevent the escape of the moths which may have passed the winter as larvæ in barrels or elsewhere.

But, as before suggested, the all-important method of control is spraying with a poison. Authorities differ as to just the type of spray that is best. Many western experimenters insist on a coarse, forcible spray which shall force the poison into the calyx cup. Others believe in a fine, mist-like spray which shall reach all parts of the tree. This is the type of spray which is most in favor. All agree that the spraying should be very thorough and that it is best to make the first spraying within a week or ten days after the petals fall from the blossoms, using 3 pounds arsenate of lead to 50 gallons of water. A second spraying is usually made three or four weeks later. In sections where several broods are produced it is necessary even to spray three or four times for this insect.

Avoid Spraying When Trees Are in Bloom.—Another important point is the desirability of avoiding spraying while the trees are in bloom. Authorities differ as to just how serious a matter it is, but there seems to be considerable evidence to show that the bees may be killed by such a spray. It is also probable that the pistils may be injured if the spraying is done just when they are in the most tender condition, which is when the trees are in " full bloom." In any event there seems to be nothing gained by spraying when trees are in bloom, over spraying just after the petals fall. It is certainly worth while to avoid any chance of injuring either the bees or the blossoms.

Aphis.—This is the most discouraging group to fight, of all the "bugs." So far as winning the fight is concerned the writer had far sooner tackle the San José scale. With the latter there is a well-defined course of treatment, and if one follows this carefully there is no question about success. With the aphis one never knows quite what to do, and when the best possible has been done, the result usually leaves much to be desired.

The life history of the aphis is as follows: It passes the winter in the egg state and these eggs will be found as little, shiny black objects looking much like weed seeds, clustered about the buds on last year's growth. They hatch very early in the spring, usually before the buds open, into little, dark green, almost black, lice which will be found on the expanding buds, and, later, on the under side of the leaves. The leaves soon curl up and protect the insects almost perfectly. The later generations of the young are produced alive, and as it requires but a few days to reach maturity and as each adult female will produce several young in a day, they increase with great rapidity. This makes their control a serious matter.

Control.—Now, what shall be done to check this insect? As already suggested, in the general discussion, this is a sucking insect and must be killed by a contact poison; that is *every insect must be hit to be killed.* When we remember how well they are protected and how rapidly they increase, the difficulty of controlling them may be realized. It is realized still more fully after we have tried to fight them. Nothing but the most thorough treatment will be effective, for if only a few individuals are left after a spraying they will increase so rapidly that in a very few days things are as bad as ever.

The best time to fight the aphis is in the early stages, before the leaves have become much curled. Indeed, if some treatment could be devised to destroy the eggs in winter, that would be the ideal method. It has often been suggested that the winter spraying with oil or lime-sulfur might be effective, but there is much doubt in regard to this. Orchards which had been sprayed every year for four years with both oil and lime-sulfur were as badly infected with aphis as the most neglected orchard in the neighborhood.

The best treatment seems to be to spray with lime-sulfur at the rate of one gallon of the commercial preparation to about 25 of water just as the buds are breaking and after the aphids have hatched. If the right time can be selected after all the aphids are hatched and before the leaves are out enough to be damaged, and if the work is done thoroughly enough to destroy this first generation, then there will be no future generations. Later treatment, when needed, must consist in using some one of the contact sprays, either as a separate spray or combined with the arsenical sprays which are given for codling moth. On the Pacific coast, where these insects are troublesome and where there is a form which does not curl the leaves, it is the usual custom to combine a tobacco preparation with the poison and the fungicide of the regular sprayings and thus kill both types of insects and the fungous diseases.

But when all is said and done, the aphis is still a very difficult insect to control and it is fortunate that bad outbreaks of it do not occur more frequently.

Curculio.—Both the plum and the apple curculios work on the apple, but the former is a far more serious pest. They are both " snout " beetles, but the plum curculio is of a dark, brownish-gray color and has a short snout, while the apple curculio is reddish-brown in color and has a long, slender snout. For present purposes, however, they may be considered together.

Life History.—They hibernate as adult insects in the grass or trash about the orchard and emerge in the spring about the time that the trees bloom. They feed for a time on the buds, leaves and even blossoms, but soon attack the fruit, and the females begin laying eggs in small punctures in the skin of the young apples, the plum curculio cutting, in addition, a crescent-shaped incision above the incision where the egg is deposited. On apples most of the eggs do not develop and the damage results from the scars, which cause the fruit to become misshapen and unsalable. With plums and peaches the larvæ usually do develop and produce the white " worms " of the fruit, all too common in many orchards.

The most effective treatment for the curculio is spraying with arsenate of lead, using 3 pounds to 50 gallons of water, within a week after the petals fall from the blossoms. This is the same spray which is most important for the codling moth, so that one kind of treatment will control these two serious pests.

Bud Moth.—This is a very interesting insect from the standpoint of its life history, which is quite unusual. The egg hatches in the summer and the little " worm " is dark brown with a shiny black head. It grows to perhaps an eighth of an inch in length and then prepares a little nest for the winter. This little nest or burrow is usually located in some crevice of the bark near a bud, and considerable experience is necessary to find it, as it is very difficult to detect. About the only indication of its whereabouts is a bit of leaf, or a small scale of bark, attached to the branch. On poking about with a pin, however, the searcher will find a little web and soon is rewarded by finding the little silk-lined tunnel and in it the rascally little "worm."

As soon as the weather begins to warm up in the spring, and the buds begin to break, this little fellow crawls out of his winter quarters and establishes himself in the center of the expanding cluster of leaves and blossoms from some terminal bud. Here he develops, feeding on the leaves and blossoms and drawing them together in a rather compact bunch by fastening the ends together with silk threads.

Spraying.—Once the larva gets inside this cluster it is perfectly safe. No amount of spraying can touch it, as it feeds on the inside. The only time when it is feasible to attack this enemy is when it goes from its winter quarters to the opening buds and leaves. The larva eats its way into this cluster of leaves, and if the trees can be sprayed just before it crawls from winter quarters it can be poisoned. But the poison must be strong. Five to ten pounds of arsenate of lead to fifty gallons of water will be none too strong. And the spraying must be thorough; every bud-cluster must be reached.

The amount of damage which this insect does in some seasons is very great, but the insect is so inconspicuous that its presence is usually not even suspected. Practically the entire crop of certain varieties is sometimes destroyed by the bud moth and the loss attributed by the growers to unfavorable weather at blossoming time.

Canker Worm.—There are two types of canker worm, differing principally in the fact that in one case the eggs are laid in the autumn and in the other case in the spring. In both types the insect pupates in the soil and the wingless adult females crawl up the trunk of the tree and deposit their eggs in clusters or sheets upon the branches. Here they hatch about the time the leaves are well expanded into small "measuring-worms" and begin feeding.

Their presence can usually be detected by shaking the branches of the trees, when each little "worm" will drop from the leaves and hang by a thread. Another good method is to go under the trees and look up through the tops, when the small holes eaten out where the little larvæ have been feeding will be readily seen.

Ordinarily canker worms are not troublesome, frequently they will not be seen for years, but when they do come in force, look out for trouble. It will require sharp, efficient work to keep them in check.

Methods of Combating.—There are two principal ways in which these insects may be combated. The best way, by all odds, because it fits in with the fight against other insects, is to spray with arsenate of lead or some such poison. Usually the spraying for codling moth will attend to the canker worms as well. And yet instances are seen where the most energetic and up-to-date orchard men have been literally swamped by a bad outbreak of this pest.

Where, for any reason, one expects such an especially severe attack from them, it is well to band the trees with some sticky substance to catch the wingless female insects as they crawl up the trunk. If no crack is left underneath the band through which the female can make her way, and if the bands are kept sticky for a long enough time, the method is decidedly effective. For the fall canker worm October and November, and for the spring species March and April, are likely to be the months during which the females move up the trunk.

In this connection it is worth calling attention to the fact that the stirring of the soil in cultivated orchards makes it difficult for canker worms to pupate with any degree of comfort and security.

Tent-caterpillar.—This is a leaf-eating caterpillar of the "first magnitude." A few nests of them in an apple tree will strip it of leaves about as completely as the cold of winter can do it.

The eggs are laid in the summer in curious bands which may be discovered about the twigs during the winter when the leaves are out of the way. These eggs hatch with the first warm days of spring and the little bits of black, hairy caterpillars may be found clustered about the expanding buds in the vicinity, waiting for the leaves to come out enough to give them a "square meal." Getting such an early start as they do and being provided with an insatiable appetite, they come very near to keeping up with the leaves when there is a bad attack of them. This makes it necessary to use drastic measures with them when they once get a start in an orchard. Few insects can make an apple tree look more desolate.

Remedy.—Where trees are attacked badly by this insect it will usually be necessary to give a special spraying with arsenate of lead before the blossoms open, else they may get so large that it will be difficult to kill them with any ordinary dose. If they have been allowed to get a start in the orchard it is simply a question of using poison strong enough and they can be killed. Half to three-quarters of a pound of Paris green, or four to six pounds of arsenate of lead to fifty gallons of water will be found none too strong.

The Railroad Worm or Apple Maggot.—There is not much satisfaction in discussing this insect because, up to date, there has been so little discovered that can be done for it.

Life History and Habits.—The adult insect is a little fly which deposits its eggs just under the skin of the apple. This egg-laying is likely to occur at any time during the summer and on hatching the little maggot burrows through the flesh of the apple. If there are several maggots in one apple the fruit may be completely riddled. An affected apple has a peculiar pitted appearance on the outside, the sunken areas being of a different color from the balance of the surface. On cutting open the apple the flesh will be found to be a net-work of little tunnels. The first tunnels made by the little worm after hatching, usually close up and appear merely as little hard threads running through the flesh. The later tunnels remain open. An apple attacked by this insect is practically worthless as human food, but may be fed to stock.

It is a curious fact that the apple maggot seems to have very decided preferences for certain varieties. In a general way those varieties which are soft in flesh and mild in flavor seem to be especially acceptable to it. Such varieties as Hubbard-ston, Porter and Tolman Sweet may be badly attacked, while adjoining trees of other varieties are little injured.

Destroy the Wind-falls.—About the only generally accepted thing to do for this pest is to destroy the wind-fall apples. If one has any number of trees and attempts to do this by hand it is a good-sized contract. But if it can be arranged to run hogs or sheep in the orchard they will effectually clean up the wind-falls. The one objection to these animals in the orchard is that they do not always wait for the apple to drop before they eat it, and they are likely to clean up not only apples but leaves on low-hanging branches. In many old orchards, however, where there are no branches near the ground this objection does not apply. Hogs are especially adapted to this purpose. They not only dispose of the drop apples, but by their rooting they furnish a good substitute for cultivation and their droppings will enrich the soil. They are particularly good in old orchards on lands too steep and rocky to be cultivated. Occasionally they make some trouble by barking the trunks and branches, but this does not often happen if they are kept well watered and fed.

Effect of Spraying.—The one other hopeful suggestion in connection with this insect is that it seems to do relatively little damage in orchards which are well sprayed. Some of the most recent experiments seem to show that it may be possible even to do some special spraying for it, using some poison combined with molasses to make a sweet poison which, when sprayed upon the leaves, shall attract and kill the adult flies in the same way that poison fly-paper kills our house-flies.

Cultivation.—It is also worthy of note that early spring plowing, followed by thorough cultivation, seems to reduce considerably the damage from this pest.

Borers.—The apple grower is likely to be troubled by two species of borers, the flat-headed and the round-headed apple-tree borers. They differ principally in the fact that the latter requires much more time to reach maturity than the former, but either one will stay in the tree long enough to make it look sick. All parts of the trunk and main branches are liable to attack, but especially the lower part of the trunk. The larvæ burrow in the wood, principally in the sap wood, and in bad cases they may completely girdle the tree.

Clean Culture.—Trees standing in sod, or with weeds about the trunks, are especially liable to attack, much more so than in well cultivated orchards. Take the case of a single young orchard which was examined on account of some of the trees being badly attacked by borers. The land was under cultivation, but several patches were very weedy. Other parts were entirely free from weeds; and without exception the trees attacked by borers were those standing in weeds. This suggests one of the best methods of fighting this pest in sections where it has been found troublesome—thorough cultivation.

Careful Examination.—The presence of the borers may be detected usually by the castings or dust which is thrown out by the larva as it bores through the wood. In badly affected trees it is also shown by the sickly appearance of the tree, but no one should ever wait for this sign. In sections where this pest is likely to be troublesome the trees should be examined carefully at least once a year, the best time being early autumn.

Dig Out Borers.—When a tree is found to be affected the only thing to do is to cut out the borer. A good sharp knife and a stout wire are the usual equipment. Cut into the burrow and follow it up until the borer is found. Sometimes the wire is used to push into the hole and kill the borer without getting it out of the burrow. This is all right provided one is certain that the borer is killed, and of course it saves some cutting of the tree.

Prevention.—It seems unfortunate that some really satisfactory method of prevention has not been devised. Various schemes have been suggested and some of them are certainly worth trying. A piece of wire screen, if put on carefully so that the female insect can neither crawl down behind it, nor deposit the egg through it where the screen rests against the bark, will prevent any attack on the trunk, where most of the trouble occurs. Another plan worth trying, in sections where these insects are known to be plentiful, is to wash the trunks with soft soap or whale-oil soap, made the consistency of thick paint. To this is added some crude carbolic acid, an ounce to each gallon of the wash.

Another borer which is worth mentioning here is the shot-hole or pin borer, a small, cylindrical insect of the size of the lead in an ordinary pencil. It makes many small holes in the trunk and main branches, but, so far as known, never attacks a thoroughly healthy tree. If this insect is found, therefore, it is an indication that the trees have been damaged in some other way, and the cause of and remedy for this injury should be investigated

INSECTS ATTACKING THE PEAR

The pear is attacked by much the same list of insects as the apple. The San José scale is even more partial to it than to the apple, the codling moth attacks it, so does the curculio, and the canker worm is by no means averse to a pear diet. Of course the treatment for all these insects is the same as when they attack the apple. Two other insects, however, which have not been mentioned may be given here.

Pear Psylla.—This insect prefers the pear and it frequently becomes so serious as to practically ruin an orchard. Cases are known where men were actually driven to cut down their pear trees because of the difficulty of keeping the psylla in check.

Life History.—The adult insect is very small indeed, perhaps a tenth of an inch in length, and is likely to escape notice entirely unless a systematic search is made for it. The adults are very active, jumping and flying readily, and from this are often called "jumping lice." They pass the winter in this stage, in cracks and crevices or under scales of bark on the trees. With the first warm weather the eggs are deposited, principally upon the twigs. The young soon hatch and begin feeding, which they do by sucking the juice of the tree, attacking principally the leaf stems. The insect gives off a "honeydew" similar to that of the aphis, which coats the whole tree, trunk and all, with a shiny, and later a blackish, varnish. So abundant do they become by successive broods, that the trees are seriously weakened, making little growth and sometimes dropping both leaves and fruit.

Control.—The psylla may be largely controlled by spraying with lime-sulfur and in bad cases there should be an application of this wash just as soon as the leaves are off the trees in the autumn. This ought to be followed by another application in the spring and both of these should be of such a strength as to do thorough work. If the specific gravity hydrometer test is made, 1.03 is the proper strength after diluting. About one gallon of commercial lime-sulfur to 9 or 10 gallons of water will usually produce this strength. Where the dormant spraying has been neglected, or if the insects are plentiful in spite of winter spraying, some summer applications must be made. Any of the contact sprays are likely to be useful, but some of the tobacco extracts seem to be most efficient. If this summer spraying can be done just after a rain has washed off the honeydew so much the better.

Leaf Blister Mite.—Another pest which is frequently troublesome on both pears and apples is the blister mite. This is not a true insect, but is related to the red spider of plants and to the mite which causes "scab" in sheep. It is entirely too small to be seen without the aid of a microscope, so that the orchardist is never likely to see it, but if he lives in an infested district he is likely to become altogether too familiar with its work.

Habits and Injuries.—The winter is passed in the adult stage under the scales of the buds, where the mites collect in large numbers. As soon as the leaves begin to expand in the spring they are entered by the adults and the eggs are deposited in the leaf tissues. The eggs soon hatch and the old and young feed upon the cells of the leaf, causing the galls or blisters which are very characteristic.

These are at first light-colored in the apple and reddish in the pear, but later turn brown when dead. This is the most noticeable and distinctive stage of the injury and is easily recognized by anyone who once becomes familiar with it. The small brown blisters are scattered somewhat regularly over the surface of the leaf, giving it a peculiar and very characteristic appearance. In serious cases, however, the most of the leaf is affected and sometimes both leaves and fruit may drop as a result of the injury to the leaves. The fruit is itself also attacked, though much less commonly, and the injury is less severe and much less conspicuous.

The principal injury comes through the interference with the functions of the leaf. The mites remain in the leaves until autumn, when they seek the buds and work in under the outer scales for the winter.

The most convenient treatment is to spray with lime-sulfur in the early spring. This catches them in their winter quarters among the bud scales. Any of the forms of this wash which are used for the San José scale will be effective, and fortunately one application is usually all that is needed for both pests. In the event of a very serious attack Professor Parrott of New York, who has carefully investigated the blister mite, recommends two applications, one in the autumn and one in the spring, using kerosene emulsion diluted with five parts of water. The autumn application is likely to be most effective, since the mites have not yet secreted themselves in the bud scales. This double treatment, however, is rarely necessary. The mite has seldom been serious in orchards which are carefully sprayed for San José scale each year, while it is often seen both in neglected orchards and in those where the spraying is done carelessly.

The Pear Slug.—The foliage of the pear, plum, quince and cherry is likely to be attacked by a shiny, olive-green little slug with a brownish head. Frequently the first intimation one has of any trouble is to notice that some trees in the orchard are turning brown as though from the effects of dry weather. A closer examination will show these little slugs scattered over the upper surface of the leaves. They eat out the tissue of the leaves till only the ribs and the epidermis of the lower surface remain. The leaves turn as brown as in winter and are later sometimes replaced by a new crop. The slugs spend the winter as larvæ in the soil and emerge in late spring or early summer.

The pest is easily controlled by spraying with arsenate of lead or any similar poison. Contact poisons may also be used and even fine dust or water is effective.

INSECTS ATTACKING THE STONE FRUITS

There are not nearly so many serious insect enemies of the stone fruits as of the pome fruits. Probably this is due in considerable part to the more pungent taste of the foliage of most of the stone fruits. However, there is no real dearth of insect enemies, even of the stone fruits.

The peach, like the rest of its relatives, is attacked by very few insect enemies. The San José scale, the plum curculio and the aphis are all likely to attack it, especially the first named, but about the only " specialty " in the insect line is the borer.

Peach Tree Borer.—Most people who grow peach trees are familiar with this pest. Its presence in the tree is shown by a sticky gum which is thrown out in large quantities at or near the surface of the ground.

Life Cycle.—The adult insect, which one rarely sees, is a very pretty moth, looking, however, much more like a wasp. It is variously marked with black, brown and several shades of yellow, and the two sexes are quite unlike. The eggs are laid throughout the summer on the bark and usually well down on the trunk. The larva, on hatching, burrows into the inner bark and sap wood, where it feeds, causing the copious production of gum just mentioned. Here it feeds for nearly a year, ceasing operations only during the winter, and emerges during the early part of the summer to begin the round of life again.

Dig out the Borers.—The orchardist is likely to have little difficulty in identifying the work of this insect. The gum already mentioned is the first indication. On digging into this the brownish castings of the larva will be found, and a little searching with a knife will soon disclose the burrow and later the larva itself. Sometimes the larva will even be found outside the tree in the mixture of gum and castings. A small, sharp-pointed trowel will be found an excellent implement to work with. It can be used to dig away the gum and some of the surface soil, and may even be used to follow up the burrows and locate the borer itself. Usually a fairly heavy wire is a useful addition to the equipment and a good knife ought also to be included. Experience seems to differ as to the best time to dig out the borers, but autumn is usually preferred for the work. In southern peach districts the "worming of the trees" takes place twice a year, say about April and October.

This is the remedy on which the greatest reliance must be placed and is frequently the only one used. Mounding up the trees with earth early in the season, wrapping the trunks with building paper and using various washes are all recommended, but are, after all, only makeshifts.

The plum curculio perhaps deserves some further mention in connection with its work on plums and peaches, though it has already been discussed under apples. The larva is the white "worm" so often found about the pits of plums and peaches. The injured fruit usually drops prematurely, sometimes when very small and green, and at other times they merely ripen prematurely. Often this dropping is not a serious matter, as it serves merely to relieve the tree from an overburden of fruit. But when the tree has set a light crop, the loss from curculio may be a very serious matter.

The spraying already discussed is generally all that it is worth while to attempt in the way of remedies. The jarring of the trees to make the insects fall upon a sheet and thus give an opportunity to destroy them, while an entirely effective method, is too slow and expensive to be warranted under most conditions.

The Cherry Aphis.—The cherry has a special aphis of its own which attacks especially the tips of vigorous shoots and often does very spectacular work, especially on the big, sweet cherries. On young trees, which are making long, vigorous shoots, each shoot will be terminated by a cluster of curled leaves which later turn brown. The insect itself is dark brown or black and large compared with other aphids. But the general treatment is the same.

QUESTIONS

1. Contrast insects with biting mouth-parts and those with sucking mouth-parts.
2. What three things make the San José scale especially dreaded by orchardists?
3. What kinds of plants are attacked by this insect?
4. What are the principal remedies used to combat the scale?
5. Give reasons why the spraying for scale should be especially thorough.
6. Give some idea of the damage done by the codling moth or apple worm to the American apple crop.
7. What methods should be used in combating this insect?
8. Outline the life history of the aphis.
9. Give methods of controlling the aphis.
10. Describe the damage to the apple from attacks of the curculio.
11. Outline the life history of this insect.
12. What remedies should be used?
13. Describe the life history of the bud moth.
14. How is it combated?
15. Tell what you can of the canker worm and its work.
16. How is it controlled?
17. Tell how to combat the tent-caterpillar.
18. Describe the life history of the railroad worm, or apple maggot.
19. What methods are recommended in fighting this insect?
20. Give directions for controlling borers.
21. Give a list of insects attacking the pear.
22. Which of these is most destructive in your section? Give methods of controlling it.
23. What are the serious insect enemies of the stone fruits?

CHAPTER XII

DISEASES OF FRUIT TREES

As in the case of insects, the writer makes no claim in the present chapter to anything like a complete list of the fungous troubles which may beset the orchard owner. He merely hopes to give some suggestions, taken principally from personal experience, which may help the student and the orchardist in recognizing the more common pests and in deciding what to do for them.

Importance of Knowing Why.—To the student, the fungous diseases of fruit trees form an extremely interesting group of organisms, one that he likes to examine and to study. To the orchard owner they are a pestiferous collection of annoying troubles against which he must be constantly on his guard. But even with the practical orchard man it is very desirable that he should give them sufficient study to know what methods are best and why they are best. This later point has received much study. It has always seemed that almost anyone ought to do better work if he knew *why* he did it in a certain way rather than in some other way. If the man who sprays understands that when he leaves live San José scales on the tips of a lot of branches he is likely to have the entire tree reinfested because the scales breed all through the season and crawl down onto the part he sprayed; if he understands this he is far more likely to do good work than if he is merely told to spray thoroughly. If in cutting out fire blight, he understands just why he cuts as he does and why he disinfects his shears, he is much more likely to do his work properly than if he is merely "shown." So it seems worth while to understand something of the life history of these fungous diseases that cause so much extra work to the orchardist and to know just how the fungicides affect them.

Nature and Types of Fungus.—The fungus is merely a very low form of plant life. It does not manufacture its own food,

163

as the apple tree does, out of air and water and various other ingredients, but it allows the tree to do this and then it comes in and steals the manufactured foods. It is a robber pure and simple. And in order that it may absorb these manufactured foods such as sugar and starch, it has to establish a very intimate contact with the host plant (and a very unwilling host it is).

Sometimes it grows on the surface with very slight attachment to the host, as in the case of mildews, and such a disease may be treated by the use of dry sulfur dusted upon the leaves after the fungus has become established, because practically all of the fungus is spread out there open to attack.

Again, the fungus has a much more intimate connection with the host, although still growing on the surface. Such a type is the apple scab. In this case a large part of the fungus is imbedded in the host, and treatment, after the fungus has become established, is of relatively little value.

Lastly we have a type of fungus which grows wholly or largely within the host. The black knot of the plum is such a fungus. Here the fungus is entirely safe from attack after it once enters the host and until it emerges in the black knots of the fruiting stage.

The most rational treatment for all fungous diseases is that which attempts to prevent their ever gaining a foothold on the host, and we are enabled to give our trees this kind of protection because men have discovered certain substances which are harmless to the host plant but which will kill the fungus. Frequently the margin of safety is very slight and a substance to be effective against the fungus must be of such a strength or such a composition as to come very near to injuring the host plant.

Sometimes varying conditions of weather or of the plant cause the fungicide to pass the margin of safety and become injurious to the host as well as to the fungus. Bordeaux mixture is one example of this. As sprayed upon the apple tree it is probably in the form of copper hydroxide, or some similar compound, and in this form it does not hurt the apple tree but does destroy the apple scab. But under certain weather conditions the chemical form of this fungicide undergoes a change which makes it dangerous to the apple and we have the apples on the tree "russeted" and the leaves of the tree damaged so that they turn yellow and fall.

Action of a Fungicide.—Most fungicides become effective against the fungus by entering its cells and destroying its tissues. For example, the spore of the fungus becomes lodged upon the leaf of the host plant and, the conditions of heat and moisture being favorable, it germinates much as a grain of wheat might do, sending out a little germ tube which grows about over the surface of the leaf and finally enters the tissues, either by way of one of the breathing pores or by actually working its way through the tissues. Now if the germ tube is able to do all this without encountering any injurious substance, it establishes itself within the host and goes on thriving. But if the tree has been properly sprayed, then the little germ tube in its wandering prior to entering the host comes in contact with some of the fungicide, absorbs it into its tissues and is thereby destroyed.

This is the whole story in a few words and the aim of the man who sprays should be to do his work so thoroughly that no wandering fungus can escape coming in contact with a particle of the fungicide used, whether this be lime-sulfur or Bordeaux mixture or plain copper sulfate.

SPECIFIC DISEASES

Now let us consider a few of the more important specific diseases. They may perhaps be considered in two sections, those attacking the pome fruits and those attacking the stone fruits, because it so often happens that a particular disease attacks both the apple and the pear, for example, or the peach and plum.

DISEASES OF POME FRUITS

Scab.—This list may be very appropriately headed by the scab or black-spot, which stands in about the same relation to apple diseases as the codling moth does to apple insects. It attacks fruit (Fig. 71), leaves and twigs. On the fruit it produces very characteristic spots which are a peculiar olive green in the early stages but soon become blackened, the skin usually breaking about the margins of the spot. In very bad cases the spots coalesce and the fruit may crack open nearly to the core (see Fig. 90). On the leaves the spots are usually nearly circular in outline, at least in the beginning, and are of a peculiar light green color which gradually changes to brown as the tissues die. In many cases the leaves wrinkle in a peculiar manner, due to the growth of the surface being retarded irregularly. The scab passes the winter upon the old leaves in the orchard and the spores reinfest the trees the following spring from these old leaves.

Fig. 71.—Scab, or black-spot of the apple. This is the most serious of all the apple diseases, but can be controlled by thorough spraying.

Susceptibility to Scab.—There is a very marked difference in the relative susceptibility of different varieties of both pears and apples. Among pears the Flemish Beauty is peculiarly liable to attack and the crop is frequently ruined, many specimens being cracked nearly to the core, while adjoining trees of Bartlett may be relatively little affected. With apples the Fameuse, Rhode Island Greening, McIntosh and Spy are among those which are especially subject to attack.

The treatment for scab, in either pears or apples, consists in spraying with lime-sulfur or Bordeaux mixture, and the number of applications varies with the locality, the season and the variety. If a bad attack is expected the trees should be sprayed before the blossoms open, just after they fall and once or twice thereafter at intervals of two to four weeks. The relative importance of these sprayings will vary with the season. If the weather is dry during the early part of the season and wet at the last part, a single late spraying may give better results than two or three early ones.

Rust.—Similar forms of this disease attack the apple, pear and quince. It is one of those peculiar diseases which at one stage lives on one host plant and at another stage on another host. In this case the second host, with all three forms of the disease, is the cedar tree. On this it forms the peculiar rough brown knots known as "cedar-apples," and authorities agree (and common experience bears them out) that one of the first things to do, where it is at all possible, is to get rid of the cedar trees.

On apple leaves the rust appears as small roughened spots, generally in the form of a distinct ring. The tissue of this ring is thickened and on the under surface of the leaf there are numerous little protuberances, while on the upper surface the tissue turns yellow and finally a bright orange. On the fruit the disease is less conspicuous, but appears about the same as on the under surface of the leaves.

Varieties of fruits differ greatly in their susceptibility. Among apples the Wealthy is conspicuous for its liability to the disease, and the bright orange spots will be found on the leaves of this variety if there is any of the disease in the neighborhood.

When the disease cannot be controlled by destroying the cedar trees, the only thing to do is to resort to spraying and the same applications given for the scab are usually sufficient to keep this disease in check, though they will not entirely eradicate it.

Blotch.—This is a relatively new disease and is much more common in the Middle West than elsewhere, but is sometimes found in most apple sections. It resembles the scab very closely and is often mistaken for it, but on the fruit it is apt to be scattered rather uniformly over the entire surface, while the scab is confined to one side of the fruit. The blotch also makes a less compact growth on the areas affected. It produces cankers upon the twigs and branches and peculiar light brown spots upon the leaves. It works later in the season than the scab, necessitating, where serious, one or two sprayings after the last spraying for scab.

Cankers.—There are a number of diseases which attack the twigs, branches and even the trunks of apple trees (and less frequently of pears and quinces), producing ugly roughened brown areas. Sometimes the diseased section is very well defined with a distinct line marking its boundary where the diseased tissue has shrunken and broken away from the adjoining healthy tissue. In other cases, as the European canker, there are many concentric rings or folds where the tree has repeatedly attempted to heal over the wound and each time the fungus has,

Fig. 72.—Apple canker. There are several different diseases which pass under the general name of canker and some of them are quite serious.

during its season of rapid growth, gotten the upper hand (Fig. 72).

Treatment.—These cankers vary greatly in the organism which causes them and in the appearance, but the general line of treatment is much the same. There are three ways of fighting such diseases.

First, all affected twigs and branches which can be spared should be cut out and burned.

Second, in case the branch is too valuable to be spared, or in the event of a canker spot on the trunk, the diseased tissue should be cut out carefully and then the wound painted over as in the case of wounds made in pruning. For the preliminary work of cutting out, a light, sharp hatchet will be found very satisfactory, and the smoothing up of the wound may be done with a knife or a heavy chisel.

Third, the trunk and branches of the trees should be carefully sprayed whenever an application of any fungicide is made to the orchard. In particular they should be given a thorough spraying before the buds start in the spring.

These three lines of attack will generally keep things fairly well under control, though cases are found where the attacks are so bad as to make the task of cleaning up the trees almost hopeless.

Sooty Blotch and Fly Speck.—These two diseases are very similar, the difference in appearance being that suggested by the names. Some observers have even considered them as two forms of the same fungus. They are both superficial, with very little attachment to the host, and can frequently be entirely rubbed off with a cloth. They injure the appearance of the fruit so as to render it unsalable. There is usually little or no trouble with them in orchards that are sprayed for scab, but occasionally a later spraying may be necessary.

Fire Blight.—This is one of the most serious diseases of the pome fruits, both because it injures the trees so severely and because the methods of eradicating it are so expensive. It attacks pears, apples and quinces, as well as many allied plants, such as mountain ash, hawthorns, and crab apples. The disease is most noticeable where it attacks the tips of vigorously growing shoots. Here it works rapidly, killing both leaves and twigs and causing them to turn brown and eventually nearly black, especially on the pear. It will also, on bearing trees, attack the fruit spurs, where it does more serious, though less spectacular, damage, because new terminal shoots are easily grown, but new spurs are grown with great difficulty. By following down the spur or twig the disease frequently becomes established on the main branches or even the trunk, where it produces what is popularly known as "body blight."

The Cause.—The disease is caused by a bacterium which works in the tender parts of the twig, largely in the cambium layer, and during the actively growing stage the organisms may be found some distance below where there is any outward sign of the disease. It winters over in the old, diseased tissues and is spread in the spring to the growing shoots, largely through the instrumentality of insects, particularly bees. Bearing apple trees may often be seen with one-quarter of the fruit spurs dead, and in every spur the infestation came through the blossoms, doubtless having been carried by the bees in their visits to the blossoms.

There is a marked difference in the susceptibility of varieties, the Wealthy and Rhode Island Greening, among apples, and the Bartlett, Clapp and Flemish Beauty, among pears, being especially liable to attack, while the McIntosh and Baldwin apples and the Anjou and Seckel pears are much less so.

The Remedy.—The disease cannot be influenced by spraying. The only satisfactory remedy is to cut out the diseased parts, and the best time to do this is in the autumn. If all the diseased areas can be cut out and burned during the dormant season there will be no outbreak in the spring. Of course this cannot be done, but systematic effort will go a long way towards it. If the work can be done in the autumn before the leaves fall, so much the better, as the affected areas are more easily located then. The diseased shoots should also be cut during the growing season, though this is a less efficient time than the other. Great care should be taken to get well below the diseased portion in this cutting so as to be sure that all the bacteria are removed.

The shears or knife with which the cutting is done should be disinfected after every cut to prevent any germs being carried to healthy tissue; otherwise this cutting may really spread the disease from branch to branch. For this disinfecting a solution of corrosive sublimate is used (1 part to 1000). A cloth or sponge dipped in this may be used to wipe the shears, or it may be carried in a can and the shears dipped into it. In the winter work all affected parts which are cut out should be gathered up and burned. This is not so important in summer work, since the parts removed are soft and soon dry up and kill the bacteria.

In addition to this active work of control it is well to keep the trees in only moderate growth. Withhold nitrogenous fertilizers and cultivation, perhaps seed down the orchard and do not prune heavily in winter.

DISEASES OF THE STONE FRUITS

Brown Rot.—This attacks practically all of the stone fruits but especially the plum and peach. It is most conspicuous on the fruit, causing it to turn brown and shrivel and eventually to dry up. The fruit also becomes covered, as the decay advances, with a powdery material, the spores of the disease. Fruit in clusters is especially liable to attack, and thinning should be practised so that no two fruits may touch. The disease may also attack the blossoms and even the spurs, following down from the fruit or blossoms. Damp and warm weather is especially favorable to its spread and the rapidity with which it works when the trees are not carefully sprayed and when all the conditions are favorable for the disease is something alarming. It passes the winter largely in the mummied fruits which frequently remain hanging to the trees until the following season.

Efforts to control the disease should be along two lines. In the first place all of these mummied fruits should be destroyed if possible. They may be shaken off the trees and then either gathered up and destroyed or else buried or plowed under. The second line of attack is by spraying. The trees should be given a thorough spraying with lime-sulfur, at the winter strength, applied shortly before the buds swell in the spring. Strong copper sulfate solution is satisfactory, if more convenient, and may be used if there is no San José scale in the orchard. Then the trees should be sprayed later with self-boiled lime-sulfur. When a bad attack is feared, three applications should be made: The first perhaps three or four weeks after the blossoms fall, again two or three weeks later, and a third time two or three weeks after this. Under less serious conditions one spraying may be all that is needed and this should be probably six weeks to two months after blossoming.

In any case care should be taken not to spray these fruits, especially peaches, so late that the spray will still be on them at picking time.

Peach Scab.—This is a very common disease on many varieties of peaches, producing small, blackish spots which may be so plentiful as to make practically one whole side of the fruit black. The growth of the side attacked is retarded so that the fruit becomes one sided, and in bad cases this side frequently cracks open. Fortunately the treatment just outlined for the brown rot will also entirely check the peach scab.

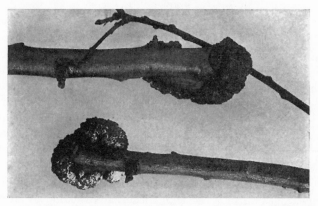

Fig. 73.—Black-knot of the plum, showing how new knots will start from the old stubs when these are not cut back far enough.

Leaf Curl.—This is a very striking disease and one which it is very easy to recognize. It attacks all parts of the tree, leaves, branches, flowers and fruit, but is so inconspicuous on all parts but the leaves that it usually escapes notice. The leaves thicken, curl up, and are often highly colored in certain parts and in others of a light yellowish green. As the disease advances the leaves turn brown and soon fall, causing a severe loss of vitality to the tree, which not only loses the food which the leaves would have produced had they remained healthy, but also is further exhausted by being obliged to put on this second crop of leaves. The spores of the disease live over winter on the bark and gain entrance to the buds when growth starts in the spring. The spread of the disease is markedly favored by cold, damp weather in the spring.

It may be controlled practically by a single spraying with lime-sulfur at the winter strength applied just before the buds break, or just as they are breaking, in the spring.

Black-knot.—This is another very striking disease and attacks both the plum and the cherry, principally upon the smaller branches but often upon both main branches and trunk.

Fig. 74.   Fig. 75.

Fig. 74.—A plum tree badly affected with black-knot.

Fig. 75.—The same plum tree as shown in Fig. 74 after the knots have been cut out. It is possible to recover trees which are very badly affected if the knots are cut out and the trees sprayed.

The spores gain entrance to the tree during the spring or summer and grow for a season entirely within the branch. The following spring the affected part of the branch begins to swell and soon the well-known knot develops. At first it is soft in texture and light brown in color, but gradually turns darker and becomes harder in texture. During late spring and early summer the knot is covered with a velvety appearance, which is caused by the production of summer spores. Later these disappear and the surface becomes hard and roughened.

The knots may develop in new positions or by the side of old knots (Fig. 73). It is very common for them to break out where a small twig joins a branch, the fungus having apparently gained entrance in the angle between the two where the bark is probably less impervious. The disease lives over in the tissues adjoining the old knots and breaks out again either above or below the knot.

The most practical remedy is to cut out and burn the knots (Figs. 74 and 75). This is especially important in the spring before the spores are produced, but should be kept up through the season. Care should be taken to cut well below the knot, otherwise the disease may break out again as shown in Figure 74. Spraying, particularly just before the buds break, is also effective. This may be supplemented by an earlier application in late winter and by others during spring and summer if the outbreak is serious.

QUESTIONS

1. What is a fungus?
2. Describe the action of a fungicide.
3. Describe the apple scab.
4. What methods are recommended for combating the apple scab?
5. What remedies are recommended for rust?
6. Tell what you can of the disease known as blotch.
7. Outline the methods of fighting canker.
8. Describe the work of the fire blight. How may it be controlled?
9. Describe peach scab.
10. Describe leaf curl. How is it controlled?
11. What is the most practical method of controlling the black-knot of plums and cherries?
12. What are the worst fruit diseases in your district?

CHAPTER XIII

SPRAYING APPARATUS

IT has already been said that it pays to have a good equipment with which to work. There is as great a difference between an ordinary spray pump and an exceptionally good one as there is between a No. 3 Baldwin and an Extra Fancy Baldwin. And usually the best pump does not cost much more than the medium.

FIG. 76.—Using a bucket pump on a bearing apple tree. This is a very efficient little pump for the money and is entirely satisfactory for a few trees.

It is the same with buying a spray pump as with buying a suit of clothes. Get a good one and it will last for years and be a satisfaction all the time. Buy a poor one and you are sorry for it from the start. Moreover, the styles in spray pumps do not change much.

A good spraying outfit consists of a pump at one end and a nozzle at the other, with more or less hose and extension-rod between. We will begin with the pump.

175

Spray Pumps.—There are quantities of them on the market. Some are better than others, but most of them are good. A few of them are worthless or nearly so. Of course the type of pump one ought to have depends on whether he has six trees, or sixty, or six thousand; also on whether his trees are old or young, peach or pear, dwarf or standard. There are five general types of good pumps which it seems worth while to mention.

I. *The bucket pump* is shown in Figure 76. This is for the man with the six trees. And it will surprise anyone who has not tried it to see what an efficient little pump it is. The writer has never been able to figure out where it gets its pressure, but it certainly develops one. The good points are: (1) That it develops this high pressure and will, therefore, deliver a good spray; (2) that it is very cheap, so that anybody can afford one; and (3) that it is very simple in construction, and consequently easy to repair and to operate. We do not mean from all this that it will do as good a job as a power sprayer, but it is not a toy, by any means.

Fig. 77.—Knapsack sprayer. This is an excellent pump for rough ground or wheresoever it is difficult to get about, but is rather heavy when one has much spraying to do.

Its shortcomings are (1) that the operator has to be constantly going back to the base of supplies after more spray material; (2) that it is inconvenient to move about; (3) that there is no agitator; and (4) that the pressure runs down quickly. And yet for all this it is entirely adequate for a few trees.

II. *The knapsack sprayer* is shown in Figure 77. This is not adapted to very tall trees nor to very large operations, but is the most convenient thing made for the man with a garden and dwarf or otherwise small trees. It is also especially good where a man wants to go over the trees in a young orchard in search of occasional trees affected with the tent-caterpillar or with the red-humped apple caterpillar. It is handy to get about with, one man can handle it, it agitates the liquid well and maintains a good pressure. On the other hand, it is heavy to carry about, particularly in the late afternoon if one has been using it all day; it requires filling rather frequently, and it has an unpleasant

Fig. 78.—A barrel outfit with a collapsible ladder; excellent for working among old trees which hang low.

habit of slopping and wetting the operator in the small of the back. On the whole it is a very efficient little pump, but, like most sprayers, it is more comfortable to "use it by proxy."

III. *The barrel pump* (Figs. 78 and 79) is by all odds the most generally satisfactory of all the spraying machines. It is adapted to more different circumstances, and a good one will always give a good account of itself. If a man has only a few trees he can combine with one or more neighbors and the cost of the barrel pump will not be great for each one of them, while the satisfaction in using it will be great. On the other hand, a barrel pump will be satisfactory for a goodly number of trees and if the owner of the large orchard gets enough outfits he can handle any size of orchard with them.

The following are some of the important points in a good barrel pump.

1. It ought to be mounted on the side. It is singular how few pumps are mounted this way, because there seem to be good practical reasons for preferring it to the end-mounted pump and

Fig. 79.—A barrel spray outfit with two extra barrels of water; a device that will save much time where the water supply is far from the orchard.

no reasons or none of importance for the other plan. The advantages of the side-mount are: (1) That it brings the pump itself lower, thus reducing the danger of catching on trees; (2) that it brings the center of gravity of the whole outfit lower, thus reducing the danger of tipping over (Fig. 79); and (3) that the sediment in the spray mixtures (and there is usually more or less of this) naturally works down under the pump and is drawn out instead of collecting about the corners as it does in the end-mounted pump.

2. It ought to have a good-sized air-chamber. This does not mean that the air-chamber should be conspicuously placed on top of the pump as is often the case. It can be as low down as desired, but it will keep the pressure much more uniform.

3. There should be as few and as small openings about the pump as is compatible with the free working of the plunger and agitator. The splashing of the liquid through these openings is bad enough at best; a prize awaits the manufacturer who develops a pump which does not splash the operator.

4. The pump ought to have a good agitator. As already suggested, most of our spray materials carry more or less solid material in suspension, and these ought to be distributed evenly with the liquid. With an inefficient agitator the operator gets nearly all the poison on the first few trees and the balance are sprayed with plain water, or nearly so.

5. There ought to be a good strainer at the bottom of the pump. Even with the most careful preparation of the materials and the most thorough straining there is always danger of something getting into the pump that will clog the nozzle. The strainer is an additional safeguard. If it can be such as can be readily taken off and cleaned so much the better. And if the actual straining area is on the bottom instead of on the sides of this strainer it will come nearer to emptying the cask.

6. The pump should have all brass working parts. In these days of strong corrosive materials the best of pumps will wear out soon enough.

7. The valves should be simple and easily accessible. It is astonishing how often a valve will get stuck, even when the pump receives reasonably good care. The operator should know just where it is and how to get at it and the manufacturer should put no unnecessary difficulties in the way.

8. The type of packing ought to be simple and the method of renewing it or of tightening it should be easy. This is an extremely important point. The packing is bound to wear and allow leakage, and no one wants to be obliged to resort to a machinist or a high-priced (and low-speed) plumber to get his pump fixed.

9. There ought to be an opportunity for two leads of hose if they are wanted.

10. There should be a pressure-gauge. This can be dispensed with, but it helps one to keep track of what the pumper is doing and it stimulates him to do better work.

IV. *The large, double-action hand pump* attached to a large tank is shown in Figure 80. Many of the points discussed under the barrel pump apply with equal force to this type of pump. It has the great advantage over the barrel that it will carry more

Fig. 80.—A large, double-action, hand pump with 200-gallon tank. An excellent outfit, but it is a man's job to do the pumping.

liquid. This is especially important where the orchard is some distance from the water supply. The chief disadvantages of this type of pump are that it requires a good, strong man to work it, and it requires an equally good team to haul it, if the orchard is on a side hill or if the land is rough or soft.

V. *The Power Sprayer.*—There are four different types of these and many variations under some of the types. We have in the first place the *traction power sprayer.* Here the power is generated by the movement of the wagon wheel, which, by means of a sprocket wheel and chain, works a pump that compresses the air in a large chamber. This compressed air, in turn, forces the liquid out of the tank. The great objection to this machine is that the pressure runs down as soon as the wagon stops. And since it is absolutely necessary to stop in order to do good spraying on trees of any size the best orchardists have ruled this machine out of their list. It is all right with small trees where the outfit travels a considerable distance for every gallon

FIG. 81.—Gas power sprayer. An excellent type in some respects, but it is too difficult to clean out the tank.

of liquid put out, but most orchardists cannot afford so expensive an outfit for this one type of spraying.

In the second place, there is the *gas sprayer,* shown in Figure 81. This consists of an air-tight steel tank which holds the spray material, and a tube containing carbonic acid gas under pressure. The tube of gas is connected by suitable pipes and valves with the tank of liquid and when one is ready to spray he simply turns the valves and lets the gas into the tank. This, of course, exerts a pressure on the liquid and it is forced out through the hose. In some respects this outfit is admirable. It is relatively

small and light and it requires no extra man to run it. The
two difficulties which orchardists have with it are that the
cost of power is relatively high and that such materials as
Bordeaux mixture and lime-sulfur tend to coat the inside of
the tank and then peel off in flakes which constantly clog the
nozzles. As the tank is required to stand a heavy pressure there
is only a small opening into it and it is well-nigh impossible to
keep it thoroughly cleaned out.

The third type of power sprayer uses *compressed air* as a
source of power. It is, therefore, essentially like the type just
discussed, except that it uses air instead of carbonic acid gas.

Fig. 82.—A gasolene power outfit. The most efficient power sprayer. The cut also shows
an excellent arrangement for filling the tank and mixing the materials.

The air is compressed by a special apparatus which has to be
installed on the farm, and this makes the first cost high. There
is also the same objection in reference to scaly coating from the
inside of the tank clogging the nozzles.

The last and by all means the most important type of power
sprayer at the present time is that run by a *gasolene engine*
(Fig. 82). The best of these engines have been perfected until
they give relatively little trouble in running and the pumps are
also admirably adapted to the work. Of course the great advantage of any power sprayer over other types of pumps is the
high and relatively constant pressure that it develops. With

FIG. 83.—A small gasolene power sprayer. This is an efficient machine and moderate in cost, so that the small orchardist can afford to own one. It can be run by one man if labor is scarce.

the gasolene type the owner may also easily adapt it to doing other kinds of work, such as pumping and sawing wood. There are many different styles of gasolene outfits, from one costing one hundred dollars and using a one and one-half horse-power engine and a hundred-gallon tank, up to a twelve hundred dollar machine with a ten horse-power engine and a three- or four-hundred-gallon tank. Of late several good forms of the small machine have been developed which seem to give promise of great usefulness (Fig. 83). They are especially acceptable where

FIG. 84A.   FIG. 84B.

FIG. 84A.—Old style of vermorel nozzle. This type has the serious weakness that the ejectors are constantly catching on the branches of the tree.

FIG. 84B.—Angle vermorel nozzle. This type has great advantages over the last; it has no ejectors and it delivers the spray at an angle.

good, reliable labor is scarce. With one of these machines a man, if "put to it," can do his spraying alone, and they are light enough to get about on relatively rough land and cheap enough so that the small orchardist can afford to buy one. One of these machines will easily take care of two or even three small orchards, so that if a man is on sufficiently good terms with his neighbors there is nothing to prevent his clubbing in with one or two of them and thus bringing the cost of his power outfit nearly down to that of a good barrel pump.

Nozzles.—Next to the pump in importance, in fact more important in some ways, is the nozzle. The number and variety of them on the market would bewilder a novice, yet they may nearly all be reduced to three or four principal types.

The Vermorel Type.—This is a relatively small nozzle and delivers a small amount of liquid as compared with other types. This shortcoming is usually gotten around by making them in clusters of two or more, but of course such a nozzle is heavy and therefore hard to use (Figs. 84*A* and 84*B*). This type gives a very fine, mist-like spray, but the small size of the orifice renders it very liable to clog, and this in turn makes it necessary to have some kind of ejector to push out the clog. This means a double annoyance, first because one must constantly stop and clean the nozzle and second because the ejector is liable to catch upon the branches and twigs when one attempts to spray the inside of the tree. For

Fig. 85*A*.   Fig. 85*B*.

Fig. 85*A*.—Bordeaux nozzle. Useful in spraying tall trees, as it will throw the spray material a long distance, but it makes a relatively coarse spray which is frequently objectionable.

Fig. 85*B*.—Disc nozzle. This is rapidly displacing other types for most work. It seldom clogs, does not catch on branches, makes a fine spray, and delivers a large amount of material in a given time.

these reasons the vermorel has largely gone out of use except with smaller pumps like the knapsack, where it is still the main type used.

The old Bordeaux nozzle is still largely used in many sections. It throws a relatively coarse spray, which is not suited to many kinds of work. It will throw a long distance, which is very important for high trees, and for such spraying as the winter application of lime-sulfur it is excellent. It is not likely to clog, and can be adjusted to throw anything from a solid stream to a fairly fine spray. The Bordeaux nozzle has a distinct place in any orchard man's outfit, though it is not well to use it for such work as codling-moth spraying (Fig. 85*A*).

The disc type of nozzle is shown in Figure 85*B*. This has been on the market a relatively short time but is rapidly displacing the other types for most kinds of spraying. It has three advantages that will appeal to any man who has ever sprayed: First, it does

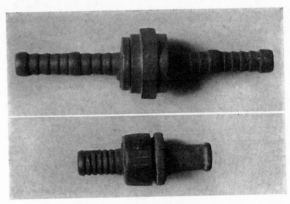

Fig. 86.—Long- and short-tailed hose couplings. The former are much to be preferred, as they do not allow the hose to pull apart so easily.

not catch on the branches of the trees; second, it throws a relatively fine spray and lots of it; and, third, it seldom clogs. For most spraying the orchardist should certainly choose this type of nozzle.

The Angle of Delivery.—Any nozzle, of whatever type, is very much more efficient for most work if it delivers the spray at an angle of 45° instead of straight ahead. Many nozzles are made this way by the manufacturers, and others can be changed into this type by introducing a small angle connection between the nozzle and the extension rod. The advantage of the angle nozzle is that the direction of the spray may be changed by simply twisting the extension rod, while with the straight nozzle the whole rod must be moved.

The Hose.—A third important feature of the spraying outfit is the hose. It has little effect on the kind of spraying done, but it does make a difference to the man who does the spraying.

The writer is very strongly in favor of a reasonably small hose, preferably about one-fourth inch in diameter. It is true there is some loss of pressure as compared with the large hose, but the greater ease and comfort of doing the work will far more than offset this loss. The following table gives the weights of various kinds and sizes of hose. If anyone who is accustomed to using the large size will once try the small size he will never go back again. It is like play in comparison, and anything which makes spraying seem playful, even in the remotest degree, ought to be adopted.

TABLE V.—*Comparison of Weights of Hose of Different Sizes*

Length	Size	Kind of Hose	Weight Empty	Weight Full
			lbs.	lbs.
25 ft.	3/4 in.	Rubber	10.87	13.56
25 ft.	1/2 in.	Rubber	6.66	9.16
25 ft.	1/4 in.	Rubber	4.11	4.45
25 ft.	3/16 in.	Special cloth-covered	1.00	1.75

When buying hose get plenty of it. The ordinary spray outfit equipped with 8 to 15 feet of hose is a "delusion and a snare." The operator has to adjust his machine almost as carefully as he would a cannon in order to even hit the tree. Twenty-five feet is the least any outfit ought to have, and if two leads of hose are used let one be twenty-five or thirty feet and the other fifty. With the small hose this is not unduly heavy and the spraying can be done with an ease and comfort and thoroughness impossible with the short lengths (see types of couplings, Fig. 86).

The Extension Rod.—In addition to these more important parts the outfit should have an extension rod on each lead of hose. This may be either an iron rod or a bamboo, lined with a brass tube. The latter is preferred because it is much lighter and its larger size makes it easier to handle, but the iron rod is certainly much cheaper and does not break as easily. There should also be at least one, and preferably two cut-offs for each lead of hose. It is absolutely necessary to have one at the base of the extension rod so that the operator may shut off the liquid at will, and it is very desirable to have a second one at the pump, if there are two lines of hose, so that in case of accident to one line it may be shut down for repairs, while the other may continue to operate.

QUESTIONS

1. What are the good and bad points of the bucket pump?
2. Discuss the knapsack sprayer.
3. What can you say of the barrel pump?
4. Give the important points of a good barrel pump.
5. What are the advantages of the double-action hand pump?
6. Name the different types of power sprayers.
7. Give the special advantages of each type.
8. Describe the Vermorel type of nozzle.
9. What are the advantages of the disc type of nozzles?
10. Why is an angle nozzle preferred to a straight one?
11. Give some points to be considered in the purchase of spray hose.
12. What type of extension spray-rod would you prefer? Give reason.
13. What power sprayers and what type of hand sprayers are used in your section?

CHAPTER XIV

SPRAYING MATERIALS

The selection of spray materials is just about as confusing to the beginner as is the choice of spray apparatus. There are many manufacturers in the field and each one is putting on the market his own special brand of each of the different materials, so that there are almost innumerable things to be had. If the orchardist wants a spray made from a copper salt he has his choice between Bordo-lead, Sal-Bordeaux, Pyrox, Tiger Brand Bordeaux and a dozen other patent preparations. If he wants to use sulfur in some form he is embarrassed by an even longer list of possibilities. He can buy commercial lime-sulfur of a dozen different manufacturers, or he can make his own concentrate or make the home-boiled wash, or use self-boiled lime-sulfur. Or, again, he can use atomic sulfur, soluble sulfur, sulfocide or various other special forms. The list of any of these principal sprays is so long that even the old stager is sometimes in doubt. Is it any wonder if the novice feels like giving up in despair? Yet if we will study into the matter it is not as bad as it seems on the face of the returns.

Doubtless new materials, and new combinations of old materials, will continue to come along, so that what was the best thing possible this year may be out of date a few years to come. This is going to make it necessary to do some experimenting all the time and to keep in touch with the Experiment Stations and the Fruit Growers' meetings. But all orchardists should do this anyway. When the list of spray materials in vogue at any one time is sifted down it will be found that there are really only a relatively small number that have to be considered. If a man buys from reputable manufacturers he is not apt to go far wrong, even though he may not get absolutely the best form.

Commercial Mixtures vs. Home Mixing.—There are two or three general questions that ought to be discussed before we

189

speak of specific remedies. The most important of these is the question of buying the mixtures already prepared or of buying the materials and preparing the mixtures on the farm: commercial mixtures *vs.* home mixing. There are certain things like arsenate of lead which cannot be made as well at home as they can by the manufacturer. Moreover, the price for these is relatively low because so many firms are manufacturing them. It seems, therefore, much better for any grower, large or small, to buy ready-made stock of such materials.

On the other hand, there are certain other things such as the various substitutes for Bordeaux mixture which often come at a high price to the orchardist and which it is relatively easy to make on the farm. It would seem that such mixtures might be prepared by the grower, at least when he is operating on a reasonably large scale. If a man has only a few trees probably it is better for him to pay the manufacturer his extra price for doing the mixing, rather than to bother to "post up" on methods, and then go to all the trouble of getting the different ingredients and combining them. But for the man who has as much as ten acres of orchard the writer is very strongly of the opinion that it pays to prepare these mixtures at home.

Classify Spray Materials.—Another point which has already been mentioned is the need of getting all these remedies classified in one's mind so that he understands which are insecticides and which are fungicides and which are a combination of both.

Dry vs. Liquid Sprays.—A third general question, though one which just at the present time seems to be settled, is the question of the dry *vs.* the liquid spray. Up to the present time no very satisfactory method of applying spray materials in a dry state to fruit trees has come into general use. But it seems so desirable to get rid of the expense and annoyance of hauling around so much water and sprinkling it on our trees that the writer cannot help thinking that American ingenuity will some day solve the problem of satisfactory powders which can be put on dry.

Copper Salts.—We come now to a consideration of some of the principal spray materials which are used by the fruit grower.

Among the fungicides the two principal substances used are some copper salt and some form of sulfur.

Copper Sulfate.—Of the copper salts by far the most important is copper sulfate, which is used either in the form of a plain solution on dormant trees or as Bordeaux mixture. This plain solution has the advantage of being as easy to apply as water, and where the grower does not have to fight any scale

Fig. 87.—Spray injury on apples. Any copper salt is likely to cause this under certain conditions of weather.

insects, especially San José scale, it makes an excellent dormant spray. It is usually applied at the strength of 3 or 4 pounds of copper sulfate to 50 gallons of water.

Bordeaux Mixture.—Where it can be used without danger, Bordeaux mixture is still probably the most efficient fungicide on the list. There seem to be two dangers from its use. On apples, in certain seasons, especially where there are many rains or a great deal of foggy weather, it may produce a russeting of the surface of the fruit that injures its appearance and sometimes its keeping quality (Fig. 87). This damage is sometimes very severe, in particularly bad cases even cracking the fruit open. It affects some varieties more than others. In some sections where there is not much trouble from the apple scab, more harm than good is often done to the fruit by spraying with Bordeaux. Another trouble that is sometimes experienced with it is that it aggravates the tendency, frequently seen in fruit trees, for the leaves to turn yellow or brown and to fall.

Yet with all its faults Bordeaux is such an efficient fungicide that it ought to be used whenever it can be without too much danger. For example, it ought to be used on all such fruits as grapes, currants and gooseberries because here it does no damage and these fruits are especially liable to damage from fungous enemies. Many good orchardists prefer to use it, particularly on those varieties not seriously injured by it, where apple scab is especially troublesome, because a considerable russeting of the skin is to be preferred to even a small amount of scab.

Formulas for Bordeaux.—There are two formulas for Bordeaux mixture which are in general use at the present time. One which is used most generally is as follows:

> 4 pounds copper sulfate,
> 4 pounds lime,
> 50 gallons water.

For those fruits or varieties which are most susceptible to injury, such as Japanese plums, peaches, and certain varieties of apples, a weaker formula is used, made as follows:

> 3 pounds copper sulfate,
> 3 pounds lime,
> 50 gallons water.

Stock Solutions for Bordeaux.—Where Bordeaux is to be used in any quantity it is much better to use in preparing it what are called "stock solutions." These are prepared as follows:

Weigh out 50 pounds of copper sulfate and dissolve it in 50 gallons of water, by hanging it in a cotton bag in the top of a barrel of water. It will dissolve much more quickly in this way than if thrown into the barrel. In fact, it never will dissolve if merely thrown into the barrel, as the water immediately surrounding the crystals soon becomes saturated and as this solution is heavier than plain water it remains right in the bottom of the barrel. The amounts mentioned give us one pound of copper sulfate to each gallon of water.

The "stock solution" of lime is prepared in the same general way. Fifty pounds of lime is slacked in a barrel, taking care to use enough water to prevent the lime from "burning," as it is called, which makes it flaky so that it is likely to clog the nozzles. After it is slacked enough water is added to make 50 gallons.

With the stock solutions thus prepared the making of a cask of Bordeaux mixture is a very simple matter. The ideal way is to have two half barrels, into one of which we measure four gallons of the copper sulfate solution and into the other four gallons of the lime water. Then add to each enough water to make 25 gallons. Next pour the diluted lime into the spray cask, add the copper sulfate solution, agitate thoroughly and the mixture is ready to apply. Or, better yet, the two solutions may be allowed to run into the cask simultaneously. A man may introduce several variations in the procedure and still be quite successful, but the thing which must be avoided always is mixing the lime and copper sulfate in concentrated solutions. This invariably leads to trouble, a thick, cheesy precipitate being formed which will clog the nozzles and will not stick to the trees, and is unsatisfactory in various other ways.

Now is there anything so complicated in this operation of preparing Bordeaux mixture that a good, intelligent orchardist cannot master it? The writer would vote most emphatically "no" and has no patience with those who argue that ready-made Bordeaux should be bought because the farmer cannot prepare it properly. There may be something in the argument of saving time and bother, but not in the argument of "lack of ability."

The Various Forms of Sulfur.—Just at the present time there seems to be a very marked interest in sulfur sprays. New forms are constantly being introduced by manufacturers and many growers are using them to the exclusion of most other sprays. There are four forms which it seems worth while to discuss at some length.

1. The Commercial Lime-sulfur Solutions.—These come as more or less clear, amber-colored liquids which mix readily with water, giving a yellow liquid. They come at various strengths, varying about 30° to perhaps 35° Beaumé (hydrometer test), the test supposedly varying with the amount of sulfur in solution. As a matter of fact a handful of salt or various other cheap materials will raise the strength as indicated by this hydrometer test just as surely as more sulfur will, so that the only reliable standard is the per cent of sulfur in solution.

In preparing these commercial lime-sulfur sprays for use in the orchard the common method is to dilute them by taking a certain number of gallons of water to each gallon of the concentrate. This is not a reliable method because, as already suggested, the concentrate may vary from 30° to 35° Beaumé. The latter would give the proper strength for San José scale by diluting with 9½ gallons of water, while the former could take only 7½ gallons of water to each gallon of the concentrate.

A hydrometer should therefore be used to test the concentrate and again to test the spray when ready to apply to the trees. The hydrometer is a simple instrument, consisting of a graduated glass tube weighted with shot at the lower end. This is immersed in the liquid to be tested and the lighter the liquid the more deeply the hydrometer sinks. The reading is taken at the surface of the liquid. Most hydrometers give both the specific gravity and the Beaumé strength. Anyone can therefore tell by the use of this instrument, and by knowing what strength he should have for a certain pest, just exactly how much water to use, provided that he has confidence in the manufacturer and knows it is sulfur and not salt in the solution. This is quite a proviso, but most manufacturers, no doubt, intend to be honest and if the buyer selects a reputable brand he is not likely to get into any serious trouble.

The Saving and the Cost.—The great advantage of the commercial lime-sulfur solutions is that they save all the annoyance

and messiness of home preparation. And this is a great deal.
They are also very simple to use.

On the other hand, the buyer pays considerably more for a
hundred gallons of spray by this method than he does to prepare
his own concentrate.

2. Home-made Concentrate.—This is the same material, in a
general way, as the commercial, but it does not run as high in
sulfur content. The great advantage of this form is that it can
be made up on the farm during the winter when work is slack
and when the labor expense is relatively small. The general
method of preparation is as follows, though formulas and
methods are still undergoing changes:

> *Formula.*— 50 pounds rock lime,
> 100 pounds sulfur,
> 50 gallons water.

It seems to be immaterial whether the sulfur is the flour
(finely ground) or the flowers, but the lime should be good
and should preferably have little magnesium in it.   Slack
the lime in the kettle in which the cooking is to be done and
when the slacking is well started add the sulfur and mix
thoroughly.   Then add enough water to make a thin paste.
Continue boiling vigorously until the sulfur is all dissolved,
which will usually take from forty-five minutes to one hour.
When the boiling is finished the concentrate may be put into
barrels and stored. If these barrels are perfectly tight and are
filled full, no other precaution is necessary than to cork up
tightly. If these conditions do not obtain then the concentrate
must be covered with oil. Any oil which will not injure the
trees and which does not take fire at the boiling point of water
will do. The various miscible oils are used with entire satisfaction.   There is sometimes considerable sediment, but this does
not seem to be a serious objection.

The proper degree of dilution either with the home-made or
the commercial, as measured by the specific gravity scale on the
hydrometer, seems to be about as follows: For San José scale,
blister mite, peach leaf curl and other spraying when trees are

in dormant condition, 1.03. For apple and pear scab and similar diseases, summer spray, 1.01. For peach scab and brown rot, summer spray, 1.005.

3. The Home-boiled Lime-sulfur Wash.—This was the original home-prepared lime-sulfur spray material and was at one time used very extensively. But the two forms already discussed have largely driven it out of use. It is still used by many growers who consider it the only really satisfactory form. The great objection to it is that only a small quantity can be prepared at a time, usually a single cask, and that, too, only as it is wanted for use, being applied hot, as a rule.

The formulas used vary greatly in both ingredients and run all the way from

　　　15 pounds lime, 15 pounds sulfur, 50 gallons water

　　to 22 pounds lime, 20 pounds sulfur, 50 gallons water.

The process of making is as follows: Put the lime and sulfur into a large kettle with about 20 gallons of water and boil for one hour. Then add enough water to make 50 gallons, strain into the spray cask and apply at once. Authorities differ as to the objection of allowing this mixture to cool; for example, to stand over night. Frequently it is very convenient to prepare the night before what is to be put on the first thing in the morning, and enough success attends this plan so that we need not hesitate to do it.

4. The "self-boiled" lime-sulfur is that in which the heat of the slacking lime is relied upon to cook the mixture. It is a very mild form, being little more than a mechanical mixture of sulfur and slacked lime, and is useful only as a summer fungicide. But for that purpose, particularly for use against the brown rot of stone fruits, it is very efficient.

The usual formula is as follows:

　　　　　8 pounds sulfur,
　　　　　8 pounds rock lime,
　　　　　50 gallons water.

An old oil cask is a good receptacle in which to prepare it. The lime is placed in the bottom of the cask, and it is imperative that it be good, *hard rock lime* and not air-slaked lime, since the heat for cooking is to come entirely from the lime. On top of the lime place the sulfur. Then add hot water slowly until the lime is slacked, stirring carefully, as needed, to prevent the "burning" of the lime. After slacking is complete allow the mixture to stand and cook for fifteen minutes, keeping the barrel covered with an old burlap to keep in the heat. Then add enough water to make 50 gallons, strain into the spraying cask and apply at once. Remember this is merely a summer fungicide and has no value for San José scale and relatively little as a dormant fungicide.

Soluble Sulfur.—At the present time the most interesting of the special forms of sulfur on the market is known as "soluble sulfur." It comes in rather coarse granules which dissolve readily in water. If further experiments shall show that it is efficient under all conditions and does not injure foliage it ought to prove a valuable form.

"Atomic sulfur" is a second form. This is a very finely divided form of pure sulfur which seems promising, but at the present writing needs further testing.

INSECTICIDES

There are two general classes of insecticides: The food-poisons, which are used for chewing insects and are usually some form of arsenic; and the contact sprays used for sucking insects.

In the first of these classes, at the present time, the arsenate of lead is used much more generally than any other form, with Paris green as a second. Several others are on the market and are used to a limited extent, but from the commercial orchard standpoint they may be ignored.

Arsenate of Lead.—The great advantages of arsenate of lead are (1) that it is very adhesive, remaining on the leaves through the entire season; (2) that it is finely divided, remaining in suspension much longer than Paris green; and (3) that it is usually harmless to foliage. This is a strong combination and it is small wonder that arsenate of lead is so generally used. It is, however, sometimes injurious to trees, and one should take every precaution possible to avoid trouble.

There are two forms on the market, one of which, known as the tri-plumbic form, has a higher percentage of lead and no hydrogen; while the other, known as the standard, has a higher percentage of arsenic but also has some hydrogen in it. This latter form, while more effective pound for pound in killing insects, is also more dangerous to plants. On such tender foliage as Japanese plums and the peach it is sometimes injurious.

Paris Green.—The only advantage of Paris green is that in some sections it is more easily secured than arsenate of lead; and possibly we might add a second, that it has a very distinctive color which prevents its ever being mistaken for anything else. There is now little danger that it will be adulterated, but if anyone wishes to test it he may easily do so. Put a small quantity of Paris green in a glass tube or bottle and pour on it some strong ammonia. If the Paris green is pure it will all dissolve, if not there will be some sediment. The value of this test rests on the fact that the materials generally used to adulterate Paris green are not soluble in ammonia, while pure Paris green is soluble in ammonia. When some cheap material which is soluble is discovered the test will lose its value. However, with our present laws and methods of enforcing them, there is relatively little danger from adulterated materials.

It is usually recommended to use Paris green at the rate of four ounces to 50 gallons of water, but many orchardists use it at the rate of five or six ounces to 50 gallons on the theory that poison is cheaper than labor, and at the latter strength they are sure of killing the insect enemies. It is well to add an equal weight of lime when the Paris green is not used in combination with a fungicide. The lime combines with any soluble arsenic which may be present.

Contact Insect Sprays.—There are four contact insecticides which are very commonly used, each one of which has its good points.

Miscible Oils.—First of all there are the soluble, or, more properly, the miscible, oils. There are several of them, but they all agree in being made from crude petroleum and in mixing more or less readily with water. They are intended for use only on dormant trees and in particular for fighting the San José scale, and for this purpose the writer has found them very satisfactory indeed. They have the advantage over lime-sulfur that they are much less disagreeable to apply, which is certainly an important consideration. They will also "creep" on the surface of the branch, thus insuring a somewhat better distribution. While these oils are usually bought already prepared, they can be easily made at home and frequently at some saving in cost. However, the commercial forms are usually so satisfactory and they are sold so cheap that it is doubtful whether it would pay the grower to make his own. It certainly would not except where he is in the orchard business in a large way.

Whale Oil Soap.—A second material frequently used for sucking insects is whale oil soap, which comes as an ill-smelling, sticky, brown soap. Only very distant relatives of the whale enter into its manufacture, as any cheap fish-oil is used in making it. For orchard use it is well to prepare it beforehand by boiling the soap with a certain quantity of water. This gets it into a condition where it will readily mix with water when wanted for use, and if this "stock solution" is made at the rate of two or three pounds per gallon it is a very simple matter to prepare a batch of spray for use in the orchard. It is generally used at the rate of one pound of the soap to about 8 to 10 gallons of water.

Kerosene emulsion is another very efficient remedy for such insects as the aphis. The chief objection to it is that it requires a special operation to make, but that is certainly not a serious matter. The formula is as follows:

> ½ pound of hard soap,
> 1 gallon water,
> 2 gallons kerosene.

Cut up the soap and dissolve it in the water by boiling. Then remove from the fire and add the kerosene and agitate the mixture violently. A good way to do this is to have a small pump, and pump the liquid back into itself until a creamy white mixture is produced. This is a "stock solution," and ought to keep for weeks or even months without the oil separating out. It is diluted for use according to the insect to be attacked. With aphids, which have very soft bodies, one part of the stock solution to ten or even fifteen parts of water may be strong enough. For those insects which are more difficult to kill, such as the San José scale, it may require one part to four or five of water.

Tobacco Extracts.—There are a number of tobacco extracts on the market which are very satisfactory for sucking insects, especially for the aphids. In the Northwest it is customary in many sections, where the aphis is plentiful, to include some form of tobacco extract with the regular sprayings for fungous pests and chewing insects so that the spray kills sucking and chewing insects and fungous diseases at one operation.

QUESTIONS

1. Discuss the importance to the orchardist of a knowledge of spray materials.
2. Under what conditions is it best for the orchardist to prepare his own spray mixtures?
3. What are some of the objections to the use of Bordeaux mixture?
4. Describe the preparation of stock solutions for Bordeaux. What is the advantage of these solutions?
5. Describe the making of Bordeaux mixture from these stock solutions.
6. What is commercial lime-sulfur? How is it used?
7. Describe the home-made lime-sulfur concentrate.
8. Tell how to make self-boiled lime-sulfur.
9. Give the advantages of arsenate of lead as an insecticide.
10. Give directions for the use of Paris green.
11. What are miscible oils?
12. Why are oils especially valuable in killing scale insects?
13. Give the formula for kerosene emulsion and describe the methods of preparing and using it.

CHAPTER XV

THE SPRAYING CAMPAIGN

Disagreeable but Necessary.—If anyone were to take a vote of the orchard men of the country as to which is the messiest and most thoroughly disagreeable operation connected with growing fruit, spraying would be elected unanimously to the position. There is no question about that. Neither is there any question that it is more important than any other one operation. We may neglect to prune our trees, we may fail to fertilize them and we may grow them in a hay field and still we may frequently grow some very good fruit. But the man who can proudly boast that he did not spray his orchard and still had a crop of fine fruit is in a hopeless and ever-dwindling minority. He is still to be found; occasionally he even gets into a fruit meeting, but his days are numbered. The advent of each new pest makes the non-spraying orchardist more rare, until he will soon be worthy of a place in a dime museum.

Now since spraying is so disagreeable and yet so indispensable, the thing for the orchardist to do is to use the best machinery and the most approved materials and then to fix his mind on the good he is doing and not on how disagreeable the work is. After all, if the operator does use the best apparatus and does protect himself as fully as possible with gloves and a hood he can get through the job with a fair degree of comfort, particularly if, as suggested, he thinks about the wormy apples he is not going to raise. While the writer thoroughly believes this, and is satisfied that anyone who once gets at it will find that it is not as bad as it might be, still he has a great deal of sympathy with the novice who feels rather appalled at the prospect of undertaking the work.

As the beginner looks over even the condensed list of enemies given in this book, and as he notes that this one requires spraying after the blossoms fall and that one before the buds swell; and then as he attempts to select a satisfactory spraying outfit from the bewildering array in even one catalogue (and usually he has half a dozen catalogues at the very least), it is no wonder that he feels as though it was a hopeless undertaking. And yet as he sifts matters out he finds that most of the spraying outfits are a good deal alike, and that most of the pests are accommodating enough to group themselves in such a way that a relatively few sprayings will control them all. So that while spraying is undoubtedly bad enough, and while the necessity for it may properly be catalogued as one reason why the orchard business will not be over-done, yet any good, intelligent man will very soon master the essential details of the work.

Good spraying consists in selecting the right materials, in getting these onto the trees at the right time, applying a uniform strength to all parts of the trees and in doing the work easily and economically and with reasonable comfort.

Making up and Applying.—We have already discussed everything except the work of making up and applying. Let us see what can be said to assist in this operation.

In the first place, the orchardist should *have every convenience* to make as easy as possible the work of preparing the mixtures and getting them into the spray tank. Few people realize how much time and money are wasted by failing to provide for this. To begin with, have a platform sufficiently raised to allow the materials to run by gravity into the spray tank. On this platform are located the stock solutions and other paraphernalia used in the mixing. Know just where to find everything that is wanted, instead of having to hunt all over the place for the arsenate of lead or the strainer. A very convenient outfit of the kind is shown in Figure 82. Then have a convenient and abundant water supply. It is nothing uncommon for a spraying gang to spend more than half the time loading up, and most of this is often spent in getting the water. Sometimes this is unavoidable, but frequently a little time and money spent wisely in advance will completely obviate the trouble. To offset the money so spent it must be remembered that the time of a spraying gang is worth money and whatever conserves that time is worth doing.

The ideal plan is to have a large storage tank, such as is shown in Figure 82, with a ball-cock to control the water running into it. This tank fills up while the gang is in the orchard and is all ready when they come in to fill the spray tank. A large gate on the storage tank allows the water to run from this into the spray tank in a very few minutes, frequently in less time than it takes to prepare the arsenate of lead and lime-sulfur, or whatever is being used for spraying.

Get Things in Readiness Early.—Order the sulfur and lime and arsenate of lead and all the other materials and have them on hand. Go over the outfit and clean it up and repair it. This is good work for winter or for rainy days, and will save any amount of annoyance when spraying actually begins.

Have a good repair kit to take into the orchard while spraying. This outfit ought to contain wrenches of several kinds (particularly a stilson), pliers which will cut wire and wire for them to cut, washers, nozzles and extra small parts of every description. A few dollars invested in such a kit will save ten times the cost the first season in the time it will save running to the house, or, worse still, to the repair shop in town.

Make the Work Comfortable.—In this matter of getting ready for the work, have as good an equipment as can be found to make the work comfortable for the men and horses. The principal thing in this line will be gloves for the men and blankets for the horses. A pair of heavy leather gloves well oiled is perhaps as good as anything. Good rubber gloves are possibly a little more effective, but they cost much more, and a good rubber glove is a difficult thing to find. Any light blanket for the horses will be satisfactory. It protects both the horses and the harness, and, while not indispensable, is worth using, at least in lime-sulfur or Bordeaux spraying. Some men wear a sort of hood for the winter lime-sulfur work, which will frequently be found an acceptable thing, particularly if one's skin is tender.

Fundamental Principles.—In the actual orchard work a few cardinal principles ought to be kept in mind.

1. Have a Definite Object in View.—Know what you are spraying for. Know what your pests look like, how they work and what will kill them. Perhaps it may seem hardly worth while to mention this, but a very large proportion of the men who spray do not have this clear notion of why they do it. How often a man is heard to say that the aphis is less abundant than it was last year and he thinks it is because he sprayed so thoroughly with arsenate of lead. As a matter of fact, arsenate of lead does not have the slightest effect in the world on them. Or he may say that he must do something this year for the big ants which attacked his apple trees the year previous when in reality the ants were not hurting his trees in the least, but were after the honeydew given off by the aphis. Or that he is considering the use of Bordeaux mixture this season for canker worms, when he should know that Bordeaux is regarded merely as a tonic by any canker worm in good health. Examples like these might be multiplied indefinitely and that, too, among good, intelligent orchard men. So that it seems quite reasonable to urge the importance of having a clear idea of what to do.

2. Spray in Time.—Many of our orchard pests are not affected in the least by any spraying which is not done promptly. The codling moth and the bud moth are good examples of this class. No amount of spraying after they once gain entrance to the apple or the bud, respectively, will have any effect on them. With a great many other pests spraying is of relatively little value if done late, and with only a few is there any objection to doing it considerably beforehand.

3. Spray Thoroughly.—This has already been spoken of more than once, but it will bear repeating, as no other one point is of more importance. A common way of regarding spraying is to consider that it is like a medicine; if the tree gets a certain quantity of it, it will be cured of its diseases. But the proper way to regard it is to think of it as we would of painting a barn. Painting one side of a barn has no effect in preserving the other side. Neither does spraying one side of an apple affect the other side. The case is even stronger than this, because such pests as the San José scale may migrate to the parts that were sprayed if we have left scales undisturbed in some places by our poor spraying.

4. Let the Wind Help.—In spraying when there is a wind blowing if one will get at just the right angle with his tree he can spray into the tree and wet one side of a branch and then the spray will be blown back onto the other side and so the whole tree is reached quite as thoroughly as though there were no wind blowing and one sprayed from each side. Some men make a practice of spraying one side of their trees with one wind and then waiting a few days and spraying the other side with a wind

Fig. 88.—Proper condition of apple blossoms for spraying before they open.   This is often a very important spraying when scab is troublesome.

from the opposite direction. This is all right if the winds are accommodating enough to come that way, but even then it takes more time to go through the orchard twice than if it can be done at one operation. In spraying bearing trees of good size some wind is even desirable, as it keeps the leaves in motion and the spray is apt to reach both sides more thoroughly.

Effects are Lasting.—If the orchardist sprays year after year he is almost certain to find that conditions in the orchard improve from year to year. In other words, the effect of spraying is cumulative. We get some of the benefit of our 1913 spraying in 1914. This is a comforting thought and ought to stimulate the owner to keep up the practice regularly. It is still more likely to be true if a whole neighborhood or section takes up the practice. A few poor, shiftless non-sprayers in a section can do a lot of damage to the whole region by keeping up the supply of insects and fungous spores.

Spraying is Insurance.—In this connection the fruit grower ought to keep in mind a fact, which is often urged but frequently forgotten, that spraying is really an insurance. He can not always tell beforehand exactly what pests he will have, but he knows somewhat definitely. He must, therefore, map out his program and spray accordingly, knowing that one year with another such a program is going to pay. And in particular he must not become discouraged and give up spraying because in some season Jones, who didn't spray, gets just as good results. A man does not become disheartened and condemn fire insurance because his house does not burn down and give him the benefit of the insurance. And he ought to regard spraying in the same light.

The Question of Danger to Animals.—Another point which is often asked about is the question of the danger to animals which eat grass that grows under sprayed trees. And less frequently there is some concern as to the danger of the sprayed fruit as human food. On the first point, danger to stock, the situation may be thus stated: With any ordinary fruit tree sprayed in any ordinary way with poison there is no danger whatever to animals which eat the grass growing under the tree, either in a fresh state or as hay. The Michigan Experiment Station investigated this matter very thoroughly a number of years ago, pasturing sheep under trees which had been heavily sprayed and in other cases cutting the grass and feeding it to horses, and no injury resulted in either case. On the other hand, there have been cases where animals have fed on grass growing beneath street trees that had been sprayed, and such animals have been either killed outright or made seriously sick. But the case here is very different from any ordinary fruit tree. With these street trees the operator stays in the tree for a long

Fig. 89.—Gravenstein apples sprayed for scab. Compare with Figure 90.

Fig. 90.—Gravenstein apples not sprayed. Compare with Figure 89. The matter of spraying was the only difference in the treatment of these apples. One lot is almost worthless and the other nearly all No. 1 apples.

time and uses a very heavy stream so that there is a tremendous drip of poison onto the grass beneath. The farmer need have no hesitation in using the grass in any orchard which has been sprayed in the ordinary way. In this connection it ought to be said that too great care can not be exercised to prevent animals from getting at the poison. This does not often happen and yet it occurs often enough to make extreme caution desirable. In particular, the empty kegs ought to be destroyed after the poison has been used. Cases are known where such kegs have been left about the orchard and have caught rain water and animals drinking this water have been killed. All poisons should be kept under lock and key and should be taken out only as they are wanted for use. It is a very easy thing to become careless about this where men are using such materials constantly.

The question of the effect of sprayed fruit on human beings was also investigated by the Michigan Experiment Station. Grapes sprayed with Bordeaux mixture were chosen and it was found that even though all the spray materials used were to remain on the fruit a person might eat 300 to 500 pounds at one meal without getting enough copper sulfate to be dangerous. In testing the matter of arsenic, apples sprayed with Paris green were examined, and it was shown that a person might eat eight or ten barrels at one time without being in danger from the *arsenic*. These figures seem fairly reassuring, even for a person with a robust appetite, and we may therefore conclude that it is safe enough to eat sprayed fruits. Nevertheless, it is poor practice to have anything on the fruit which can be seen at the time it is marketed. If it becomes necessary, therefore, to spray late in the season use a material that does not show.

The spraying program is sure to vary somewhat in different seasons and in different localities; yet it is possible to map out a fairly constant program for each of the different fruits, and it may be of interest and value to suggest such a general scheme here.

For apples and pears the usual sprayings would be as follows:

First spraying in the autumn after the leaves have fallen, using one of the miscible oils—about 1 gallon of oil to 12 gallons of water—or using lime-sulfur at the winter strength, say 1 to 9 or 10. This spraying is principally for the San José scale and may be omitted altogether where the owner is lucky enough not to have that pest.

Second spraying in the spring before the buds swell, using lime-sulfur at winter strength. This is for the scale, principally, but is also of value for certain fungous troubles. It is generally advisable to apply this spraying, though there may be exceptions.

Third spraying, within a week after the petals fall from the blossoms, using arsenate of lead, 3 pounds to 50 gallons of water, with about a gallon of commercial lime-sulfur added for fungous diseases. This is primarily for the codling moth, but it is also very helpful with the curculio and is the most important single spraying in the calendar. It ought to be stated here that some people have had trouble at times with the combination suggested above and some authorities have even gone so far as to recommend not using the combination but applying each one separately. This, however, is too much trouble and if this combination will not work we must get one that will. The writer has never had any trouble with the combination, though he has used it for a number of years.

Fourth spraying, three or four weeks after the third, same materials used. This is especially important for the codling moth, but is also useful in checking fungous troubles like the scab, the sooty blotch and other diseases.

These four sprayings will usually go far towards protecting the orchard from attacks, and, as suggested, the first may sometimes be omitted, though if the orchardist lives in a San José scale district he should always do more or less autumn spraying in case the spring work rushes more than anticipated. On the other hand, in some sections it frequently becomes necessary to spray several times in addition to those outlined. Where there are several broods of the codling moth it may be necessary to spray four or five times for that insect alone. Or if the scab is especially troublesome it may be necessary to spray before the blossoms open.

For peaches and plums it is not usually necessary to spray in the autumn, but the program would be as follows:

First spraying, lime-sulfur of winter strength before the buds swell, for San José scale, leaf curl and brown rot.

Second spraying, with self-boiled lime-sulfur when the fruit is the size of the end of one's thumb, principally for the brown rot. In sections where this brown rot or monilia is particularly bad it is recommended to make three sprayings for it with the self-boiled lime-sulfur, the first about a month after the petals have fallen, the last about a month before the fruit is ripe, and the second about half way between these two.

Cost of Spraying.—It remains to say a word about the cost of spraying. This is an item which varies so much that it might show better judgment to omit the discussion of it altogether. But it is hoped that the following figures, like others that have been given, may be at least suggestive.

A block of 53 bearing Baldwin trees, probably thirty years old, was sprayed for San José scale, using an outfit consisting of a team and three men at a combined cost of 87½ cents per hour.

Time, 7½ hrs. @ 87½ cents (cost of labor)...................... $6.56
Materials 431 gal. spray (Oil 1 to 12 = 32½ gal., @ 35 cents) 11.38

Total cost $17.94
    Labor cost per tree ....12½ cents
    Material cost per tree ....21½ cents
    Total cost per tree 34   cents

It should be said in explanation of these figures that the work was done with great thoroughness, as it was especially desired not to let any of the scales escape.

The same block of fifty-three trees was sprayed for codling moth at the following cost:

Time, 6½ hours (3 men and team) @ 87½ cents (cost of labor).... $5.69
Materials 250 gal. spray (3 lbs. arsenate of lead to 50 gal.) = 15 lbs. arsenate of lead, @ 8 cents 1.20

Total cost $6.89
    Labor cost per tree .... 10¾ cents
    Material cost per tree .... 2¾ cents
    Total cost per tree 13   cents
    Total cost per barrel of apples, about 4   cents

A block of 1,487 four-year-old apple trees was sprayed for San José scale at the following cost:

Time, 41 hours (3 men and team) @ 87½ cents (cost of labor).. $35.88
Materials 720 gal. spray (Oil 1 to 12 = 55½ gal., @ 35 cents).... 19.43

Total cost $55.31

    Labor cost per tree .... 2.41 cents
    Material cost per tree .... 1.30 cents
    Total cost per tree .... 3.71 cents

QUESTIONS

1. What can be done to make spraying convenient and comfortable?
2. Discuss the importance of knowing why we spray.
3. Why is it important to spray in time?
4. Why is thoroughness especially important in spraying?
5. In what sense may spraying be considered as an insurance?
6. Under what circumstances is there likely to be danger to animals from spraying?
7. Outline the seasons spraying for apples and pears.
8. How should plums and peaches be sprayed?
9. Discuss the cost of spraying.

CHAPTER XVI

RENOVATING OLD ORCHARDS

In all the older orchard-growing sections of the country there are many old orchards which have been neglected for years and are practically worthless as they stand, sometimes worse than useless, since they harbor every imaginable pest, and yet which may be brought back into vigor and made to grow fine crops of fruit if rightly handled. Orchards have been changed from absolute worthlessness into thrifty growth and remunerative crops in from two to three years. So easily and quickly can this change be made that an old orchard, which is not in too bad condition, offers better and quicker returns than the setting of a new orchard. It seems worth while, therefore, to devote a chapter to this subject, since in many respects it is quite different from ordinary orcharding.

Is Cutting Down Better than Renovation?—There are cases so bad that the best thing to do is to cut down the trees and put them on the wood-pile. It may be remarked in passing that they make fine wood for an open fire-place. Anyone who has not used well-seasoned apple wood in his fire-place has something to look forward to. The first question to decide, therefore, is whether the orchard is sufficiently promising to warrant the necessary outlay to bring it back into good condition again or whether it should be used for fire-wood. Of course it is impossible to make rigid generalizations on the subject, for so much depends on the owner and the farm.

Age and Vigor.—There are three or four considerations which seem to be of special importance and which would apply to almost any case. The first of these is the age and vigor of the trees (Fig. 99). The younger they are the better, because the owner has just so many more crops to look forward to. Trees up to fifty years are certainly worth considering if they are thrifty. Trees of seventy-five or one hundred years are sometimes seen that should be considered by no means hopeless.

212

Vigor is far more important than age. The vigor should be in the roots and trunk. Indeed, if the roots are poor the outlook is rather hopeless. But with a good root system and with a sound trunk and main branches it makes little difference how much dead wood there may be among the smaller branches. We can judge of the root system by the amount of growth being thrown out by the top. If the original branches are killed by San José scale but the roots remain sound, the tree will at

Fig. 91.—A good type of tree for renovating. If the dead wood is cut out and the sucker removed from about the trunk it will very soon develop into an excellent tree.

once throw out a large number of water-sprouts to take care of the food being sent up by the roots. Water-sprouts are, therefore, always a hopeful sign in an old, neglected tree. They indicate vigor and are useful in forming the future top, as will be explained later (Figs. 94, 100 and 102).

The Stand of Trees.—Having decided favorably as to the age and vigor of the trees, the next question of importance to the owner is the stand of trees in the orchard. Where there are many gaps in the orchard its value is very much reduced. Of course it is possible to set out young trees where the old ones have died out, but this is seldom entirely satisfactory. In the first place, the young trees so set are not apt to do well and often refuse to grow at all. In the second place, even though they do grow, it is a long time before they come into bearing. With a poor stand of trees the profits are bound to be less, the reduction depending on how poor the stand is, for many

FIG. 92.   FIG. 93.

FIG. 92.—Rather a difficult tree to renovate and one which will require several years to work over. It is headed so high and there are so few small branches low down that the operation will have to proceed slowly.

FIG. 93.—A difficult type of tree to renovate, but one which has little value as it stands. It is so high that it cannot be sprayed properly and all other operations are costly. But it can be renovated, as will be seen by referring to Figure 96, which shows the same tree three years later.

operations in the orchard cost just as much for a poor stand as for a good one. Plowing, cultivating and cover crops, for example, are "per acre" items and not "per tree." Even such operations as spraying cost considerably more per tree if the trees are scattered. It is, therefore, far more likely to be worth while to undertake renovation with a good stand of trees than with a poor one.

The Question of Varieties.—The third point on which the fate of the orchard hinges is the question of what varieties it contains. Our old family orchard with one tree each of forty different varieties is far less likely to prove profitable than a good block of Baldwins. And, on the other hand, an orchard of Ben Davis, or some such variety where the consumer will need to "take a glass of water" with his apple in order to get it down, would certainly appeal to any practical orchardist less, even though it were all of one variety, than an orchard made up

Fig. 94.—A poor type of orchard for renovating. The trees are so tall and there are so few small branches low down that it will take several years before it can be brought into anything like a profitable condition.

of several varieties but all of them good. So the variety question is important. Of course, even large trees can be grafted over, but that is a long and rather expensive operation, for "grafting" is costly in other places than New York City.

Pests in the Old Orchard.—A last question which is worthy of some consideration, though it is not nearly so important as those already mentioned, is the matter of what pests are in the orchard. San José scale, for example, complicates the situation and adds very decidedly to the cost of bringing the trees back to health. So do cankers. The orchardist would seldom, perhaps never, turn down the proposition merely on account of the pests in the orchard, yet coupled with other difficulties they may turn the balance against the orchard.

Having decided that the orchard is worth undertaking, the renovating will usually fall under the following six heads:

1. Pruning.
2. Grafting.
3. Fertilizing.
4. Plowing and cultivating.
5. Cover crops.
6. Spraying.

Some of these are more important than others and the second item, grafting, can usually be omitted from the list altogether and yet it is best to be prepared for the whole six. Let us consider each one as briefly as we may and still get a clear idea of it.

1. Pruning.—This is usually the first thing done and requires more study and a greater variation than any of the others. Each tree is going to be a problem by itself. Some will require severe treatment and others only normal pruning. The type of treatment depends on how badly the top has been killed, on whether the tree is so high as to make a lowering of the top desirable, and on how many water-sprouts there are in it. Depending on these three questions a tree may be pruned normally, or it may be pruned severely, or it may be "de-horned"; that is, the top cut back very severely. Serious mistakes are often made in choosing the type of treatment. If a tree needs to be de-horned the pruner wastes time and money if he gives it merely a light pruning; and, on the other hand, trees are sometimes killed outright by being de-horned when they should have been given merely a severe pruning.

Suppose that the type of top is satisfactory, that is that the tree is not over-tall and there is not much dead wood in it, then it may want only a normal pruning.

If the top is very high so that it ought to be lowered and yet there are very few water-sprouts lower down, then the top ought to receive a severe pruning to start more water-sprouts in order that it may be de-horned later. It would be a mistake to de-horn at once, because there are not enough water-sprouts to take care of the food sent up by the roots. And it would also be a mistake to give it only a light pruning.

If the top is poor and high with plenty of low-growing water-sprouts then the thing to do is to de-horn at once and start a new top.

A common mistake among those who undertake this sort of work is to de-horn trees which are really too good for such drastic treatment. If a tree has a reasonably good top it is much better to do the work gradually, taking several years, perhaps, to accomplish the desired result. The owner thus secures some returns from his orchard each year, and still the trees are improving all the time.

Having decided on which of these three types of treatment is to be meted out to our tree we begin the pruning. A safe rule to follow is to go over the entire top and take out all dead wood (Fig. 99). Frequently, far too frequently, this is all that the tree will stand, and in any case one can judge better what more ought to be done after the dead wood has been taken out. Next should follow diseased branches. Branches affected with blight should come out altogether. Those having such diseases as European canker may be kept for a few years if they seem to be needed and either taken out altogether, later on, or the diseased areas treated, if the branches are too important to be sacrificed.

In most cases where these old trees are not de-horned it is very important to lower the top more or less. This can be done gradually, year by year, taking out relatively small branches from the top of the tree, and in a surprisingly short time the tree will be down where it can be sprayed and picked with comfort and dispatch and yet there will have been little loss in the crop. The King tree shown in Figure 93 is a good example of this. Before the work of renovation began it stood forty feet high with the bearing wood at the ends of the branches and most of the fruit borne so high that the cost of spraying and picking the fruit was simply prohibitive. Now it is down, as shown in Figure 96, where the work on it can be done with comfort. It had been neglected too long to form a model tree, yet no

FIG. 95.—An old orchard before the work of renovating began; full of dead wood and the foliage small and sickly.

FIG. 96.—The same orchard as shown in Fig. 95 after three years' treatment. Many of the trees are almost models in form and foliage, and all are greatly improved.

one would ever recognize it as the same tree shown in Figure 93.

In this renovation work the operator has to be very careful about the wounds which are made in pruning. Many of them are large in size and the trees, of course, are less vigorous than younger ones, so that everything possible has to be done to facilitate the healing process. In particular, no stubs should be left and the painting or tarring of the wounds should be very carefully attended to. Even with the best of care these large wounds are going to be a menace to the tree. The pruner is fortunate also if he does not find a lot of old stubs on the trees, left by former pruners, which have already started to decay and have gone too far ever to be entirely recovered. It is a problem to know just what to do with them. If the decay has extended into the main branch it can be stopped entirely only by chiselling out all of the decayed wood and filling in the hole, but this is usually too costly a process to be undertaken on a commercial scale in an orchard. About all that one can do is to resaw the stub, dig out as much of the decayed wood as can be done conveniently and quickly and then fill in the cavity with cement. This is only a make-shift, and delays but does not stop the decay. It merely keeps out the water and air, rendering the conditions less favorable for the organisms causing the decay.

In most cases of renovation work it is best, at the start, to save all the water-sprouts in the tree. This becomes increasingly important as the pruning is more severe. Where trees are dehorned every sprout should be carefully preserved, and unless the pruning is relatively light (what we have called "normal pruning") there will be few of these sprouts that can be spared to advantage. The second year a large number of them may be removed, but not in the beginning, for the tree will need all the leaf-surface possible to take care of the relatively large amount of plant food that will be sent up by the roots. It will be a revelation to those who have never had experience in this work to see the luxuriant growth which these old trees will develop even during this first season (Figs. 96, 98 and 102).

This is about all that need be said in regard to the pruning proper. There may be parts of the remaining top that will need some thinning, but frequently not, and in any case it is a relatively unimportant part of the work.

Scraping.—Another operation which ought usually to accompany the pruning is scraping off the rough bark. This is regarded by some as of doubtful utility, but it is usually very desirable. It helps to get rid of a large number of insects, eggs and fungous spores. There can be no question about that. And where the orchard is affected with San José scale this scraping is imperative, since live scales will be found hidden away under the old scaly bark and these can never be reached by the spray

FIG. 97.   FIG. 98.

FIG. 97.—Beginning the work of renovating an old apple tree; a high top full of dead wood. Compare with Figure 98.

FIG. 98.—The same tree as shown in Figure 97 after three years' treatment. It is now an excellent tree.

mixtures unless the old bark is removed. More than this, it has always seemed from pure theory that the bark will expand better and the whole tree respond better to the efforts in its behalf if this old, mossy, scaly covering that it has carried for so many years is removed.

2. **Grafting.**—If the trees in the orchard are of satisfactory varieties the owner is saved this expense, but it usually happens that a few trees are of poor sorts, and sometimes a large number have to be worked over. This matter of grafting is really a

subject in itself and can be treated only very briefly here. One
of the chief points to be secured in the remodelled tree is a low
top, and it is also one of the most difficult points. There are
two ways of doing it: Either the new grafts or buds must be
put on water-sprouts which come out low on the trunk or main
branches, or else we must use what is known as the crown or
bark graft. The former method is much to be preferred, and
where water-sprouts are already available or can be developed,

FIG. 99.   FIG. 100.

FIG. 99.—An old apple tree before beginning renovation. Two-thirds of the top is dead
and the rest sickly.

FIG. 100.—The same tree as Figure 99, de-horned after one year's treatment.

there need be no difficulty in changing over the top. It is
simply a question of budding, if sprouts are small, or of cleft
grafting, if the sprouts are large. For budding we should have
a branch not over half an inch in diameter, and the ordinary
shield-bud method is used.

The more buds we put in the more quickly the new top can
be grown, and it is such a simple operation that the extra cost
amounts to very little. In such a tree as is shown in Figure
100, fifty buds might be used and the tree changed to the de-

sired variety with very little loss of time. If the same tree were to be worked over by cleft grafting it would simply be necessary to insert cions in all of the main shoots shown on this tree, perhaps ten in number.

When water-sprouts, or other relatively small branches, can not be had then we may resort to crown or bark grafting in order to lower the top. In this method the branch to be grafted is sawed off at the desired height, which may be well down toward the trunk, and the cions, cut to a thin wedge, are pushed down

Fig. 101.   Fig. 102.

Fig. 101.—The same tree as Figure 100 after one season's growth. Notice the vigor of the foliage.

Fig. 102.—The same tree as shown in Figure 99 after three years' treatment. It will soon be a model tree.

between the bark and the wood. There is no splitting of the branch, as in cleft grafting, and consequently very much larger branches may be worked over. A six-inch, or even an eight-inch branch, may be used. And the cions, being pushed right into the cambium layer of the stub, are almost sure to grow. The objection to the method is that it takes several years for the cions and stock to unite firmly, considerably longer than with cleft grafting, and during this time the cions frequently blow out if the orchard is in a windy location.

3. Fertilizers.—On the matter of fertilizers for the renovated orchard the writer has rather decided opinions, based on his work in several orchards and on observations in several others.

No Nitrogen.—In the first place, there ought to be no nitrogen of any kind applied the first year. This comes as near to being a rule without exceptions as we are likely to run across. Just think for a moment of what has been done to the orchard. If all that has been outlined (with the addition of cultivation and spraying) has been carried out thoroughly it will be the most surprised lot of trees in the state, without the addition of an ounce of nitrogen. We have taken away from one-fourth to nine-tenths of the top, which alone would induce a vigorous growth; it has been freed from insect and fungous attacks and the soil has been stirred up so as to supply it with all the water it can use, something it probably has not had for years. Incidentally this soil treatment seems to give it about all the plant food that it can use and it puts forth a rank,

Fig. 103.—Trunk of a tree damaged by too much nitrogen. The cambium layer has been killed and the bark is separating from the wood.

dark green growth that would do credit to a green bay instead of a green apple tree. A glance at Figure 102 will show the type of growth to be expected.

Now suppose that more nitrogen has been added, particularly slowly available nitrogen, like barn manure or tankage. The tree is bound to make a still more rank growth and it is going to be practically impossible to check it in the autumn in time for it to ripen its wood before winter comes on. The result is almost certain to be more or less damage to the cambium layer and consequent killing of the adjoining bark. If the damage is "less" we are likely to find injury around the trunk of the tree, as is shown in Figure 103. In this case the bark was killed only part way around and the tree survived, but it is like a man with one lung so far as getting down to work is concerned.

Fig. 104.—An orchard damaged by too much nitrogen. The trees have grown late in the autumn and have not been able to withstand the cold.

When the damage is more severe the tree may be killed outright or so severely damaged that it is practically out of the race.

Figure 104 shows a case of this kind. It was in an orchard in the Annapolis Valley, Nova Scotia. The trees had been rather neglected for several years, being kept in sod and no fertilizer used. Then the owner had a "change of heart" and decided to do better by his trees, so he plowed the orchard and applied a heavy dressing of barnyard manure. The soil was not very fertile, and the past neglect had made it less so, with the result that the trees had made long, straggling roots in search of moisture and plant food, as it is well known that trees will do in a poor soil like this. Then comes this entire change of conditions. The soil is plowed up and supplied with an abundance of both moisture and food, particularly nitrogen. The large, spreading root system at once develops an abundance of feeding roots throughout its entire length, as it is also well known that trees will do when conditions are favorable. The result is that the trees are worse off than trees accustomed to good care from the start. They "over-eat," over-grow and are not able to withstand the cold of winter.

Therefore, if you are tempted to use nitrogen in a renovated orchard resist the temptation, under most conditions.

Damage from this source is usually first shown by the trees having a sickly appearance as they leaf out in the spring. An examination of the bark about the base of the trunk will frequently show that it is loose and separates readily from the wood over considerable areas. In severe cases practically the entire cambium layer is killed and the bark may be pulled off in long strips. When the cambium layer is killed all around the trunk there is nothing to do but cut the tree down. But where the damage is less severe we may cut away the injured bark and paint over the wound and the tree will probably recover.

On the potash and phosphoric acid side, the case is quite different. There is certainly no danger of damaging the trees and probably every reason to expect that you will benefit them. Consequently, the orchardist should use from 400 to 600 pounds of basic slag and from 200 to 300 pounds of high-grade sulfate of potash per acre. Doubtless these amounts could be varied still more and yet give good results, but the amounts suggested have been used on different orchards with entire success.

4. **Cultivation.**—It is assumed that the orchard is not going to be kept in sod. Most of these old orchards of the type under consideration have long been in sod and occasionally it may be possible to renovate them by sod culture, but usually not. If they are to be cultivated the first problem is to get them plowed, and sometimes it is a very difficult problem. A steady team is needed, a very strong plow, and a man who has a good grip on his temper. With these essentials and with plenty of time and

perseverance almost any orchard may be plowed. It is sometimes recommended to use a disc harrow first in case the orchard has long been in sod and the roots are close to the surface, but this is entirely unnecessary. Some large roots will have to be cut, a great many in fact, and they will keep working out of the ground all through the first season, but the tops have also been severely pruned and some loss of roots will do no harm. It is a good plan to do this first plowing away from the trees to facilitate getting out the sod from about their trunks. This will require

Fig. 105.—An old, neglected orchard when renovation was begun. The foliage is thin and poor and the trees generally unthrifty.

some work with the mattock or grub-hoe after the plowing is done, but it is worth while in order to make a thorough job.

After the plowing is done the land should be put in the best condition possible. Usually a disc harrow is a good implement to use after the plow and it ought to be run the same way the land was plowed to avoid turning up the sod. The disc harrow may be followed by anything else in the harrow line that is available. The orchard should be cultivated up to about July 10 and then sown to some cover crop.

5. **Cover Crops.**—There are no important special directions for cover crops in a renovated orchard unless it be to use buck-

wheat the first year on account of its rotting the sod and leaving the soil in such good physical condition. If the soil is reasonably good to start with there is usually little difficulty in getting a good growth of cover crop this first year, because the sod furnishes plenty of humus and the fertilizers applied, with the subsequent cultivation, leave the land in fine condition.

6. **Spraying.**—Here again there is no marked difference in the program for a renovated orchard. If the trees are affected with San José scale, which is one of the most common causes of

Fig. 106.—The same orchard as shown in Figure 105, after five years' treatment. There were fifty-three trees in the orchard and it yielded as follows: 1908, 43 bbls.; 1909, 45 bbls.; 1910, 205 bbls.; 1911, 50 bbls.; 1912, 175 bbls.

the decline of these old orchards, two very thorough sprayings will be necessary, one with oil in the autumn just after the leaves are off; and the other in the spring, with lime-sulfur, just before the buds swell. These two sprayings, with two for codling moth, are generally all that are necessary. A thing which will interest and please the man who does the spraying is to see how much easier the spraying becomes year by year as the trees are gradually reduced in height by the successive prunings. It is the tops of these tall trees that take the time and the materials.

Renovation Practice.—As already suggested these theories of renovation have been tried out on many different orchards. The history of one of these orchards may be worth stating briefly to show what can be accomplished in such old, worn-out orchards as we are considering.

The block consisted of fifty-three trees on about an acre and a quarter of land (Fig. 105). The trees were in such bad condition that the advisability of cutting them down and planting a "real" orchard was considered seriously, but it was finally decided to see what could be done to bring them back into usefulness again. The methods just outlined were followed. During the first summer the orchard appeared as shown in Figure 105. This first year was the bearing year and the block produced forty-five barrels of apples, "the first really good crop it had ever borne," one of the neighbors said. As the trees were mostly Baldwins the following year was the "off year" and the orchard produced only forty-three barrels. The third year it bore nearly *two hundred barrels,* the fourth year about fifty, and the fifth year one hundred and seventy-five barrels. This last year the apples were thinned, which reduced somewhat the total crop but greatly improved the general quality. In fact, there were very few No. 2 apples in the orchard. The trees now look, after five years' treatment, as shown in Figure 106.

QUESTIONS

1. Are renovated orchards likely to be profitable?
2. What points should one consider in deciding whether to renovate an orchard or not?
3. Give some idea of the importance of varieties in such an orchard.
4. How would you prune an orchard that is to be renovated?
5. Why is scraping recommended?
6. Discuss the fertilizing of a renovated orchard.
7. What tillage should be practised in such an orchard?
8. Can you describe any methods in the renovation of old orchards which you have seen?

CHAPTER XVII

PICKING AND HANDLING FRUIT

THIS is where the real fun of fruit-growing comes in. The other work is, much of it, pleasant and most of it interesting, but for downright pleasure go out and gather a basket of Carman peaches or pick a basket of McIntosh apples.

Thinning the Fruit.—While it does not strictly belong here, being half way between pruning and harvesting, this is perhaps

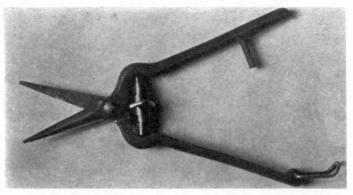

FIG. 107.—A pair of thinning shears. The long pointed blades enable one to get at the stems in a cluster of fruit.

the best place to discuss the thinning of fruit. It is another western custom that is bound to become more general. The sooner our eastern growers can be brought to realize its importance the sooner they will see a marked improvement in the grade of fruit produced. No one thing will so change the size and appearance of a crop of apples as the simple operation of removing about half of them from the trees (Fig. 109). Thinning is profitable for many different reasons, but the following are some of the most important.

1. It maintains the vigor of the tree. The development of the fruit is the most serious drain that the tree has to undergo

229

and the production of the seed in the fruit is much more exhausting than any other part of the fruit. So that, while a thinned tree may produce nearly as many bushels of fruit as one that is not thinned, the number of fruits is so much less on the thinned tree that it is left in far better condition.

2. It prevents the breaking of branches due to overloading (Fig. 110). This is a very important matter on trees that are bearing a full crop. It is not advisable to thin a tree so much

Fig. 108.—Boys thinning Japanese plums.

that no props at all are required to help the tree to carry its load, but there is no question that with proper thinning the number of props may be greatly reduced and still leave the tree reasonably free from danger of breaking.

3. It enables us to get rid of fruit infested by insects and fungous diseases. This is especially true of the codling moth and the railroad worm, but applies to a number of other pests. This not only relieves the tree from the drain of maturing these fruits, but it helps to hold the pests in check and, perhaps most

important of all, it relieves the owner of the moral responsibility of deciding what to do with these inferior specimens when packing time comes.

4. The fruit is of better size and color. The improvement in these respects will be a revelation to the man who has never thinned. The fruit seems to swell right out after the tree is thinned and runs a very even grade at picking time (Fig. 109).

Fig. 109.—Branch of an apple tree that was thinned twice. Even now there are some apples left that should have been taken off. The most difficult thing in thinning is to get the men to take off enough fruit.

5. The trees will bear more regularly. This seems to be the universal testimony of those who have tried it for a sufficiently long period. Of course a single year will not demonstrate it, nor is it probable that old trees which have formed the "habit" of biennial bearing can ever be brought entirely to annual bearing. But there seems to be little doubt of its efficacy on young trees, though it is probable that with fruits like the apple and pear, which bear on spurs, it will be necessary to remove all the fruit from some spurs in order to induce this annual bearing.

This seems like a goodly array of advantages and ought to be sufficient to at least warrant a fruit grower in making a start. Once the start is made the practice will probably be kept up.

The actual operation varies greatly with different fruits, with different men and under different conditions. Most authorities seem to favor the use of a pair of shears for taking off the fruits, though others are rather partial to a good pair of hands. A point that is very important is to go systematically over the tree

Fig. 110.—Boys thinning apples. It cost 40 cents per tree to thin trees of this size twice, and they averaged about four barrels of apples at harvest time. That is ten cents per barrel for thinning and the owner was offered $1.00 per barrel more than his neighbors.

in thinning. If he does not do this the operator never knows when he is through. Begin by removing all defective fruits, such as wormy or diseased ones, those that are under-sized and those that show limb-bruises or other similar defects. Then try to thin down to a reasonably uniform distance apart, for uniform distance gives uniform fruit. This is going to vary, of course, but the usual error is not to take off enough. When a man gets through with the thinning and looks at the ground he is sure he has taken off too many. When it comes time to pick he almost always wishes he had taken off more. Western orchardists are by far the best authorities in the matter, and many of them recommend thinning apples to as much as 8 or 10 inches apart. If this seems like too much, begin by taking off all the apples but one from each spur. Then gradually increase the distance as confidence and courage increase. With peaches and plums a good rule to begin on is to thin until no two fruits touch each other. Of course this really means that the fruit will average a fair distance apart and this can be increased as suggested for apples. The main thing is to get the practice introduced.

The Cost.—What discourages many from thinning is the notion that it is an endless job and that the cost is very high. Of course it does cost, but one should reflect that it costs little more to pick an apple by *thinning* in July, than it does to pick it by harvesting it in October. The writer kept careful account of the cost of thinning an orchard of fifty-three bearing Baldwin trees one season. They were gone over twice, once the fore part of July and a second time the fore part of August, and the total cost was about forty cents per tree. It was the orchard shown in Figure 106, and the trees would average about four barrels per tree, which made the cost of thinning about ten cents per barrel. As no check trees were left without thinning, it is impossible to say how much the fruit was increased in value, but it was certainly a beautiful crop and an apple buyer offered for it what he claimed was a dollar a barrel more than he was paying for most fruit, because of their uniformity and size. This would make the profit due to thinning one thousand per cent.

HARVESTING THE CROP

Coming now to real picking, several questions of importance present themselves: First, what equipment is needed for picking; second, when fruit should be picked; third, how it should be picked.

Picking equipment.—For most fruits this consists of some type of ladder and some kind of receptacle, usually a basket.

There are all kinds of ladders on the market, but two kinds especially commend themselves. In step-ladders the kind shown in Figure 111 is preferable. It has only one leg in front, which enables the operator to establish it firmly on the ground much more quickly than can be done with the four-legged kind, and incidentally it is much more firmly established. The spread of the ladder proper at the bottom also helps to make it a very stable ladder.

Then for old apple trees or other large-sized trees the best ladder is what is generally known as the orchard type of ladder, where the two side-pieces come together in a point. This makes it much easier to establish the ladder firmly against the tree than is the case with the other type of ladders in which the two side-pieces run parallel or nearly so. Both types of these ladders are shown in Figure 115.

Fig. 111.—Picking cherries. Notice the type of step-ladder, broad at the bottom and with only one leg in front.

A very satisfactory picking receptacle is a smooth oak picking basket such as is shown in Figure 112. For perishable fruits it ought to be lined. Another good picking receptacle which is strongly recommended by many western fruit growers is the galvanized iron pail. Besides being a perfectly rigid affair with no tendency to allow the fruit to squeeze down along the edges of the receptacle, as it will do in a flexible one, the pail possesses the additional advantage that the foreman can tell by the sound when a picker throws an apple into it. This last point appeals to any man who employs a number of pickers. Never buy the rough type of picking basket shown in Figure 113. They cost just as much and bruise the fruit far more. Another type of picking receptacle which is very objectionable is the picking bag (Fig. 114). There are various types of these, from a home-made contrivance made from a grain sack and designed to sling over the shoulder, to the cross between a pail and a bag. With a very careful picker they may work very well,

FIG. 112.   FIG. 113.

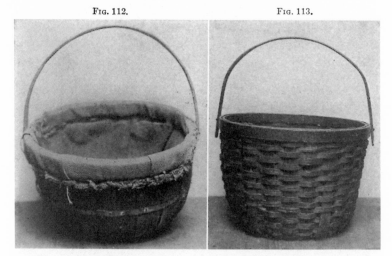

FIG. 112.—A good picking basket. The smooth surface does not bruise the fruit and the padding helps still more to reduce this type of damage.

FIG. 113.—A poor type of picking basket for fruit, yet one often used. The rough sides are sure to bruise the fruit.

though even then it is difficult to see how fruit can escape being bruised more or less as the operator moves about in picking. With the usual help that must be employed when there is much picking to do, it is simply out of the question to avoid a lot of serious injury. It probably will not show itself when the fruit is emptied into the box or barrel; frequently it may not show when it is packed, but it certainly will in the long run. Such fruit cannot keep as well as that which has not been subjected to this treatment.

A word also ought to be said in regard to the containers which are used to carry the fruit from the orchard to the packing house. If possible these should not be the packages which are to be sent to market. Some very large peach growers make a practice of taking the regular basket in which the fruit is to be shipped right into the orchard, but in most cases this is not done. And where it can be avoided it is certainly better not to use them, for the baskets are bound to get soiled and broken

Fig. 114.—Picking apples into bags. These may be all right with very careful men and have the advantage of leaving both hands free, but the fruit is almost sure to be bruised with the least carelessness.

more or less in their trip from the storehouse to the orchard and back again. For the smaller fruits, like plums and peaches, the picking basket shown in Figure 116 is excellent for transporting the fruit from orchard to packing house, and it will last much longer if oiled. For apples and pears either a heavy orchard box should be used or else barrels. In either case it is much better if these receptacles are kept expressly for this purpose. Second-hand barrels are entirely satisfactory and the heavy orchard box makes an excellent receptacle to store apples in and will last a long time if handled with reasonable care.

When and How to Pick.—We come now to the second of our picking questions. When to pick the fruit varies, of course, with circumstances and with fruits. It varies all the way from peaches, which are never quite so good as when allowed to get thoroughly ripe on the trees, to pears, which practically ought never to be allowed to ripen on the tree. The distance the fruit has to be shipped is an important factor in determining the proper degree of ripeness for most fruits. The farther one has to ship the "greener" must the fruit be when picked. That is one of the advantages which the local grower has over the man who has to ship long distances. Watch the way prices jump up when the first "native" or local peaches or strawberries come on, and you get an estimate as to how much it improves them to ripen on the tree or vine.

As there is considerable variation in handling the different fruits at picking time it may be well to suggest a few points as to picking each particular fruit.

Apples when grown for market are seldom allowed to get fully ripe on the tree, though it probably does not reduce their quality any to do so if they mature early enough. Gravensteins, for example, that have ripened on the tree are certainly fully as good as if they had been picked earlier and allowed to ripen in storage. Of course the winter varieties are not really ripe until long after they are picked, and even the early sorts, though they are more nearly ripe, are usually pretty "green" when picked.

The proper degree of maturity is judged in various ways. The amount of red color is frequently a fair index. The appearance of the cheek, whether it is still a dead, even, hard green or whether it has begun to ripen up and look edible, is very important. The ease with which the stem separates from the tree is also an excellent index of maturity. So long as either the stem or the spur is likely to break instead of the joint between the two, the apple may safely be left on the tree, except where one is shipping very long distances. But when this joint separates easily, when some of the apples even begin to fall, then there is little danger of their being too green. The color of the seeds is another point usually given, but it is really seldom resorted to. If the seeds are examined they should be a good brown color, as a rule, before the apple is fit to pick. There are exceptions to this rule, for some varieties are still immature when the seeds are brown and others are fairly edible while the seeds are still very light colored, but these exceptions are rare.

FIG. 115.—Picking apples from well-loaded trees. Apple trees carrying a full crop cannot be thinned enough to carry their fruit without danger unless they are propped.

In the operation of picking the apple, if the thumb is placed beside the joint between the stem and the spur, and then the fruit is bent towards the thumb with a quick motion, the joint will usually break readily. This requires a little practice, but once acquired the good picker will harvest very few spurs. The apple should always be picked with the stem on, as where the stem is pulled out it breaks the flesh and allows disease germs to enter. This is a point frequently overlooked by careless pickers and ought to be insisted on by the foreman. It is frequently a good plan to make more than one picking of a variety. With early apples this is especially true, but it will hold with even as late varieties as the Gravenstein and the McIntosh. One gets much better fruit in this way, and it is surprising how the smaller apples which are left on the tree will fill out in size. Of course this is especially important with such varieties as Wealthy and McIntosh, which tend to drop before they are fully ripe, yet it is often worth trying even with varieties which hang on well.

Pears, as already suggested, are picked decidedly green, in fact greener than any other fruit. If allowed to become too ripe on the tree all sorts of difficulties are likely to develop. Some varieties rot at the core, many develop the hard, gritty granules, so disagreeable to the consumer, of an otherwise fine pear, while still others become mealy. Most of the indications discussed under the apple, except red color, apply to the pear, but the really important indication is the appearance of the cheek of the fruit. When this changes from a dull, unattractive, green to a more yellow and inviting appearance the fruit should be picked. Of course, greenness can be over-done, even in the pear, in which case the fruit will wilt and shrivel instead of mellowing, but there is relatively little danger of this. Pears should be picked very carefully, more so than almost any other fruit. Bruises are peculiarly disastrous with a fruit which must remain in storage so long and which has a flesh that is so soft and melting.

Peaches ought to remain on the tree just as long as possible and still get to market in good condition. This accepted rule practically means that it is impossible for anyone to advise the owner as to when to pick. It all depends on how far he is from his market, and it will probably require some experimenting on the part of the man who is not familiar with the business. The all-important indication with the peach, as with the pear, is the appearance of the cheek of the fruit. When this looks mature and is attractive in color the peach is ready to pick. Do not pay much attention to the question of red color. This is largely a varietal question and depends also on how dense the top of the tree is. Moreover, red frequently develops on a peach weeks before it is ripe. We frequently see the advice given to judge by feeling of a peach whether it is ready to pick or not. This is absolutely unnecessary and very detrimental to the fruit. It may be necessary at the start to test a few specimens in this way in order to get at the relation between appearance and maturity, but that is all. The man who cannot pick peaches without pinching and punching them in this way had better be put to picking potatoes, which will stand that sort of treatment. Moreover, it is an unnecessary waste of time. The picker who stops to feel of every peach he picks will not pick many. Another point worth mentioning is the fact that cling-stones

Fig. 116.—Peaches picked into oak picking baskets, to be packed out into other baskets for market.

and semi-cling-stone varieties may be allowed to stay on the tree much longer than those which are perfectly free. The real cling is not much in evidence these days, but the semi-cling is fairly common. Peaches are, of course, always separated from the very short stem, and this ought to be done by as straight a pull as possible, as this bruises the edge of the cavity less than if they are pried loose.

Cherries.—There is no great art about picking cherries except to be sure to get the stems. In fact, the fruit itself should not be touched any more than can be helped. Do the work with the stems alone. They should be allowed to get as ripe as possible before being gathered, as they do not improve much after picking. And still they are not allowed to get fully ripe except for very nearby markets. Taste is the standard by which to

FIG. 117.—Attacking an old-timer. The cost of picking such large trees is much greater than from low trees.

judge ripeness that is usually suggested by those who write on this subject, and it is probably as good as any, though if it is adopted there is danger that some pickers will require to have their judgment refreshed rather often. Cherries ought always to be picked into baskets or some other rigid receptacle and this should be rather small, as too large a body of fruit is likely to lead to injury.

Plums are generally picked before they are ripe; for distant markets, long before. Yet like all stone fruits, they will respond in improved quality if they can be allowed to stay on the trees till fully ripe. The writer has had some experience with Burbank and Red June plums which was interesting to him and may be helpful to others. Both of these are Japanese varieties, a

Fig. 118.—A load of apples on the way to market. This is a good type of wagon for hauling barrels. It is low, making it easy to load, and it will carry twenty-five barrels easily.

class usually singled out by authorities to recommend picking green. The trees under discussion were thinned carefully and the fruit was then allowed to hang until it was fully ripe. We started picking once or twice and quit because there was not enough fruit that was sufficiently ripe. We made repeated pickings, taking only the really ripe plums, and, though these two varieties are not usually rated as of high quality, these particular specimens were certainly delicious. They were put up in strawberry quart baskets and sold at 9 to 10 cents wholesale. But it was the quality that accomplished the results, and it was the ripeness that gave the quality. Plums ought always to be picked with the stems on if possible. With some of the American varieties it is sometimes difficult to do this, as they separate from the stem very readily.

Management of Pickers.—It remains to say just a few words in regard to orchard methods which apply pretty generally to all the different fruits. The first of these, and by all means the most important, is the question of managing the pickers. Various methods are in vogue, but, with few exceptions, the only proper way is to pay by the day and not by the piece. With small fruits this may not be so generally true, but with the orchard fruits, which we are considering, where the orchardist wants good work he can get it only by absolutely owning the men's time. It is desirable to get as good help as possible. And if the owner can have enough regular men, or men who have worked on the place enough to have an interest in things, so that he can put one or two of them with the raw recruits, it is a great advantage. It is also well not to have too many men in any one gang.

Fig. 119.—Distributing barrels in the apple orchard.

Some method must also be adopted to relieve the picker of the necessity of holding his basket, so that he may have both hands free. A very common and handy device is an iron hook fastened to the handle of the basket which may be hooked over a limb of the tree or a rung of the ladder. Sometimes the basket is hung to the belt or over the shoulder.

The sooner the fruit can be gotten under cover after being picked the better. Do not allow it to stand in the hot sun. Of course this is more important with the perishable classes, like cherries, but it holds to a greater or less extent with fruit of any kind.

For hauling the fruit from the orchard some type of low

wagon will be found very useful. If it can be such as will turn in a very short space so much the better. A low wagon becomes almost imperative where apples are brought from the orchard in barrels (Fig. 118). The amount of energy that is wasted in lifting barrels of apples into high wagons or carts and then lifting them down again would have built the Panama Canal. Good equipment for all the different operations is half the battle in handling the fruit economically and well (Fig. 119).

QUESTIONS

1. Give the principal benefits from thinning fruit.
2. Describe how it is done.
3. Give some idea of the expense.
4. What should be the equipment for picking the different fruits?
5. Discuss the stage of maturity for the picking of apples.
6. Same for peaches and plums.
7. Same for pears. For cherries.
8. Give special points and cautions to be observed in the picking of each of these fruits.
9. Discuss the management of picking crews.
10. Describe the picking of fruits as you have seen it and discuss the good or bad features.

CHAPTER XVIII

STORING FRUIT

IT is rare that a fruit grower is supplied with abundant and efficient storage room. Frequently the only storage available on the farm is the cellar of the dwelling house or, worse yet, of the barn. While the late varieties of apples may keep surprisingly well in these old cellars, there is no hope of holding the earlier and more perishable fruits.

Advantages of Good Storage.—The principal advantages which the orchard man secures by having adequate and efficient storage are the following:

1. Prevents Forced Sales.—It puts him on an equality, or nearly so, with the buyer. Frequently the great advantage which the buyer has over the fruit grower is that the latter has no place to store his fruit and the buyer knows this. He therefore offers as little as his conscience will let him, knowing that the orchard man, realizing his precarious position, will accept the offer rather than run the risk of failing to find another buyer. Now suppose that the grower has plenty of room in which to store his fruit and that this storage is efficient so that his fruit will keep in good condition for a long time. He is in a very different situation from the former case. He knows that his fruit will be perfectly safe for a number of weeks or months and he therefore feels quite independent about selling. If the price offered is satisfactory he will take it, and if not he will wait. Good storage facilities, therefore, put the transaction just where it belongs. Neither buyer nor seller has any advantage over the other. If they can agree on a price the fruit changes hands, and if they can not it does not.

2. Good storage prevents gluts of the market by allowing the producer to hold back a part of his crop. This is especially true of the more perishable fruits. For example, in New England there is what is known as "Elberta week," when this variety comes on with a rush. It so happens that it usually comes the week of Labor Day, when most people do not want to labor. The result is that prices usually collapse. But if even the large growers were so situated that they could put some of their peaches in storage for this week they would not only be saved the necessity of selling this part of the crop at a sacrifice, but the mere fact that they took some of the fruit off the market would help to keep the price up.

3. Good storage increases consumption by keeping the fruit in better condition. This is a self-evident fact but one frequently overlooked. If a consumer gets a barrel of apples in poor condition, one barrel will perhaps be all that he will buy; whereas if his first barrel comes to him in fine shape he may be induced to use two or even three barrels. Few people realize how much difference there is in selling capacity between a fruit which is merely not decayed and one which has been kept in prime condition.

4. Good storage improves the price by allowing the grower to delay his marketing. It almost always happens that the price of any fruit is higher at either end of the season than it is in the middle of the season. Therefore if a grower can keep the fruit which he would ordinarily market in the middle of the season until this rise in price occurs he is going to realize considerably more for his crop.

5. Good Storage Avoids Mental Strain.—It seems worth while to add another advantage of good storage, and that is the influence it exerts on the grower himself. Few people who have not had the experience realize what a mental strain it is upon a man to market a large crop of fruit. A good share of this strain comes from his anxiety lest the fruit shall deteriorate before he can sell it. The reassurance which a good storage would bring to such a man would increase his comfort and prolong his life.

The Ideal Storage Plant.— With all these benefits to be secured from storage it is worth while next to consider what constitutes an ideal fruit storage plant. It ought to have the following characteristics:

1. Low Temperature.—A satisfactory storage must be able to give relatively low temperatures. Just what these shall be depends on the kind and condition of fruit, but they must be low. Usually fruit keeps best when the temperature approaches the freezing point. With apples it is generally considered that the best temperature is from 30° to 32° F., but it is quite possible that this idea may be modified with further experimentation. The low temperature prolongs the keeping of the fruit for two reasons, first because it prevents or retards the work of the organisms of decay and second because it slows down the life processes of the fruit so that it lives a slower life and therefore lasts longer.

2. Little Variation.—The storage room should have as constant a temperature as possible. Variations are always objectionable and become more so as they are rapid and extreme. The writer once had experience with a small storage room where the insulation was very poor. The first winter he managed it he attempted to get around the difficulty by putting a small oil stove in the room. As this could not be left burning all night, the temperature was run up to perhaps 60° during the day and then fell to nearly freezing during the night. This was repeated each day of the very cold weather. It is needless to say that the fruit kept very poorly that winter, so much so that it was decided that something would have to be done to improve matters. The following year furring strips an inch thick were nailed against the walls and then the room was lined with building paper, thus giving an inch air space and the additional layer of paper over the entire wall surface. The result was that the following winter the temperature was very constant and the fruit kept surprisingly well.

3. Getting Fruit In and Out.—The storage should be arranged so that it is convenient to get fruit into it and out again. Just what this arrangement will be will vary with circumstances, but if it is at all possible to get a wagon into the storage it will save tremendously in the cost of getting the fruit in and out. An elevator and an outside bulk-head are two common methods, but neither is as expeditious as the wagon method, and the bulk-head method is not much more efficient in conserving the cold temperature of the storage house.

4. Not too Expensive.—The storage must be reasonable in cost. Just what may be considered as a reasonable cost varies. The cost of the same house in different localities will vary and the price which a grower can afford to pay and still make a profit on his investment will vary. If an orchard man is selling his apples to a fancy trade at $5 to $10 a barrel he can afford to put more money into a storage house than the man who is selling on the general market for $1.50 to $2.00 a barrel. In estimating the capacity of a room or building it is customary to allow ten cubic feet per barrel, and two and a half cubic feet per bushel box. These amounts allow for alley ways for getting at the different lots in the storage. It is generally considered that a refrigerated storage house can be put up for from $2.50 to $3.50 per barrel of capacity. If an orchard man is expecting to put his fruit in cold storage he can probably put up his own building, provided he is a reasonably large grower, cheaper than he can hire his fruit stored in a commercial storage plant.

The usual price charged for storing apples is 40 to 50 cents per barrel for the season. Now if a grower is producing say one thousand barrels of apples, and putting them in refrigerated storage, he pays $500 for the season. This is the interest at five per cent on $10,000, which at the estimates given above would put up a building with a capacity of from 2,900 to 4,000 barrels. Of course it is going to cost the owner something to run it, but even so he is going to save money and he is going to have the advantage of a satisfactory storage right on the place (Fig. 120).

5. Proper Moisture.—A storage room should carry a relatively high percentage of moisture. Just what the best moisture content is has not yet been accurately determined. Mr. Madison Cooper, a recognized expert in such matters, suggests for apples 80 per cent of a saturated atmosphere. One thing is certain, it is very easy to get the storage room too dry. While it is undoubtedly possible to also get it too moist, this is a far less common difficulty. The writer recalls the methods used by two growers in the Annapolis Valley, Nova Scotia, who were noted for their success in keeping apples. One of them had a stream of water running through his storage cellar and the other made a practice of wetting down his cellar with a hose. It is apparently particularly objectionable, from the moisture standpoint, to have a cement floor in the building unless some provision is made to supply the needed amounts of moisture.

Fig. 120.—A good type of farm storage house. This building will hold about two thousand barrels of apples and has ample room for empty barrels in the loft.

In one house the requisite moisture supply has been kept up in a room which has a cement floor, by having a small channel cut in the cement along two sides of the room and keeping a small stream of water in this from a faucet which is allowed to drip slightly.

6. *Good Size.*—The storage ought to be ample. The cost per barrel is less on a large plant than on a small one and it therefore adds relatively little cost to increase the capacity of the house considerably. And where new orchards are coming along, more and more room is going to be needed. It is there-

fore much better to build a good-sized plant to begin with. It can never be done as cheaply afterwards.

7. *Operation Inexpensive.*—The building must be operated cheaply. This is imperative. The more simple the method of operating the better. A method requiring expensive machinery that is likely to get out of repair and which needs the attention of expert and high-priced men, while it may be all right for the large city plant, is certainly not usually the best for the farmer.

The various types of fruit storage may be classified as follows:

1. Refrigerated storage, in which ammonia, carbon dioxide or some other gas is used for cooling the room. This is the most common type with large establishments and has the advantage that it is usually very accurate in operation. It is possible to regulate the temperature to a degree, which is often very important. The objections to it are that it is expensive and that the machinery required to operate it is rather complicated and when it gets out of order requires an expert to fix it up again. There are three different methods of cooling storage rooms by this gas system: (*a*) The gas, after being liquefied under pressure, is conducted in pipes to the storage room which is to be cooled, and there allowed to expand and take up the heat of the room; (*b*) the gas is allowed to expand in pipes which are immersed in brine and this cooled brine is then conducted to the room to be cooled; (*c*) the air of a certain room (or rooms) is cooled down and then is put in circulation by fans and carried thus to the storage rooms.

2. We have refrigerated storage where ice is used for cooling. This is the type of storage which is often used for fruit, and it has proved an exceptionally satisfactory method for this purpose. The method is briefly as follows: At the top of the building are vats in which are located coils of pipes filled with chloride of calcium brine. This brine is 25° Beaumé density and will not freeze at 3° F. These coils, known technically as the primary coils, are connected by pipes with other coils in the rooms to be refrigerated, known technically as the secondary

coils. To cool the rooms, broken ice and coarse salt are put into the vats and the ice in melting takes up the heat from the primary coils, thus cooling the brine in them. This makes the chloride brine heavier and it flows, by gravity, down through the connecting pipe into the secondary coils. Here it takes up the heat of the room and thereby becomes lighter again, and so the flow is kept up. The temperature of the refrigerated rooms is controlled principally by varying the amount of salt used with the ice, but there are valves on the pipes by which the flow may be stopped altogether when desired or shut down as much as may be wished. The great advantages of the system are: The cheapness with which it can be run, requiring no high-priced labor whatever; the fact that one or more of the rooms may be run without the others, thus reducing the cost proportionately; the fact that there is no intricate machinery to get out of order, and repairs at their worst are made by a plain plumber, and, most important of all, the fact that it works well in practice.

3. There is the frost-proof type of fruit storage. This depends on the temperature of the outside air for cooling the rooms. It is not as efficient as either of the others, but neither does it cost as much, either to build or to operate. The old-fashioned barn or house cellar is the crudest form of frost-proof storage. The building shown in Figure 121 represents the highest type. Where storage is required principally for winter varieties of apples and where the autumn temperatures are relatively low, the frost-proof house is likely to prove very satisfactory. Where the more perishable fruits are grown it is by no means so useful. Such a building or room is operated by opening it up when the outside air is cooler than that of the room and closing it again when the outside temperature rises. With a little attention, and leaving it open during the cold nights of early autumn, the temperature may be forced down fairly low quite early in the season.

Construction.—It may be worth while to give next the type of construction used in the two buildings here described.

Fig. 121.—Storage building at the Massachusetts Agricultural College. This building is equipped with a gravity brine system of refrigeration which is well adapted for farm use.

In the refrigerated building, shown in Figure 121, the walls are relatively very complicated and are correspondingly efficient. Particularly on the outside walls of the refrigerated rooms the insulation is very perfect. These walls consist of the following materials, beginning on the outside: (1) Brick veneer, (2) air space, (3) water-proof building paper, (4) inch boards, (5) 2 by 10 inch studs, the space filled with shavings, (6) inch boards, (7) water-proof paper, (8) inch hair felt, (9) water-proof paper, (10) inch hair felt, (11) water-proof paper, (12) inch boards.

Fig. 122.—Type of apple storage house found in the Annapolis Valley, Nova Scotia.

An excellent feature of this building, which every storage building should possess, is an ample storage room in the third story for empty packages.

The frost-proof storage house has been brought to great perfection in the famous Annapolis Valley, Nova Scotia, where this type is used exclusively. Some of these houses are located on the farms, but most of them are located along the railway, and are either coöperative or are built by large commission houses or by large buyers who operate in the section. One of the farm type is shown in Figure 120 and one of the other type in Figure 122. The walls of these storage houses vary considerably, but the following is a common construction. Beginning on the outside we have: (1) Shingles, (2) water-proof paper, (3) inch boards, (4) water-proof paper, (5) inch boards, (6) 2 by 4 inch studs, (7) lath and plaster, (8) inch furring strips, (9) inch tongue-and-groove sheathing.

A diagram of this wall is shown in Figure 123. Considering that it is not a very complicated wall, it is certainly a very efficient one.

Keeping Qualities of Fruits.—It remains to say a word about the factors which influence the keeping quality of fruits. Like most of the work in fruit growing, we need more light on many points connected with the storage of fruits, yet the following seem reasonably well established:

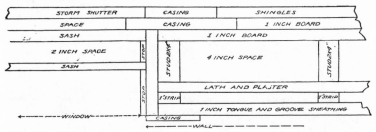

FIG. 123.—Diagram of a cross-section of the walls of the storage house in Figure 122.

The handling of fruit from the time it is on the tree until it lands in the storage house has a very important influence on the length of time it will keep. Fruit which is picked roughly, so as to bruise it in separating it from the twig; fruit which is thrown into the picking basket or poured from that into the receptacle in which it is to be stored; or fruit which is roughly handled while loading or unloading in hauling the packages from the orchard to the storage house, will not keep as well as that which is carefully handled. The importance of this cannot be over-emphasized, and every detail in the work should be carefully scrutinized to see if there is any possible chance for improvement.

The degree of maturity of the fruit at the time it is picked and stored has a very decided influence on the length of time

it will keep. It is a common impression that the greener the
fruit is when picked, the longer it will keep, but this is by no
means true. A certain degree of immaturity is desirable, but it
is quite possible to overdo it. There is some difference in this
respect with the various fruits, but in general it may be said that
fruits will keep longest if picked when they are fully matured
and well colored, but before the tissues have begun to break
down, while the flesh is still firm.

Delay in getting the fruit into storage after it is picked is
a third very important factor. It ought to be understood that
there are certain life processes which are constantly going on
in the fruit, as in any other part of the plant. These processes
have to do with the growth, maturing, and finally with the breaking down and decay of the fruit. They go forward more rapidly
under some conditions than under others. Among other things
which hasten this ripening process is the removal of the fruit
from the tree. It ripens faster after it is picked than while it is
on the tree. Therefore it should be hustled into storage as fast
as possible when once it has been picked.

Mr. G. Harold Powell has shown that Kings, Suttons and
Rhode Island Greenings picked September 15 and stored within
three days, kept in good condition until March, while the same
varieties picked at the same time and handled in the same way,
except that they were not stored for two weeks, were badly decayed by January 1. Their commercial value had been injured
from 40 to 70 per cent by delay in getting them into the storage
house.

High Temperature Before Storage.—One of the chief factors
in making delay dangerous is the higher temperature to which
the fruit is subjected in the orchard or the open shed. A high
temperature shortens the life of the fruit by hastening the
life processes in it. There is no question about that. Just what
is the best temperature and just how it ought to be varied in
ripening up the fruit, are matters still to be determined, but
there is no question that they ought to be low. The more
carefully fruit has been handled the higher temperature it
will stand and still come out in good condition. And conversely

the rougher the fruit has been handled the lower the temperature should be. We ought not, however, to expect that fruit is going to be any better when taken from cold storage than when put in. Many people have apparently overlooked this and expect the storage man to make a number one apple out of a number two while it is in his charge.

Fungous and physiological diseases exercise a very important influence on the keeping of fruit. Among the former the scab or black spot of apples and pears, and the monilia, or brown rot, of the stone fruits, deserve particular mention. Frequently they cause almost the total loss of fruit that is stored. Spraying, careful handling, and low temperature are the methods of reducing the loss, but even these cannot reduce it to zero. Among physiological diseases the scald, and the dry rot or Baldwin spot of apples, are especially important. Neither one is entirely understood, but either one will cause a tremendous amount of loss under certain conditions.

The conditions under which the fruit was grown also exert a very important influence on the length of time that it will keep. Large, overgrown specimens will not keep as well as smaller specimens with firmer flesh. This is why apples grown in sod orchards usually keep better than those grown in cultivated orchards. Fruit grown on a light sandy soil generally does not keep so well as that grown on a heavier soil, though this is probably due largely to the fact that the fruit on the sandy soil is allowed to get too ripe before picking. Fertilizers certainly exert an influence on keeping. Where too much nitrogen is used and the fruit is large and soft it will not keep so long after it has reached maturity. On the other hand, the maturing of such fruit is delayed. Good color is desirable because it means a fully developed fruit, but overcolor is not desirable because it indicates that the fruit may be past the best stage of maturity.

The type of package used in storage certainly influences the keeping quality. A tight package seems generally to give better results than an open one, and a relatively small package is better than a large one, probably because the smaller body of fruit does not generate so much heat. The weight of the fruit in the larger package may also have an influence. A bushel box of apples is often found to keep better than a barrel of the same apples.

Wrapping the fruit will usually cause it to keep better. It seems to prolong its life and of course prevents bruising and the transfer of disease from one specimen to another. Any type of "wrapping," from storing the fruit in sand or sawdust to the use of an oiled wrapper, will assist its keeping.

QUESTIONS

1. Discuss the influence of storage in preventing forced sales of fruit.
2. How does good storage prevent gluts in the market?
3. How does it increase consumption?
4. In what way does storage affect the price of fruit?
5. Give several characteristics of an ideal storage plant.
6. Describe an ammonia cooling system.
7. Describe the system of cooling with chloride of calcium brine and ice.
8. Describe the frost-proof storage house.
9. Give the wall construction of a well-insulated storage house.
10. How does the method of handling fruit affect its keeping qualities?
11. What influence on keeping quality has the degree of maturity at picking time?
12. How is the keeping of fruit affected by delay in storage?
13. Give other influences affecting keeping quality.

CHAPTER XIX

GRADING AND PACKING

THESE two operations are very intimately associated and are frequently performed by one operator at the same time. But as methods improve there is more and more tendency to separate the two and make the grading an operation by itself. While we hear much less about this grading of fruit than we do about packing it, and while fruit is frequently put upon the market without any grading whatever, yet there is no doubt that where anything like careful grading is done it requires more judgment and closer attention to the business in hand than packing does. Once a man learns the art, he can pack apples, for example, into a box without much thought, provided they have been graded and sized. It is largely a mechanical operation. But when he is grading apples into from four to six grades, varying in size and color, he must look critically at every fruit he handles.

Reason for Grading.—Another point emphasizing the importance of grading which is frequently overlooked is the poor impression which a mixed lot of fruit always gives. It is worth while to take out the large apples, and sell them separately, merely for the improvement it makes in the appearance and price of the medium-sized apples that remain. A customer will be perfectly satisfied with an apple two and a half inches in diameter, provided all the rest of the apples in the package are of about the same size. But put this size in with some of three-inch and larger specimens and he objects strenuously and thinks he is being cheated. By all means grade carefully for any sort of good fruit.

Grades for Apples.—Just what the standard for the different grades shall be, and just what names shall be used, is a somewhat mixed question at present. The grades for apples in barrels recognized by the United States and the Canadian federal laws are discussed in Chapter XXII. For boxed apples the usual designations recognized by our western growers are

258

Extra Fancy, Fancy, and Choice (grade C), which are defined as follows:

Extra Fancy.—In this grade all apples shall be sound, smooth, free from worms, worm stings, scale, water core, sun damages or diseases of any kind, and of proper shape, according to the variety. No apples smaller than 165s shall be allowed in this grade (this is the number of apples required to fill a bushel box). No apples that are of a red variety that are not at least three-fourths red, except Rome Beauties one-half red, will be taken in this grade. Yellow Newtowns, White Winter Pearmains, Grimes Golden, Bellflowers, Winter Bananas and Red Cheek Pippins will be allowed in this grade, but no other variety of yellow apples. Winter Bananas and Red Cheek Pippin must show a red cheek.

Fancy.—In this grade also all apples must be smooth, sound, free from bruises, blemishes, worms, worm stings, water core, sun damages or diseases of any kind, and of proper shape, according to the variety. No apples smaller than 165s shall be allowed in this grade, excepting apples of the following varieties, which will be accepted when packed as small as 200 apples to the box: Winesaps, Jonathans and Missouri Pippins when red all over. All apples of red varieties ranging in color from three-fourths red down to one-third red will be included in this grade. All varieties of yellow apples will be allowed in this grade.

Grade C.—This grade shall be made up of all merchantable apples not included in the Extra Fancy and Fancy grades. These apples must be sound and free from bruises, worm stings and other diseases. Skin to be unbroken, but will include misshapen apples or apples having a limb mark or other similar defect. This grade will include apples of all colors and as small as 200s, but no smaller. It is optional with the buyer whether this grade be wrapped or not.

Western Grades for Apples.—It will be seen, therefore, that as yet our grade names and definitions are in process of evolution and are still somewhat variable. Doubtless we shall see more and more uniformity in both of these matters. But the grade name and the grade definition are of minor importance compared to the grading, and if growers will grade carefully and uniformly, and will pack honestly and skilfully, there is likely to be little difficulty about names.

Coming now to the question of packing, we need, first of all, a satisfactory equipment. This means suitable packages, a packing table of some kind, usually a press, besides such accessories as wraps, stencils, stemmers for apples, and various other things which will vary with different fruits and different types of packing.

Packages for Apples.—Since the package will, to a considerable extent, determine the kind of equipment needed, we may begin with a discussion of packages in general. For apples we have principally the barrel and the bushel box. Both of these packages have their advocates and both have their place in marketing apples. The barrel is the typical eastern package, while the box is used in the West to the exclusion of all other packages. The box, however, is gaining ground, though slowly, among the eastern growers. The claims for the box, which seem to be fairly well founded, are that it carries the fruit in better condition, that it is a more attractive package, and that its smaller size makes it more convenient for many consumers. On the other hand, the barrel is an old and well recognized package (Fig. 124). Fruit can be handled in it at less cost than in boxes and it will stand rough usage in transit much better than the box. We ought not to have rough usage, but neither ought we to have a great many other things that we do have. Nothing but apples of the very highest grade ought to go into boxes. It is essentially a high-grade package, and if a customer finds poor fruit in it he feels defrauded and rightly so. The writer would meet the argument that there is a demand for small quantities of the poorer grades by suggesting that these be put in some other type of package.

There is a third class of package for apples which is just now coming into prominence and which is bound to become of more and more importance. That is the small retail package holding from a few quarts up to perhaps half a bushel. These packages are principally of two types, either baskets or cartons. They have the advantages from the standpoint of the consumer, that they can be carried easily in the hand, that they keep the fruit in good condition and that they hold so little fruit that the question of storage is not important. They thus obviate the greatest difficulty which is experienced with the barrel, and even with the box, namely that the ordinary household cannot use all the apples before they begin to decay.

Fig. 124.—An attractive face to a barrel of apples. Such a barrel of apples is sure to attract attention, and if the middle is as good as the face it is sure to make friends.

For pears we have almost the same packages as for apples, except that they are shipped quite largely in half barrels instead of in barrels, and that the pear box is of a different size from the apple box, being 18 x 11½ x 8½ inches inside measure.

Peaches are shipped principally in three types of packages: The Delaware peach basket, holding from 5 quarts to 16 quarts, usually in the latter size; the Georgia six-basket carrier; and the climax peach basket, a relatively new package. One of the climax baskets is shown, filled with apples, in Figure 145. It has the advantage of being a small package which is quite rigid so as to protect the fruit well. It also packs well into cars.

In western sections we have also the four-basket carrier and the peach box. The box is 18 inches long by 11½ inches wide and is made in three different depths—4, 4½ and 5 inches.

Plums are packed in practically the same packages as peaches.

Cherries go to market principally in two kinds of packages, either in strawberry baskets and crates or, the fancy western cherries, in boxes varying in capacity from eight to thirty pounds. Sometimes these fancy cherries are also packed in one-pound cartons.

Packing Apples.—Since the barrel must long remain the most important package for apples it seems worth while to discuss,

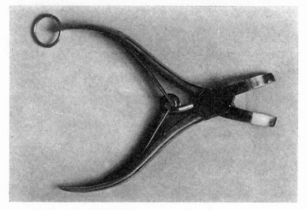

Fig. 125.—Stemmers; shears for removing the stems from the face apples when packing in barrels.

in some detail, the equipment for packing apples in barrels and the operation of so packing them.

The table for barrel packing ought to be fairly large, for, the fruit being rarely graded beforehand, the operator needs a rather large supply from which to choose. A table which is three by six feet and six inches deep (with six-inch boards around) will be found a good size, and the sides and bottom should be padded with or made of burlap or some such material to keep the fruit from bruising. A table of this size which is mounted upon two carpenter's "horses," instead of having rigid legs of its own, can be hung up on the wall out of the way when not in use. There should also be several swing-bail baskets and a press.

There are several styles of presses on the market, principally either the lever or the screw type. The screw press with a circle follower shown in Figure 127 is preferable, but the lever press is very popular with many packers and can perhaps be worked more quickly, but it may not do quite as good work. The circular follower is much better than the old bar-follower

FIG. 126.   FIG. 127.

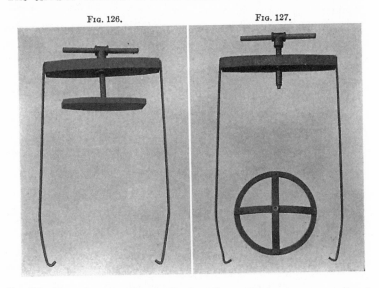

FIG. 126.—The ordinary barrel press with a bar follower. This is not nearly so good as the press shown in Figure 127.

FIG. 127.—Barrel press with circle follower. Any blacksmith can make such a follower and it is a great improvement over the old bar follower.

because it touches the entire circumference of the barrel head, thus insuring its going down more evenly than with the bar (Fig. 126). Presses with circular followers are now manufactured and may be secured from some dealers, or the follower may be made by any good blacksmith, using quarter-inch bar iron.

In addition to the above there should be a stemmer (Fig. 125) for removing the stems from the apples of the face layer, a good stencil for marking the head, and a false or padded head. The false head is merely a round piece of board slightly smaller than the barrel head and padded on one side. This is used when the barrel is nearly full, for pressing the apples down in order to get a smooth surface on which to lay the "tail" or last layer of the barrel. In packing good fruit one ought also to have corrugated pasteboard heads, paper caps and lace circles. The corrugated cardboard heads are circular and just large enough to fit into the head of the barrel and are designed to prevent bruising of the face layer of apples. It ought to be said here

FIG. 128. — Swing-bail basket used in packing apples in barrels.

that some orchard men prefer not to use these, but others believe that they serve a useful purpose. The paper cap is a similar affair except that it is of paper and may also be printed (Fig. 152), and is designed as an additional protection and for advertising purposes. The lace circle (Fig. 124) is merely for ornament, to make the barrel look attractive when opened in the market.

The operation of packing a barrel of apples in new barrels may now be given in detail. First, nail one head of the barrel, using about six five-penny nails; next, loosen the hoops at the other end and take out this head; third, drive down the quarter hoops snug and nail them with three small nails (lath nails are good), which should always be clinched on the inside of the barrel, otherwise many apples will be damaged. Put into the barrel a corrugated head with the smooth side up, a paper cap and a lace circle. Be sure that the latter is put in with the best side down so that when the barrel is opened in market that side will be seen and not the reverse side.

The barrel is now ready to be filled. Select the apples for

the face of the barrel. These should be of uniform size and color (Figs. 129, 130, and 131) and should fairly represent the contents of the barrel. The interior of the barrel may contain smaller apples than the face, but it should also contain some that are larger. Where the face apples are of uniform size it is possible to tell beforehand exactly how many it will take of any particular size to lay the face. The following table gives the numbers and arrangement of the different sizes:

TABLE VI.—*Number and Arrangement of Facing Apples in Barrel.*

Diameter of Apples	Number of Apples in Face	Number of Circles in Face	Number in Center of Face
Inches			
2¼	48	3	3
2½	40	3	1
2⅝	34	3	0
2¾	31	2	4
3	27	2	3
3¼	23	2	2
3½	19	2	1

The apples intended for the face should be placed in a basket as selected (Fig. 128), and the stem clipped out of each one (Fig. 125). If the stem is not removed it will be bent over when the apple is placed on the head of the barrel, in laying the face, and will usually break the skin, thus giving an opportunity for decay to start. When the required number of apples have been selected, lower the basket into the barrel and pour out the apples very carefully. Next begin and lay a row of apples, stem end down, around the outside of the barrel; then a second row and so on until the entire face is laid. Figures 129, 130 and 131 will give a good idea of the arrangement of the apples in the different faces. Having laid the face there are three different ways in which we may proceed. First, we may pour in the apples without attempting to place any more; or, second, we may place a second layer, or face, directly upon the first one; or, third, we may select apples which have a red cheek (provided we are packing a red variety) and place an apple, with the red cheek down, in each opening in the face already laid. This

Fig. 129.—Face of a barrel of apples using nineteen apples 3½ inches in diameter: one apple in the center of two circles.

Fig. 130.—Face of a barrel of apples using 27 apples 3 inches in diameter; three apples in the center of two circles.

Fig. 131.—Face of a barrel of apples using 40 apples, 2½ inches in diameter; one apple in the center of three circles.

last is considered by far the best method. It accomplishes two important objects. It fills up the openings in the face so that the buyer gets the impression of a full, solid barrel of apples instead of a lot of open space; and the red cheeks look well, setting off the apples of the face.

Having laid the face, we next proceed to fill up the barrel. The apples are put into the baskets and each basket, as filled, is

Fig. 132.—A good type of packing table for boxing apples. Notice the rack for holding the box and the hood for holding the wrapping paper.

lowered into the barrel and carefully emptied. After about three baskets have been put in, the barrel should be shaken or "racked" in order to settle them into place. The first racking is deferred until three baskets are in so that there may be weight enough upon the face apples to hold them in place, but thereafter the barrel should be racked after each basket is emptied until it is nearly full. Then the "false head" is put in and the barrel is given a thorough shaking and at the same time the operator exerts as much pressure by hand as he can upon this head. The object of this, as before explained, is to get a smooth surface on which to lay the "tail" or last layer of apples.

The "tailing off" of the barrel is the supreme test of good packing. The whole object is to lay a smooth surface so that when the pressure is put on it will be distributed over the entire face and not confined to a few spots, as it will be if a few apples stick up above the rest. Many packers tip the barrel

Fig. 133.   Fig. 134.

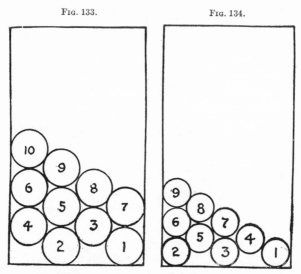

Fig. 133.—Diagram showing method of starting the 2-2 pack.
Fig. 134.—Diagram showing the method of starting the 3-2 pack.

slightly in order to slant the face and then begin to lay the apples at the lower side of this slanting surface. In this way the apples will stay in place better than if the surface is level. The proper height for this last layer is a somewhat debatable point. It depends on the variety and on the distance the fruit is to be shipped. Some varieties, such as Russets, require and will stand a good deal of pressure. Others, such as Gravenstein and Northern Spy, will not stand so much. Among many experienced packers the general opinion is that where the apples

are well racked, so as to get every one into its place and leave
no open spaces, the apples should not project more than a half
inch above the barrel even when they are to be exported.   At
this end of the barrel many packers use what is called a "cushion-
head" to put between the fruit and the head of the barrel.
This cushion-head is merely a pad of excelsior enclosed in paper
and is intended to relieve the apples from some of the bruising

FIG. 135.   FIG. 136.

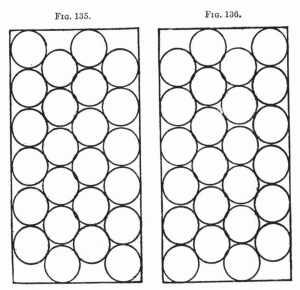

FIG. 135.—Diagram showing the arrangement of apples in the first and third layers of a 2–2
box of apples with 96 apples in the box.

FIG. 136.—Diagram showing the arrangement of apples in the second and fourth layers
of a 2–2 box of apples with 96 apples in the box.

that they would otherwise get.   They serve a useful purpose
and they are in fairly general use among growers.

Following the tailing of the barrel, the cushion-head is put in
place, then the head of the barrel, and lastly the press.   The
head is then pressed down and nailed in with six nails.   These
should be driven through the upper hoop and the staves into
the head.   Never nail the second hoop at either end of the
barrel.

Our barrel is now ready for marking, which is done with a stencil. This ought to contain the name and address of the grower and the name and grade of the apple. And above all the stencil should be of plain, large letters.

Scoring Barrels of Apples.—As an indication of the relative importance which is placed upon the fruit, packing and package for a barrel of apples it may be worth while to insert here the score card used in judging barrels at the Third New England Fruit Show, held in Boston in November, 1913.

Score Card for Barrels of a Given Variety of Apple

FRUIT.—Texture and flavor	100	
Size	100	
Color	150	
Uniformity	150	
Freedom from blemishes	150	
		650
PACKAGE.—Staves	10	
Hoops	10	
Heads	10	
Nailing	20	
Marking	20	
		70
PACKING.—Facing	70	
Tailing	60	
Pressing	70	
Racking	80	
		280
Total		1000

Packing apples in boxes requires more skill than packing them in barrels. That is one objection to the box. Still, any man who is at all "handy" will very soon pick up the principal points, and it is then largely a matter of practice. There are two principal sizes of boxes used. One is 10½ inches deep by 11½ inches wide by 18 inches long inside measure, and the other 10 by 11 by 20 inches. The first shape is preferable, but the capacity is a trifle less. The material for the ends should be ¾ inch thick, that of the sides ⅜ inch and the top and bottom ¼ inch.

A good type of packing table for boxes is shown in Figure 132. It is more shallow and holds fewer apples than the table used for barrels and there is a rack or shelf at one end to hold the box in a slightly slanting position while it is being filled. There should also be a hood for holding the wraps. A convenient type, made of galvanized sheet iron, is shown on the left-hand side of the packed box in Figure 132.

Fig. 137.   Fig. 138.

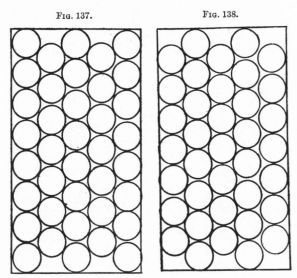

Fig. 137.—Diagram showing the arrangement of apples in the first, third and fifth layers of a 3-2 box of apples with 188 apples in the box.

Fig. 138.—Diagram showing the arrangement of apples in the second and fourth layers of a 3-2 box of apples with 188 apples in the box.

Most boxed apples should be wrapped, and various kinds of tissue and other light papers are used for the purpose. If they can be printed, at least for the top and bottom layers, so much the better. The principal advantages of wrapping the apples are that the wraps act as a padding, preventing bruises and enabling the operator to pack the fruit more tightly; that they prevent the germs of rots being transferred from one apple to another and that they prolong the life of the apples. Wraps are used in varying sizes, according to the size of the apples to be packed, but the 9 by 9 inch size will be found most useful. There should also be layer-papers, made of heavy cardboard in sheets 11 by 17½ inches, to be used between the layers of apples; and also lining papers, which are sheets 17½ by 36 inches, of ordinary wrapping paper or a similar weight. These are for lining the boxes.

It is difficult and probably impossible to give sufficiently explicit directions for the actual packing of the box, so that one who is unfamiliar with the operation can become an expert. In box packing we are all of us Missourians to the extent of "needing to be shown," but it is hoped that with the help of the diagrams (Figs. 133–139) anyone can get a start in the work.

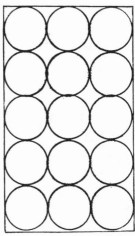

FIG. 139.—Diagram showing the "straight" pack. This pack is now little used, as it bruises the apples more than any other pack.

There are many different plans or "packs" in boxing apples, but they may practically all be classified under two heads, the "straight" and the "diagonal." There is a third type of pack, known as the "offset pack," which differs from the diagonal slightly; but it is not very generally used, and will be omitted from our brief discussion. As a matter of fact, the straight pack is now rarely used, as it bruises the apples much more than the diagonal. Most of the diagonal packs are either "three-two" or "two-two."

In starting the first layer of the three-two pack, place an apple in the lower right-hand corner, the second one in the lower left-hand corner and the third half way between these two. This leaves two spaces, one on either side of the middle apple, and the fourth and fifth apples are slipped into these spaces. This, again, leaves three spaces, in which three apples are placed; and so on, until the layer is completed. The method of starting this pack is shown in Figure 134. The second layer is started by putting an apple over each of the spaces between the apples of the first layer; that is, this second layer is started with two apples instead of three. This brings each apple of the second layer over a space of the layer below, instead of its resting directly upon an apple of that layer, as in the "straight" pack. There is, therefore, considerable "give" to this pack, and consequently much less bruising of the fruit.

The two-two pack is started by placing an apple in the lower right-hand corner and a second one in the middle of the space remaining. The next two apples are placed in the spaces left by the first two, and so on (Figs. 135 and 136).

Layer paper may or may not be used in box packing. When to use it is a point that can be learned only by experience. It is used with certain sizes and shapes of apples in order to bring them high enough to get the required firmness or compactness in the box.

The bulge or swell is a crucial matter in box packing. The apples must be put into the box in such a way that when the top is put on and nailed down, both the top and bottom of the box are

FIG. 140.—A western type of box press.

pressed out in the middle, giving a bulge. It is the pressure exerted by this bulge in the top and bottom boards which keeps the apples tight in the box. Of course the bulge is produced by having the mass or body of apples in the box thicker in the middle than it is at the ends. Different packers secure this bulge in different ways, but the three principal methods seem to be as follows: First, pack the apples a little tighter in the central part of each layer than they are at the ends. In this way, when the cover is nailed on, the apples press together more at the ends than in the middle and we get the bulge as a result. Second, selecting just a little larger apples for this

Fig. 141.—An excellent type of box press which can be made at home by anyone who is handy with tools.

middle part of each layer. Third, turn the apples on the side or end in order to bring them at the right height. Some packers will tell you that they do not do *anything* to secure the bulge, that it "just comes that way," but of course this merely means that in their cases the method is carried out unconsciously.

Scoring Boxes of Apples.—The following score card is the one used in judging boxes at the New England Fruit Show in Boston in 1913. It represents fairly accurately the relative importance placed on the various points which enter into a well-packed box of apples.

Score Card for Boxes of a Given Variety of Apples

FRUIT.—Texture and flavor	100	
Size	100	
Color	150	
Uniformity	150	
Freedom from blemishes	150	
		650
PACKAGE.—Material	30	
Marking	10	
Solidity (nailing, cleats, etc.)	10	
		50
PACKING.—Bulge or swell	100	
Alignment	20	
Height of ends	60	
Compactness	80	
Attractiveness and style of pack	40	
		300
Total		1000

The packing of fruit into the other types of packages has not been so well reduced to a system, and in many cases probably never will be. It is largely a question of getting a smooth, attractive "face" on the package that shall fairly represent the contents and still tempt the customer to buy (Figs. 145, 146, 147 and 148).

QUESTIONS

1. What are the advantages of grading fruit?
2. Name and define three standard grades of apples.
3. Mention three kinds of apple packages and give the advantages of each.
4. What packages are used for pears?
5. What for peaches?

6. What for plums?
7. What for cherries?
8. Give a list of the equipment needed in packing barrels of apples.
9. How is the barrel prepared for packing?
10. Describe the "facing" of the barrel.
11. How is the barrel then filled?
12. Describe how to place the apples of the last layer, and "head up" the barrel.
13. What are the main points considered in scoring barrels of apples?
14. Name the different kinds of "packs" for boxes.
15. Describe the packing of apples in boxes.
16. What are the points considered in scoring boxes of apples?
17. What styles of fruit packages have you seen in market?

CHAPTER XX

MARKETING

THE greatest single problem in marketing fruit is to have good fruit (Fig. 142). Beside this problem all others sink into insignificance. Given such fruit there can be developed a market for almost any quantity. In fact, it will sell itself. If this truth could only be brought home to our orchard men, and if they could only be made to adopt such methods as would

FIG. 142.—The greatest single problem in marketing fruit is to have good fruit. Fruit like that shown above, which was picked up in the local market at Amherst, will *not* tend to increase the consumption.

insure yearly crops of such fruit (and there are methods that will make this reasonably certain), there would be little difficulty in anything else. In fact, the fruit growers' millennium would have arrived. Some of the things which seem most important in bringing about this result have been discussed in this book.

The next greatest problem is to pack it honestly and carefully. This was discussed in the last chapter. The man whose fruit is invariably well packed, and who has the reputation of getting just as good, or a little better, fruit in the middle of the package than is on top, is never going to lack for customers.

The discussion in this chapter will presuppose that the orchardist has been measurably successful in growing a crop of good fruit, and that it has been properly packed for market. How shall it be disposed of to the best advantage? This is our next problem.

The Best Market.—We ought first to consider with the utmost care just what are the requirements of the particular market we intend to supply. As already suggested, under the

FIG. 143.—Boxes of western apples. The use of the box and careful, honest packing have made the western apple famous.

discussion of varieties, the general type of market should be decided upon before the orchard is ever set. Of course conditions are going to control largely whether the owner should develop a special market or retail market, or whether he is going to rely on the general market. If he is too far away from his customers it is relatively difficult to develop a special market. Yet it is surprising to what an extent a special market may be developed by proper methods when one has really fine fruit

(Fig. 143). There is not the slightest question that the special, retail market is the one which pays if it is well worked up.

Some one has said that the great difficulty with farmers is that they sell at wholesale and buy at retail; and this difficulty is nowhere better shown than in the fruit business. The less fruit you can sell a customer, at one time, the more he is willing to pay for it. Did you ever stop to think of that? Take it in apples. A man is usually quite willing to pay five cents for a single apple and sometimes ten cents for a really fine one; and he thinks he is getting a bargain at two for five. But attempt to sell him a barrel at these rates, and he thinks that you are committing highway robbery. A barrel will hold about three hundred and fifty to four hundred apples of average size. Taking the latter number, if these are sold at ten cents it means $40; at five cents, $20; and at two for five $10 for the barrel. No one would suggest that we sell apples at $40 per barrel, but we should come just as near to retailing them direct to the consumer as we can.

The following table brings out the point just discussed and is worthy of study by every fruit grower:

TABLE VII.—*Value of a Barrel of Apples when Sold in Retail Lots, Estimating 350 Apples per Barrel*

Unit of Quantity	Price per Unit	Value of a Barrel at This Rate
Single apple	2½c. each	$ 8.75
Single apple	5c. each	17.50
Single apple	10c. each	35.00
One dozen apples	25c. dozen	7.29
One dozen apples	40c. dozen	11.66
One dozen apples	50c. dozen	14.58
One dozen apples	60c. dozen	17.50
One peck apples	25c. peck	3.00
One peck apples	50c. peck	6.00
One peck apples	60c. peck	7.20
One bushel apples	$1.00 bushel	3.00
One bushel apples	1.50 bushel	4.50
One bushel apples	2.00 bushel	6.00
One bushel apples	2.50 bushel	7.50

The special market, too, will usually respond at once to any improvement in quality or pack (Figs. 144, 145, 146 and 147). If you are selling through a good grocery store, which is one of the very best methods, the consumer knows who furnishes the fruit, and if it is good he asks for more of your brand; while if you ship into the general market there is much less chance that special effort will receive special reward. Where the grower can secure such a market he should, if possible, retain control of the price for which the fruit is sold. If he is reasonably close to his market, and if he has confidence in his grocery-

FIG. 144.—Pasteboard carton for fancy apples. This package will carry the fruit perfectly, but it is too costly for anything but very high-grade fruit.

man, he can usually afford to assume any loss due to decay. When this is done the grocer is usually willing to accept really good fruit on the commission basis.

When the grower does keep control of the price he can lower it if necessary to move his crop of perishable fruit faster; and at the same time that he is getting more for his fruit the consumer is usually paying less for it.

Then if a man is to develop and maintain this special market, it is very desirable that he should keep up a continuous supply of each fruit. This was discussed under varieties, but is worth mentioning again. If your customers are watching for your brand do not disappoint them at any point in the season. The writer recalls an instance where a man actually refused a dollar a barrel more for his Spies than he could get at his regular market because he did not want to disappoint and lose his customers. To carry out this plan the fruit grower must not only have a good list of varieties but he should have good storage facilities as well.

The General Market.—Where the orchard is situated so that the owner cannot develop a retail market he must rely on the general market. In this case he sells either to a buyer at the orchard or through a commission man. There is a good deal to be said in favor of the former method. The buyer and the seller are more nearly on an equality than in the latter. If the buyer does not want to pay what the grower thinks the fruit is worth it can remain on the farm. And an additional advantage is

Fig. 145.—The climax peach basket used as a retail package for apples. This package has much to commend it. It is cheap, carries the fruit in good condition and will pack well into cars.

that one gets rid of the entire crop with relatively little worry, and he can then give his attention to other matters. He also has his money for use and is saved considerable loss from shrinkage. On the whole, there is considerable argument for selling to a buyer at the orchard. It is not as good as the retail plan, but stands next to it.

Frequently, however, the grower has to sell through a commission man. This is the poorest type of marketing, not because commission men are dishonest, but from the very nature of the method. Even the commission men themselves will admit that there are dishonest men in the business, which makes the situation still worse. It puts temptation in the path of the commission man which is unnecessary. There is the same objection to it as to the sod-culture method. It may do when properly carried out, but there is always danger that it will fail. The chief objections to this plan are two:

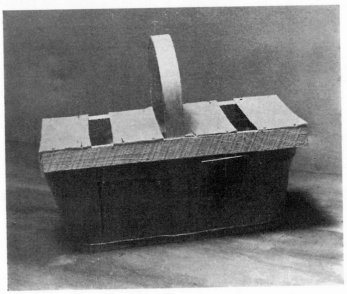

Fig. 146.—Climax peach basket with cover on. This type of cover holds the package rigid so that the fruit is not damaged.

First, the grower is practically at the mercy of the commission man. He can put down any amount he chooses in making his returns and in ninety-nine cases out of a hundred the grower will never be the wiser. Such laws as the one in New York, which is discussed in Chapter XXII, will undoubtedly help to mend matters, but they can not altogether remove the difficulty. The grower is still very largely at the mercy of the commission man.

The second objection is that by this method there is usually little chance of holding the fruit, in case the market is not satisfactory. The fruit is there, it must be disposed of, and the seller must take what he can get for it.

Under these circumstances it becomes absolutely essential to find an honest commission man. There are plenty of them. Having found one then stick to him. Do not be led away simply because your neighbor happens to get a little more for his fruit on a certain day than you did. Perhaps his fruit was better or perhaps his commission man was simply trying to draw trade.

FIG. 147.   FIG. 148.

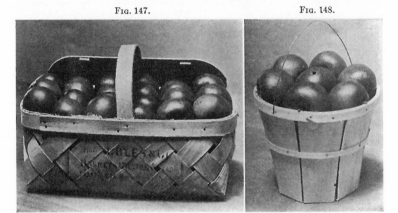

FIG. 147.—Splint basket used for apples. A store window filled with these baskets makes an attractive sight and one which it is difficult for the customer to pass by.

FIG. 148.—An attractive package for the retail trade.

It is a very common custom, and especially with the man who is not too scrupulous, to make some uncommonly good returns early in the season in order to draw trade. Do not be fooled by it. Call the attention of your own commission man to it if you like; it may spur him on. But do not leave him.

Coöperative Marketing.—The best method of marketing fruit where it can be properly carried out is undoubtedly coöperation. The western states have amply demonstrated this in the splendid results that they have secured. The chief advantages of coöperation seem to be:

1. It utilizes the best business talent of the community. This is a crucial point. It is only one man in a thousand who has the head to run such a business, and the coöperative method picks him out and lets him run the business for the community. The rest of the men are free to devote their attention to producing a crop of good fruit for the manager to sell, and anyone who has ever tried it knows that this is a serious enough proposition in itself. It is no discredit to farmers as a class to say that not many of them are good business men. Neither are many of the men in the hardware business. But the fellows who are not do not try to manage the business. They do something else—sell goods or make goods.

2. The distribution of the output is better. The members do not all ship to Boston one day and to New York the next, but all the markets are uniformly supplied. The manager looks after that. If there is an association of associations, as there usually is when the scheme is well started, the control of the distribution is just that much better.

3. The fruit is handled in large lots and therefore better freight rates can be secured. The car-load shipment is much more economical than the small lot.

4. The association can adopt methods of advertising that would not be open to the single grower. As a matter of fact, the single grower usually does not advertise at all; but even if he does, there are many kinds of advertising that he cannot afford.

5. The manager of an association can keep in telegraphic touch with the markets and thus know better whether to ship or not, and, if so, where.

Objections to Coöperation.—All these advantages and many more are claimed and usually admitted for coöperation. Then why do we not have more associations? There are probably many reasons, but the one chiefly responsible seems to be conservatism. The farmer has always run his own business and thinks he can do so still. Distrust of each other among farmers is also usually given and probably is an important reason for lack of coöperation. Someone has said that most men would rather lose two dollars than see their neighbor make one, and while this principle can hardly be endorsed, there is undoubtedly some truth in it. Another very important reason seems to be that the best growers in the community usually do not make much by joining the association and sometimes even lose something. This is because they have already been receiving the highest prices for fancy fruits. Since they are the ones who must usually take the lead in such matters, the scheme is likely to languish unless they are of a somewhat self-sacrificing turn of mind.

A further difficulty which is usually experienced is that the packing varies too much in the different packing houses. This is pretty certain to be so unless the packing is all done under one central supervision. This plan has been used in some sections of the northwest and seems to work well. An experienced packer is put in charge of each gang of hands, and he is responsible, not to the owner of the fruit, but to the association. This obviates the difficulty which one speaker expressed by saying that no man ought to pack his own apples because it is so hard for him to see a worm-hole.

Utilizing Low-grade Fruits.—It remains to say a word about utilizing the poorer grades of fruit. Of course, we may say that there should not be any such grades, and it is quite true that entirely too much of our fruit belongs in this class. But even with the best of treatment there is going to be some of this sort of fruit produced, and it is a very important question what disposal should be made of it. Usually it is put on the market and allowed to bring what it will. Most men who market these inferior grades of fruit (such as poor windfalls and wormy specimens) do not appreciate the depressing influence which this sort of fruit has on the market. Because they are getting some cash for their fruit they think it is a better bargain than to let it lie on the ground and rot. Perhaps it is looking at it from their own selfish standpoint, though even this is to be doubted, if they are growing any good fruit in addition. But if we look at it from the standpoint of the larger interest of the industry as a whole there can be no doubt whatever. These grades ought never to be put upon the market in a fresh state, but should be canned or made into jams, jellies, vinegar, and other products. Every fruit-growing community ought to have its canning plant, and the time will come when it will. Not only will such a plant take care of the poor grades at all times, but it will also take the good grades in times when the market is glutted, and thus reduce the frequency of such depressions.

QUESTIONS

1. Discuss the effect of " quality " upon the marketing of fruit.
2. Compare wholesale and retail markets.
3. Show the advantage, to the grower, of selling in small quantities.
4. What are the objections to selling through a commission man?
5. What are the advantages of selling to a buyer at the orchard?
6. What are the advantages of coöperative marketing?
7. What objections are there to this method?
8. How should low-grade fruit be utilized?

CHAPTER XXI.

ADVERTISING.

Did you ever stop to think what a tremendous amount of time, money, energy, brains, and a lot of other less important things, are spent on advertising, on getting the producer and the consumer together? And on making consumers out of non-consumers? The writer is not much of a Socialist as yet, but when he thinks of the saving that would result if this one item of advertising were cut out by eliminating competition, he is tempted to change over at once. So long, however, as the present arrangement holds and every one who has anything to sell must depend on his own efforts to get rid of it, advertising is going to be a very important factor in any man's success. So strong is this factor that it seems worth while to devote an entire chapter to the subject.

METHODS OF ADVERTISING

There are innumerable ways in which one may advertise his wares, but the following are among the best:

A Name and a Sign.—Have a name for the farm or the orchard. The more distinctive and attractive this name can be the more assistance it is going to be in advertising. But almost any name will help. It serves to locate the goods, to make the consumer remember where those fine apples came from. Having decided on a name, put up a sign on the highway. Let it be an attractive, artistic sign if you can, but even a plain, rectangular board with the name on it is better than nothing. If the name can have special local significance, and in particular if it can be such a name as is not likely to be chosen by anyone else, so much the better. The following are examples of good names: "Hillcrest Orchards," "Fairview Orchards" "Seaview Farm," "Bay Road Fruit Farm."

A Farm Bulletin Board.—Do some local advertising at the

farm by means of a bulletin board on the highway. It will surprise anyone who has never tried it to see what this will do. In these days when so many people own automobiles, the number who will pass by the farm, particularly if it is on a main thoroughfare, is surprising. A great many of these travellers are city people, to whom anything from the country that is really good will appeal. Choice fruit appeals more than anything else. Usually these customers are perfectly willing to pay a good price,

Fig. 149.—Probably the most famous fruit label in use.

too, for a fancy article, so that they really offer an excellent opportunity to the enterprising orchardist. It is true that the sign has to be decidedly conspicuous to be seen by some of them as they flash past, but the fruit grower will soon get a name for fine peaches or choice apples, so that the automobile fraternity will be on the watch for his sign. And among the more slowly moving classes of humanity who pass by there will be many a one who will want something that is for sale.

Adopt some attractive label for the package. The western apple and orange growers have worked this method more ardently and consistently than those of any other section, and no one can

compute the sales it has made for them.   The buyer is never left
in doubt as to who grew this western fruit.

As with the farm or orchard name, so with this label—the
more distinctive it can be the better.   It is not always the most
gaudy label that is remembered the longest.   Perhaps the most

A MONTANA McINTOSH

**Young Orchards Bear Profitable
Crops in Five Years. $500 to $1000
Per Acre From Bearing Orchards**

For Particulars Write to
STEVENS & JONES
Table Rock, Montana.

Fig. 150.—A good type of advertising wrapper. Half natural width.

widely known single label of this class is Mr. J. H. Hale's famous
red label, a cut of which is shown in Figure 149.

Use an attractive printed wrap for such fruits as apples,
pears and oranges.   When ordered in large numbers the printing
does not add much to the cost of the wrap, and it may frequently
be made the means of attracting the consumer's attention to the

orchard that produced the fruit.   Here is a sample of a wrap which was sent out with a Montana McIntosh apple.   Evidently those men believed in the wrap as an advertising medium, and whether we swallow all the statements on the wrap or not, we shall at least swallow the apple (if it is good as most McIntosh apples are), and we shall know where to go when we want more apples like it (Fig. 150).

Printed Matter in Fruit Packages.—Where fruit is sold in packages put some sort of advertising matter into the package.

FIG. 151.—A good type of advertising for apple barrels. It calls the attention of the consumer to the man who grew the fruit, which is a good thing to do if the fruit is good.

This is capable of endless variations, but almost any of them will be of value. In apple barrels there is the "pulp-head" or the "paper-cap." A sample of these is shown in Figure 151. They differ only in that the "pulp-head" is a light cardboard. Besides furnishing an excellent type of advertising, they serve a useful purpose in protecting the fruit and, as with wraps, the extra cost of printing is relatively small when they are ordered in large numbers.

Another type of advertising which may be included in any sort of package is a little leaflet which guarantees the pack. Nothing will give your customer so much confidence in your fruit as to find out that you are willing to stand back of it. Here are reproduced two such leaflets from the opposite sides of the continent, which are good examples of this excellent plan of advertising (Figs. 152 and 153).

Still another type of leaflet is that which takes the customer into your confidence, tells him something about your orchard and your plans and, rather incidentally, about your fruit. It takes some literary ability to get out a good one, but if the grower

THIS BOX PACKED BY
Packer No.............................
If purchaser of this box finds any ir-
regularity in the pack, kindly return
this card with any information which
may help us to make pack more perfect
in the future.
Sierra Vista Packing Co.
RIVERSIDE, CALIFORNIA

FIG. 152.—An excellent "guarantee" label from the Pacific Coast.

NOTICE!

This fruit was packed at the "Riverside" Fruit Farm, Middleton, Annapolis Co., Nova Scotia. Having large interest in growing orchards in the Annapolis Valley, I am very desirous of having my brand known abroad for its **invariable** reliability, both as to quality of fruit and honesty of packing. To insure this object, I hereby **GUARANTEE** the contents of this package to be the same from head to head, and to be fairly represented by the face end; and I further authorize my consignees to refund the money paid for fruit of my packing which is proved not to be according to brand, injury in transit only excepted.

G. C. MILLER.

FIG. 153.—Another guarantee label from an eastern orchardist.

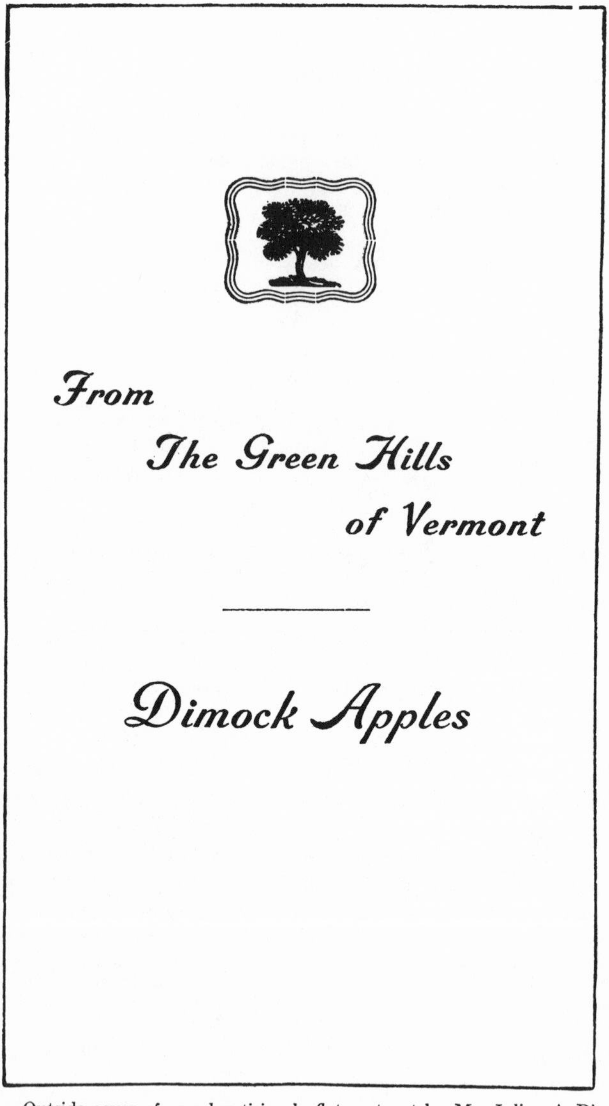

From

The Green Hills

of Vermont

———

Dimock Apples

FIG. 154.—Outside cover of an advertising leaflet sent out by Mr. Julian A. Dimock, of East Corinth, Vermont.

has that ability or can secure it in any way, it will take with an especially good class of customers. Here is one of the best of this type (Fig. 154). The contents of the leaflet follow:

We think that the apples grown in this orchard have a little the best flavor of any on earth. We wish that you could see the heavily laden trees amid the beauties of the prettiest part of old New England.

Dame Nature was in a kindly mood when she fashioned this farm. She tipped the best land to the east that it might catch the earliest sunshine, fed it with springs and protected it from the cold winds by placing it in an amphitheatre of encircling hills. The clover-covered fields stretch up over the hill-tops, while below them woodlands reach down to the little brooks in the valleys. Deer come into the fields, and, in the early mornings, stand and watch us with startled gaze. Scarlet tanagers build their nests in the apple trees and sing their love songs from the branches. Mother partridges play the old, old game of the broken wing when we come upon their little, scuttering broods.

But it was Aleck Eastman's love for his trees that built up this orchard. Forty-six years ago he and his wife settled on this farm. Even in the first year Aleck planted a few trees, for he had inherited the love of them from his father. He planted new ones and trimmed up the old ones. Every year saw a few more trees set out, while his neighbors called him crazy for using good land that might be made to feed cows for his slips of trees. But Aleck loved his trees. He imported the first spray pump that came into this county and began to kill the bugs before they came. He got up early and he worked late. He did the work of two strong men that his trees might not suffer while his farm was carried on.

Then, just when the orchard was coming into its own, Aleck awoke to the fact that it had outgrown him. His baby trees were grown to full treehood and as he became feebler the trees demanded more and more work. He could no longer climb to the topmost branches to prune and spray and pick. He had never hired help and he was too old to begin. In all his days no one had come to see his trees and show an appreciation of his work with them until I happened along. If any of his neighbors bought the place they would begin by cutting down the trees that he had spent his life to bring up. He could not carry it on any longer, so he proposed to sell the farm to me. That is why I am here to-day.

These apples that Aleck Eastman raised I am offering to you.

They are good because Dame Nature was thinking of apples when she fashioned this farm.

They are good because Aleck put a labor of love into tending his trees.

They are good because the rigors of the winters make hardy, full-flavored fruit, and the bright sunshine of the summer lays on the color so the apples are fair to see.

FAMEUSE.—Of the varieties which we grow we prefer the Fameuse (Snow), for we think it grows to perfection with us. Normally this is considered an early fall apple, but here it often keeps until spring. You know it: An early red and white, fine-flavored, crisp eating apple. Small, but full of spice.

McINTOSH RED.—This is another of the Fameuse group and perhaps the most popular. Dark red and of fine flavor for dessert.

BETHEL.—Our best winter apple is the Bethel. This variety originated within thirty miles of this farm. It matures late in the fall, is a dark red color and one of the best of keepers, and as handsome a winter apple as one cares to see. It resembles a Northern Spy, and makes a splendid eating apple.

NODHEAD.—The Nodhead is another of our favorites. A late apple, it is streaked with red and makes a table fruit of quality. It is a good keeper and should please you.

LINCOLN.—We want you to know the Lincoln. It is a trade-holder. But that is next year's story, for this is their non-bearing year.

We shall pack the fancy grades of these apples in western style as near as may be and will deliver them, freight prepaid, to either Boston or New York for $2.50 per box. We will appreciate a trial order and ask for a check with the order. Our personal guarantee goes with every box. We wish to replace every apple that arrives in damaged condition, through fault of ours, whenever this is possible.

If you insist, we will sell you a barrel of our Number One grade for $4.50, freight paid to New York. Our responsibility ends with delivery to the transportation company. We believe in our Fancy Grade and would rather sell it. We think you get more for your money.

JULIAN A. DIMOCK,
East Corinth, Vermont.

Such advertising is bound to attract an especially good class of consumers.

Recipes.—One more type of advertising leaflet may be mentioned, and that is the one which, after giving some general information about the fruit and where it was grown, proceeds to suggest ways in which it may be used. Recipes for peach ice-cream, peach marmalade, and canned peaches may be put into each basket of peaches, and the customer who bought one basket to eat out of hand may end by buying a half-dozen to put up for the winter. Here is a sample:

PEACHES.

We have more of this same grade for sale. Did you ever see finer for the money? Why don't you put up some for winter? Here are a few of the many ways in which they may be preserved. Try some of them! You'll be glad next winter that you did; not only when there is unexpected company for supper, but when you feel like having something a little extra yourself!

Canned Peaches.
4 pounds peaches.
1 pound sugar.
1 quart water.

Put the sugar and water in kettle and allow to boil a few minutes. Add peaches and cook slowly until soft. Place carefully in jars and seal.

Peach Marmalade.
10 pounds peaches.
5 pounds sugar.
½ cup water.

Put the water in a preserving kettle; add the fruit and sugar in alternate layers. Heat slowly and stir and mash the fruit, breaking it up as much as possible. Cook about two hours and put away in small jars.

Pickled Peaches.

7 pounds peaches.
4 pounds granulated sugar.
1 pint vinegar.
1 cup spice—stick cinnamon and whole cloves.

Tie the spices in little cheese-cloth bags. Put the vinegar and sugar in a kettle on the stove and stir until the sugar is dissolved. Then add the bags of spice and boil for 20 minutes. Add the peaches which have been peeled. Do not remove the pits. Boil slowly till soft. Put in stone jars.

BAY ROAD FRUIT FARM,
Amherst, Mass.

Advertise with Samples.—If you are selling apples, and possibly pears, there are great possibilities in sending a single sample fruit by mail or giving it away at any store which is handling your fruit. This is an old scheme of the cracker manufacturers and the breakfast food men and has sometimes been resorted to by the western fruit growers, who always head the procession in such matters. Of course some advertising matter accompanies the sample saying what grade it is and giving prices for this and other grades. If you are growing something like McIntosh or Northern Spy apples, that are bound to make friends when tasted, this sample method is excellent. Probably no one would expect to sell many Ben Davis apples in this way.

Window displays are capable of selling more fruit than almost any other method if they are rightly handled. To begin with, the grower must get a window in a good store in which the

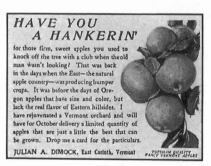

FIG. 155.—A magazine advertisement that is sure to attract attention.

public has confidence. The display must be something unusual that will at once catch the eye of the public. Fine, highly colored fruit in fancy packages, with perhaps, in the case of apples, a barrel or two with the fruit pouring out. Add to this a few photographs and a few advertising placards and you have a combination that will keep you busy filling orders for some time to come. One grower in Massachusetts put up such a display in the window of a Boston store and within two weeks received five hundred letters ordering fruit or asking for prices.

Newspaper and magazine advertising, if it is done in a businesslike way, is always good, provided the grower has fruit enough to justify it. Of course it will not pay if he has only one hundred baskets of peaches or fifty barrels of apples. But with reasonably large orchards, and especially with coöperative associations, there are great possibilities in this type of advertising. Like the leaflets it wants to be good material. The one here shown is one of the best samples the writer has ever seen (**Fig. 155**). Of course we do not all have Mr. Dimock's ability in this line, but most of us can do something if we try hard enough.

Have the Dealer and Buyer Visit the Orchard.—If you are selling fruit through a store, or even a commission house, get the proprietor and even his head clerk to come out and see the orchard. Take them out in picking season when there is something worth seeing and worth eating. Show them how the fruit is grown and handled, and if your orchard and methods are worth showing you will get these men interested and they will sell twice as much fruit as they would if they knew only the store end of the business.

QUESTIONS

1. What is the advantage of naming the farm?   Suggest some good names.
2. Of what value is the farm bulletin board?
3. Discuss the use of the package label.
4. Describe the method of advertising by means of printed material in the package.
5. Under what conditions do samples make a good method of advertising?
6. Describe the window-display method.
7. Discuss newspaper advertising.
8. What is the advantage in having the buyer visit the orchard?

CHAPTER XXII.

LAWS AFFECTING ORCHARDING.

In the recent wide extension of the legal regulation of business the orchard industry has not been allowed to escape. The first of these fruit laws aimed at the control of orchard pests, principally those carried in nursery stock, but to a certain extent those in the orchards themselves. The later laws have undertaken to regulate principally the packing and sale of fruit. While many of the first laws were crude and while some of them have been flat failures, there is no question that many of them have been of marked assistance to the fruit industry.

PESTS IN NURSERY-STOCK

Let us look first at the laws in relation to nursery-stock. These have been of two types: First, those which required the examination and perhaps fumigation of nursery-stock coming into a State or nation; second, State laws requiring the inspection of nursery-stock. The value of an examination of stock is quite variable, depending on the conspicuousness of the pest and the conscience of the inspector. Where the pest is one easily seen like the brown-tail moth for example, a thorough examination ought to prevent absolutely its entry into a State or its shipment from a nursery. On the other hand, when a pest is as inconspicuous as the San José scale, it is absolutely impossible, even after the most rigid inspection, to say that the stock is free from it. It can only be said that none was discovered. The value of such an inspection as this last rests on the fact that if the stock were badly infected the inspector would discover it.

When a pest can be destroyed by some treatment of the nursery-stock, such as fumigating with hydrocyanic acid gas for the San José scale, the treatment is of far more value than the best inspection ever given. It practically guarantees the freedom of the stock from this pest. The difficulty is that so few of our pests can be destroyed in this way.

298

Another point of great practical importance is the question of what shall be done with stock found to be infested with some serious pest. Such stock ought either to be treated so as to free it from the pest or else the stock ought to be destroyed. For example, an inspector looking for San José scale in a nursery when he discovered the scale on a tree, might break it down as an indication to the nurseryman that that particular tree was to be dug out and destroyed. But immediately adjoining trees, whose branches might interlock with those of the tree broken down, but on which the inspector failed to find any scale, might be allowed to stand and be shipped out to customers. Such an inspection is absolutely worthless. In fact it is worse than that, because if the purchaser knows of it he is thereby thrown off his guard and is less likely to discover the pest for himself.

Local Administration.—Any law dealing with orchard pests, whether it be with those in the nursery or in the orchard, is much more likely to be of value if it is administered by a State or national officer, rather than being left to a local official. The locally administered law is absolutely dependent on local support for its effectiveness. If the people of the neighborhood believe in it with sufficient zeal, then the law is carried out; if they do not, then the most zealous official is powerless. The writer has seen this well illustrated in the case of laws against the black-knot of plums. When public sentiment was not strong on the subject, black-knot flourished undisturbed even in orchards immediately adjoining the highway.

National laws are likely to be most effective both because of the fact just suggested and because such a law brings all parts of the country under uniform regulations. For example, the United States has a "Quarantine Act," by the provisions of which the Secretary of Agriculture may prohibit the importation of plants or of fruits likely to be the means of introducing into this country a dangerous pest. The following was Secretary Wilson's order prohibiting the importation of fruits likely to bring in the "Mexican fruit fly":

The fact has been determined by the Secretary of Agriculture that an injurious insect known as the Mexican fruit fly (*Trypeta ludens*), new and not heretofore widely prevalent and distributed within and throughout the United States, exists in the Republic of Mexico.

Now, therefore, I, James Wilson, Secretary of Agriculture, under authority conferred by section 7 of the act of August 20, 1912, known as "The plant quarantine act," do hereby declare that it is necessary, in order to prevent the introduction into the United States of the insect known as the Mexican fruit fly (*Trypeta ludens*), to forbid the importation into the United States from the Republic of Mexico of the following fruits:

Sweet limes	Peaches
Mangoes	Plums
Oranges	Guavas
Achras sapotes	

Hereafter, and until further notice, by virtue of said section 7 of the act of Congress approved August 20, 1912, the importation or entry into the United States for any purpose of the fruits hereinbefore named and their horticultural varieties is prohibited.

Done at Washington this 15th day of January, 1913.

Witness my hand and the seal of the United States Department of Agriculture.

JAMES WILSON,
Secretary of Agriculture.

As soon as such a notice is given the fruits affected are stopped at the port of entry.

PACKING AND SALE OF FRUITS

Canadian Laws and Regulations.—In the realm of laws intended to govern the packing and sale of fruits the Canadian "Inspection and Sale Act," better known as "Fruit Marks Act," is the oldest, the most far-reaching, and consequently the most worthy of study. Its chief provisions are as follows:

The Marking of Fruit.—320. Every person who, by himself or through the agency of another person, packs fruit in a closed package, intended for sale, shall cause the package to be marked in a plain and indelible manner in letters not less than half an inch in length, before it is taken from the premises where it is packed,—

(a) With the initials of his Christian names, and his full surname and address, or, in the case of a firm or corporation, with the firm or corporate name and address;

(*b*) With the name of the variety or varieties; and,

(*c*) With a designation of the grade of fruit, which shall include one of the following four marks, viz.: Fancy, No. 1, No. 2, No. 3.

2. Such mark may be accompanied by any other designation of grade or brand, if that designation or brand is not inconsistent with, or marked more conspicuously than, the one of the said four marks which is used on the said package.

321. No person shall sell, or offer, expose, or have in his possession for sale, any fruit packed,—

(*a*) In a closed package and intended for sale unless such package is marked as required by the provisions of this Part;

(*b*) In a closed package, upon which package is marked any designation which represents such fruit as of

(i) Fancy quality, unless such fruit consists of well-grown specimens of one variety, sound, of uniform and of at least normal size and of good color for the variety, of normal shape, free from worm holes, bruises, scab and other defects, and properly packed;

(ii) No. 1 quality, unless such fruit includes no culls and consists of well-grown specimens of one variety, sound, of not less than medium size and of good color for the variety, of normal shape and not less than ninety per cent free from scab, worm holes, bruises and other defects, and properly packed;

(iii) No. 2 quality, unless such fruit includes no culls and consists of specimens of not less than nearly medium size for the variety, and not less than eighty per cent free from worm holes and such other defects as cause material waste, and properly packed;

(*c*) In any package in which the faced or shown surface gives a false representation of the contents of such package; and it shall be considered a false representation when more than fifteen per cent of such fruit is substantially smaller in size than, or inferior in grade to, or different in variety from, the faced or shown surface of such package.

Branding Falsely Marked and Falsely Packed.—322. Whenever any fruit in any package is found to be so packed that the faced or shown surface gives a false representation of the contents of the package, any inspector charged with the enforcement of this Part may mark the words *Falsely packed* in a plain and indelible manner on the package.

2. Whenever any fruit packed in a closed package is found to be falsely marked, the said inspector may efface such false marks and mark the words *Falsely marked* in a plain and indelible manner on the package.

3. The inspector shall give notice, by letter or telegram, to the packer whose name is marked on the package, within twenty-four hours after he marks the words *Falsely packed* or *Falsely marked* on the package.

Fruit Packages.—325. All apples packed in Canada for export for sale by the barrel in closed barrels shall be packed in good and strong barrels of seasoned wood having dimensions not less than the following, namely: Twenty-six inches and one-fourth between the heads, inside measure, and a head diameter of seventeen inches, and a middle diameter of eighteen inches and one-half, representing as nearly as possible ninety-six quarts.

2. When apples, pears or quinces are sold by the barrel, as a measure of capacity, such barrel shall not be of lesser dimensions than those specified in this section.

3. When apples are packed in Canada for export for sale by the box, they shall be packed in good and strong boxes of seasoned wood, the inside dimensions of which shall not be less than ten inches in depth, eleven inches in width and twenty inches in length, representing as nearly as possible two thousand two hundred cubic inches.

4. When apples are packed in boxes or barrels having trays or fillers wherein it is intended to have a separate compartment for each apple, the provisions of this section as to boxes and barrels shall not apply.

Inspector's Right to Examine.—327. Any person charged with the enforcement of this Part may enter upon any premises to make examination of any packages of fruit suspected of being falsely marked or packed in violation of any of the provisions of this Part, whether such packages are on the premises of the owner, or on other premises, or in the possession of a railway or steamship company.

Offences and Penalties.—328. Every person who, by himself or through the agency of any other person, violates any of the provisions of sections 320 and 321 of this Act, shall be liable, for the first offence, to a fine not exceeding twenty-five dollars and not less than ten dollars; for the second offence, to a fine not exceeding fifty dollars and not less than twenty-five dollars; and for the third and each subsequent offence, to a fine not exceeding two hundred dollars and not less than fifty dollars, together, in all cases, with the costs of prosecution; and in default of payment of such fine and costs shall be liable to imprisonment, with or without hard labor, for a term not exceeding one month, unless such fine and costs, and the costs of enforcing them, are sooner paid.

2. Whenever any such violation is with respect to a lot or shipment consisting of fifty or more closed packages, there may be imposed, in addition to any penalty provided by this section, for the first offence twenty-five cents, for the second offence fifty cents, and for the third and each subsequent offence one dollar, for each closed package in excess of fifty with respect to which such violation is committed.

329. Every person who, not being an inspector, wilfully alters, effaces, or obliterates, wholly or partially, or causes to be altered, effaced, or obliterated, any marks on any package which has undergone inspection, shall incur a penalty of one hundred dollars for the first offence, together in all cases, with the costs of prosecution; and in default of payment of such fine and cost shall be liable to imprisonment, with or without hard labor,

for a term not exceeding one month, unless such fine and costs, and the costs of enforcing them, are sooner paid.

330. Every person who violates any of the provisions of sections 325 and 326 of the Act shall be liable, on summary conviction, to a penalty of twenty-five cents for each barrel of apples, or box of apples, pears, quinces, berries, or currants, or basket of fruit, or berry box, respecting which such violation is committed, together with the costs of prosecution; and in default of payment of such fine and costs shall be liable to imprisonment, with or without hard labor, for a term not exceeding one month, unless such fine and costs, and the costs of enforcing them, are sooner paid.

332. Every person who obstructs any person charged with the enforcement of this Part in entering any premises to make examination of packages of fruit as provided by this Part, or who refuses to permit the making of any such examination, shall be liable to a penalty not exceeding five hundred dollars and not less than twenty-five dollars, together with the costs of prosecution, and in default of payment of such penalty and costs, shall be liable to imprisonment, with or without hard labor, for a term not exceeding six months, unless such penalty and costs, and the costs of enforcing the same, are sooner paid.

Explanation.—The following "general notes" are also of interest as explaining and interpreting the terms of the act:

(a) *For Inspectors.*

Inspectors will not examine particular lots of fruit at the request of buyers or sellers. When not under specific directions, inspectors will use their discretion as to where they can best employ their time within the district assigned them.

Inspectors will avoid anything which would delay unnecessarily the movement of fruit or which would interfere with the interests of those concerned in the fruit trade, except in so far as action may be necessary to prevent violation of the Act.

Packages which have been inspected are to be closed by the inspector and left in marketable order after examination, unless the owner prefers to take charge of such opened packages.

(b) *For the Grower.*

If the grower sells his fruit unpacked, the Act does not apply to him in any particular.

If he sells his fruit in uncovered barrels or boxes, the Act requires only that the top of each package shall be no better than the fruit throughout the package.

If the grower packs his own fruit he accepts the responsibility of the packing, as described in the following paragraph:

(c) For the Packer (the Owner at the time of Packing).

Section 320 of the Act requires that the person who owns the fruit when it is packed in closed barrels or boxes must mark plainly on each package:

1. His name and post office address.
2. The name of the variety of the fruit.
3. The grade of the fruit, whether it is " Fancy," " No. 1," " No. 2," or " No. 3."

If he marks the package " Fancy " the fruit must be practically perfect, as described in section 321 (b) (i).

On reading subsection (b) (ii) carefully, it will be seen that the packer should aim in packing grade No. 1 to discard every injured or defective fruit, and not to deliberately include ten per cent of inferior specimens. This margin is meant to make the work of grading easier and more rapid than if absolute perfection were exacted. Ten per cent is presumed to be the margin within which an honest packer can do rapid work, using every endeavor to make each specimen conform to the general standard for the grade.

Even the twenty per cent margin in grade No. 2 must be composed of specimens not less than nearly medium size, including no culls.

The Act makes no restriction as to the quality of fruit which is marked " No. 3."

The owner at the time of packing is responsible if the face of each package does not represent the contents as required by section 321, subsection (c). Over-facing is an offence against the Act, which is most severely dealt with by the courts.

(d) For the Foreman of the Packing Gang.

Whether he is putting up his own fruit or that of another person, the man who does the packing is required, by section 4 of the Order in Council printed above, to pack the fruit in accordance with the law. He should read the whole Act carefully, but should give section 321 special attention. If he violates these requirements, he is liable to the fine specified in section 5 of the Order in Council.

(e) For the Apple Operator.

The apple operator for his own protection should see that his workmen are familiar with the Inspection and Sale Act, Part IX.

Section 4 of the Order in Council is a special protection for the apple operator against carelessness or fraudulent work upon the part of his packers.

Where the apple operator buys apples already packed, he should note particularly that the fruit is marked as required by section 320.

To avoid possible complications in case of fraudulent packing, all contracts should stipulate clearly whether the apples are purchased packed in barrels or whether they are purchased to be packed by the buyer.

Apples should not be bought or sold with the stipulation, "subject to government inspection." There is no such thing as "government inspection," meaning a "certificate" or "report" guaranteeing the quality of a particular lot of fruit.

Opinions of the Canadian Law.—There can be no doubt whatever as to the efficacy of this act. All classes of men interested in the orchard industry of Canada agree in endorsing its main provisions and in commending its effect on the fruit industry of that country. By way of evidence on this point the writer has taken pains to secure the opinions of representative men of various occupations, some of which are here given:

From the Fruit Growers.—"The Fruit Marks Act has done and is doing good work. The longer it is in operation and the better it is understood, the more good it is doing. I can safely say that apples are now much better packed than formerly."

2. "I consider the Act was one of the most necessary, the wisest and best bits of legislation bearing upon agriculture that our federal government has put through. The effect of it at home has been most wholesome and though there have been a few most foolish and short-sighted breaches of the act by fruit growers, yet generally speaking it has made them very careful and they realize that the legislation has not only been helpful to Canadian fruit as a whole but has been beneficial to their own individual work."

3. "The Act is certainly a good thing for Canada, as it has been the means of bringing up the standard of Canadian packing in the English markets."

From a Large Dealer and Buyer.—"The Act has certainly had a marked effect in improving the packing of apples by keeping farmers up to the mark, and by putting inspectors in touch with the bad packers, who would otherwise continue shipping badly packed fruit to the detriment of the good packers. It has also had its effect in warehouse-packing and checked many frauds. One of these was the marking up of the grade of fruit and another was the branding and shipping of fruit under spurious names and marks. Packers are every year having a more wholesome regard for the Fruit Marks Act, and I look for a steady improvement in the pack."

Fruit Standardized.—Turning now to the officials of the Dominion Department of Agriculture we have several opinions:

Mr. George H. Vroom, Chief Fruit Inspector for the Province of Nova Scotia, says: "The Fruit Marks Act has standardized the pack to such an extent that Canadian apples average from one to two shillings more per barrel than under the old methods. It has aided very materially in the formation of coöperative associations, which means first, last and always a better and higher grade article to put on the market. And this improved pack has been the means of opening up new markets to Canadian fruit. In short the Fruit Marks Act has succeeded beyond the most sanguine expectations."

Professor W. T. Macoun, Dominion Horticulturist, says: "While the Fruit Marks Act has not yet made every Canadian apple packer put his apples up in accordance with the requirements of the Act, yet much has already been accomplished in this direction. It has given fruit growers standards of what No. 1 and No. 2 grades of apples should be. This was not clearly understood before the passage of the Act and there was a great difference of opinion among fruit growers as to what constituted a No. 1 and a No. 2 apple. The Fruit Marks Act has made the branding of barrels much more uniform. Formerly a man could put as many Xs on the barrel as he thought would sell his fruit to the best advantage. Now the grade marks must be confined to No. 1, No. 2 and No. 3 and the packer's name and address must be on every closed package. This we consider a great step forward."

Mr. A. McNeill, Chief of the Fruit Division, says: "In my opinion the Fruit Marks Act has revolutionized the packing of apples in Canada. The effect of it has been to establish definite grades. It is safe to say that there have been thousands of dollars saved in law expenses alone by the definiteness of the definitions and the conclusiveness of them from the fact that they are a matter of law. The second benefit from the law is that the Canadian pack is more uniform as a whole than it would have been. Notwithstanding the many violations of the law, and notwithstanding the wide range of grades that may be packed within each of the grades noted in the Act, it is now being recognized quite definitely in the markets of the world that Canadian apples are in the main of the quality marked upon the outside of the package."

Mr. McNeill then quotes from a letter received from one of their Canadian Consuls in an English city who says: "From a personal interview with a dozen or more firms in this city, selected at random, it is safe to say that this English city consumes $15,000 to $20,000 worth of apples weekly during the season from October to the middle of March or April. Of this amount about three-fifths are Canadian, the remaining American. Practically all of these apples are bought of commission men in Liverpool. The tendency of the trade here is to favor the Canadian grower and packer, the reason given for this being that Canada exercises a supervision over the grading, packing and branding of its fruit that is entirely lacking in the American product."

United States Law for Apples.—This is certainly very strong evidence, coming as it does from men in so many varied lines of work, and it is small wonder that the United States has made an attempt to take up a similar line of work. The following act was approved August 3, 1912, and everyone connected with the fruit industry is watching its effect with the greatest interest. The chief objection to the law is that its standards are not sufficiently high.

An act to establish a standard barrel and standard grades for apples when packed in barrels, and for other purposes.

Be it enacted by the Senate and House of Representatives of the United States of America in Congress assembled, That the standard barrel for

apples shall be of the following dimensions when measured without disten-
tion of its parts: Length of stave, twenty-eight and one-half inches; diameter of head, seventeen and one-eighth inches; distance between heads,
twenty-six inches; circumference of bulge, sixty-four inches outside meas-
urement, representing as nearly as possible seven thousand and fifty-six
cubic inches: Provided, That steel barrels containing the interior dimensions provided for in this section shall be construed as a compliance there-
with.

Sec. 2. That the standard grades for apples when packed in barrels
which shall be shipped, or delivered for shipment in interstate or foreign
commerce, or which shall be sold or offered for sale within the District of
Columbia or the Territories of the United States, shall be as follows: Apples
of one variety, which are well-grown specimens, hand picked, of good color
for the variety, normal shape, practically free from insect and fungous
injury, bruises, and other defects, except such as are necessarily caused in
the operation of packing, or apples of one variety which are not more than
ten per cent below the foregoing specifications shall be " Standard grade
minimum size two and one-half inches," if the minimum size of the apples
is two and one-half inches in transverse diameter; " Standard grade minimum size two and one-fourth inches," if the minimum size of the apples is
two and one-fourth inches in transverse diameter; or " Standard grade
minimum size two inches," if the minimum size of the apples is two inches
in transverse diameter.

Sec. 3. That the barrels in which apples are packed in accordance with
the provisions of this Act may be branded in accordance with section two
of this Act.

Sec. 4. That all barrels packed with apples shall be deemed to be below
standard if the barrel bears any statement, design, or device indicating
that the barrel is a standard barrel of apples, as herein defined, and the
capacity of the barrel is less than the capacity prescribed by section one of
this Act, unless the barrel shall be plainly marked on end and side with
words or figures showing the fractional relation which the actual capacity
of the barrel bears to the capacity prescribed by section one of this Act.
The marking required by this paragraph shall be in black letters of size
not less than (seventy-two point) one-inch gothic.

Sec. 5. That barrels packed with apples shall be deemed to be mis-
branded within the meaning of this Act:

First. If the barrel bears any statement, design, or device indicating
that the apples contained therein are " Standard " grade and the apples
when packed do not conform to the requirements prescribed by section two
of this Act.

Second. If the barrel bears any statement, design, or device indicating
that the apples contained therein are " Standard " grade and the barrel
fails to bear also a statement of the name of the variety, the name of the

locality where grown, and the name of the packer or the person by whose authority the apples were packed and the barrel marked.

SEC. 6. That any person, firm or corporation, or association who shall knowingly pack or cause to be packed apples in barrels or who shall knowingly sell or offer for sale such barrels in violation of the provisions of this Act shall be liable to a penalty of one dollar and costs for each such barrel so sold or offered for sale, to be recovered at the suit of the United States in any court of the United States having jurisdiction.

SEC. 7. That this Act shall be in force and effect from and after the first day of July, nineteen hundred and thirteen.

REGULATING COMMISSION MERCHANTS

Another type of law which has recently been advocated is that which attempts to regulate the business of commission men. Probably no one will deny that there have been many abuses by unscrupulous men of the commission method of selling fruit and it is hoped by the advocates of these laws that some at least of these abuses may be corrected. A bill passed by the New York legislature will give an idea of what is attempted in this direction. The following are its chief provisions:

1. Every person doing a commission business in farm products is required to take out a license with the Commissioner of Agriculture.

2. The Commissioner may refuse to grant a license to a produce man whom he is convinced is not honest in his business dealings.

3. Each commission man is required to give a fidelity bond of $3000 as a guarantee of honest dealing, and farmers may collect from this bond for money not honestly accounted for by the commission merchant.

4. The commissioner is also authorized to give hearings and to examine the records bearing on the case under dispute.

Laws of this kind have long been needed and cannot fail to do good. Doubtless there will have to be many changes as the details are worked out, but it is certainly a move in the right direction.

Many people object to all these laws on packing and selling because they say, "You cannot make a man honest by legislation." Perhaps you cannot, but if you can "legislate" him so that he acts as though he were honest, it may do just as well so far as selling fruit is concerned.

QUESTIONS.

1. What two types of laws are there relating to orcharding?
2. What two types regarding nursery-stock?
3. What are some of the difficulties regarding inspection of nursery-stock?
4. Compare local administration of these laws with national.
5. Give some of the main provisions of the Canadian " Fruit Marks Act."
6. With what favor has the law been received by growers? By buyers? By officials?
7. Give the main provisions of the United States law regarding apples packed in barrels.
8. What provisions have been recommended for the regulation of the commission business?

INDEX

311

PRODUCTIVE ORCHARDING

By FRED C. SEARS, Active Orchardman and Professor of Pomology, Massachusetts Agricultural College. 157 illustrations. 316 pages. Handsome cloth. $1.50 net.

"Worthy of a place in the library of every commercial orcharder and particularly of every apple grower," S. A. Beach, Chief Horticulturalist, Iowa Agricultural Experiment Station.—"A valuable contribution to our horticultural literature from the interests of the practical orchardist as well as the college student in orcharding." Prof. J. C. Whitten, University of Missouri.—"The methods he recommends if followed intelligently can hardly fail to give success," L. R. Taft, State Inspector, Michigan State Board of Agriculture.

Every owner either of a small family or a large commercial orchard, needs this work and will find it valuable. The author, who has personally managed a successful orchard, has carefully sifted and discarded methods which will not work, and included only those of known and tried value. It is practical and authoritative for the beginner and the expert, the illustrations all have a direct message.

PRODUCTIVE VEGETABLE GROWING

By JOHN W. LLYOD, Professor of Olericulture, University of Illinois. 192 illustrations. 320 pages. Handsome cloth binding. $1.50 net.

New York State produces some sixteen million dollars' worth of vegetables annually, and State Director of Farmers' Institutes Van Alstyne says of this work, "I consider it intensely practical and of great value to both the individual who may be interested in vegetable growing and also as a text-book for students in our agricultural schools."—"I know of no work which in my judgment is better suited to the use of students as a text-book or for the practical vegetable grower." Prof. J. C. Whitten, University of Missouri.

The cultural requirements of nearly every crop are analysed in the light of many years' experience, and in a clear and logical manner every step is thoroughly explained with the help of magnificent illustrations. It places vegetable gardening on a safe and sure basis.

COMMON-DISEASES OF FARM ANIMALS

By R. A. CRAIG, D.V.M., Professor of Veterinary Science, Purdue University. 124 illustrations. 327 pages. Handsome cloth binding. $1.50 net.

"The book would make a valuable addition to the library of any farmer, stockman or student of animal husbandry," Professor Carmichael, University of Illinois. —" I consider the choice of material which has been made very good and also think it is presented in a practical and usable form. I believe it will be popular, not only with students of animal husbandry but also with farmers," Prof. E. F. Ferrin, Iowa State College of Agricultural and Mechanical Arts.

Success in farming has its foundation in maintaining good health in your animals. The author has especially emphasized the causes, prevention and early recognition of common diseases. The book is an authoritative guide to farmers but does not trespass upon the domain of the veterinarian. It is worth your while to know how to keep your stock healthy—prevention is better and cheaper than cure.

PRODUCTIVE FEEDING OF FARM ANIMALS

By F. W. WOLL, Professor of Animal Nutrition, University of California. 96 illustrations. 362 pages. Handsome cloth binding. $1.50 net.

"It is to my mind, the best arranged and most condensed treatise on the subject of feeding farm animals that has been published, "Prof. W. H. Tomhave, Pennsylvania State College.—"A helpful, timely book." Professor W. A. Henry, University of Wisconsin.—"Should be read by every student of the farming industry, no matter whether he is in the school-room and in his infancy, or out in the world and producing," S. S. Oldham, Superintendent of James J. Hill's North Oaks Stock Farm.

This subject is of more economic importance than any other single matter the agriculturist has to tackle when handling live stock on the farm. Professor Woll has sifted the mass of experimental work so that the student and the stockman has at his command a concise discussion upon feeding farm animals.